A Leap of Faith – The Spiritual Path

Allocated to The Alcoholic and The Drug Addict in The Recovery Process From God Himself

By:

Minister Wayne Beverett

A Leap of Faith – The Spiritual Path

By

Minister Wayne Beverett

Copyright @ 2018, All Rights Reserved
Printed in The United States of America

Published By:

ABM Publications
A division of Andrew Bills Ministries Inc.
PO Box 6811, Orange, CA 92863

ISBN: 978-1-931820-85-1

All scripture quotations, unless otherwise indicated are taken from the King James Version of the Bible, Public Domain. Those marked AMP are from the Amplified Bible, copyright @ 1987, The Updated Edition, by the Zondervan Corporation and the Lockman Foundation, and is used by permission. All rights reserved.

DEDICATION

I dedicate this book to The Family of God: to all of God's people with the sincere desire to be of love and service to their neighbors.

Special thanks go out to Mother Joyce Goodman.
Also, to Bishop Gale and Mother Bernadette Oliver, proprietors of Greater Light Family Church,
1600 West 3rd Street, Santa Ana, CA 92703

Thanks also go to Deacon Mel and Mother Gloria Shanks – God's people who help people who can barely take care of themselves; their love stems from God Himself!
Grace Bethel Missionary Baptist Church,
10250 Cypress Avenue, Riverside, CA 92503

There are so many other people I would like to add to this list but this book is not about them.

Last, but not least, I'm giving special thanks to my own mother, Patsy Beverett who always prayed that God would heal me.

Thank You, Ma.

TABLE OF CONTENTS

	Introduction	7
1	Volume 1	9
2	Volume 2	29
3	Volume 3	55
4	Volume 4	77
5	Volume 5	107
6	Volume 6	143
7	Volume 7	183
8	About The Author	415

Introduction

These writings were written from the pit of my soul!

Never did I flinch or turn away from the truth.

I was devastated when my Maker showed me what I had become.

Alcoholism and drug addiction are spiritual diseases.

God Himself Saved My Life!

In these passages, the reader will read about

the spiritual principles I had to learn to live by.

Every day and night, I had to learn to take steps of positive effort

to seek God and ask for His Guidance to Reconstruct My Life.

Love and service to all people is the reason

for writing these passages.

May the Living God Eternally Bless You!

Philosophical Poems and Points of Views
Timeless Realities

Volume # 1

1. It's So Old It's New

One day I looked into the sun deep and hard, and found love, bold with all colors. It floated with grace and energy as the wind blows. A great many things are conceived from this fascinating energy seed. In this life many things are hidden. That is indeed, true. But if only all people could see what is there, they would stop and think for a year or two. The signs of life are mysterious, yet often simple. It orders the people of the world to mass, and form a righteous temple unto The Most Holy One of Israel.

2. A Future With No Name

In every persons mind, there is this doorway stamped with the word TIME. It is there, in the darkness, waiting for individuals to encompass it. Sometimes when we think, we come up with great ideas; but we seldom put them into action, and they quickly disappear. Past this doorway in as much lies doom or happiness for all of us. But, if your soul is good, and your heart is filled with good intentions, then the passing through this door would be as the air you breath in

3. The Money Fever

Even in the mildest of people, there can be greed, depending upon on how long their hearts bleed. It is a death sentence, this money fever, for it makes you forever a prisoner.

You step on people left and right, yet you fell no grief, for money is in your sights. Through the years this process will continue, and in the end, you'll have nothing else to hold on to.

4. The Soft Mind

When self-dependence dies in a person, that individual is lost from the straight path of his own will. Verily I say, it is open season on his soul. Mobility is as a wrecked car and motivation is that of a far-fetched fantasy, social life is squeezed tight, nothing worthwhile seems reachable anymore. The light of day gleams through, but the height of mind falls through. At midpoint there is a feeling of hopelessness which steers the individual more into unfriendly darkness. Then anxiety sets in to accomplish a one-time dream, but it doesn't last for long; for reality is there to remind him of its pointy thorns.

5. Feelings From Within

When I look deep within my soul, my heart blooms like a gallant red rose; beating forever gently with the intentions of being friendly. When I am in this state, I am like the ocean sending waves in every motion.

These feelings are like love songs that you may keep in the corner of your mind, there for you to play back at any time. There are so many ways to describe these inner feelings, going back and forth with no ending.

6. Alone

In the middle of a crowed city, at work on a coffee break, I am alone, sitting there with feelings of despair. However, I possess the power of the light, and I overcome the rainfall of this negative posture.

Don't under estimate the power of this alone state, for it has gravity as the light, and be not weak in faith; for The Most Holy One of Israel is always there watching and handling with care! But if you happen to be cornered by the dark side, always remember this: The Most Holy One of Israel is the Beginning and the End; so please, never forget this my friends!

7. Galaxy Princess

When a man is traveling at the speed of light, there is no other thought on his mind, but that of his Galaxy Princess, the one woman who activates his emotional systems. When he holds her in his arms he has the power of a million galaxies, and that power is no fantasy, for if they join, the end result is life! Ah, the arrival of a new life is like watching the sun burn like a jewel in the sky, with compliments from The Most High.

8. Unknown Territories

Since from the beginning of mankind's existence, he has come from the simple wheel to an automobile. It's like watching a flower grow from a common seed. To uncover the total scientific soul is like venturing into a black hole to find light; at which, in this point of history, is mostly out of sight! With mankind there is always a risk, and some people use God as a Band-Aid, in order to settle their own wills at justification. There is this thought deep within our minds that pushes forward to exceed time, and in doing this, we may over-shoot and miss, but that would be just one more failure in the light of mankind's behavior.

9. Depression

It's an emotion which all of us possess, which comes to the surface when we failed to do our best. We search our feelings, looking for an answer to the failure at hand which was so disastrous! This emotion will drain you hour after hour, until there is very little mental power. Individuals mustn't let this emotion gravitate them, or it will turn their minds in!

10. Invites

There are forces unseen to the eyes of many; However, they are there, and they revolve all around us, existing in forms of non-dimensional makeups! For years they captivated my attention. I tried to determine what they were in my own understanding. Yet I could only attribute them to The Creator of all things. They seem to react with movement, in accordance to my thoughts, or feelings. They have a state of being beyond that which is known to man! And to me, no harm has come. These forces, and their appearance to me seem to be some kind of communication link attempt. Nevertheless, The Most Holy One of Israel Has His Hand upon this! I classify these shapes of non-dimensional forms as being invitational invites to The Spiritual World! A state of being which we all pass on to.

11. A Broken Heart

When love comes to an end, the bitter feelings turns a person's mind in. The burning pain this person feels doesn't let up easily, for love stands still. They say that love never dies. This is a true statement, for the choice comes from our own eyes. You may cry by day, you may howl by night. But remember, it was your own innocent heart that took the bite!

12. The Mind

The mind is a construction of highly sophisticated doorways of expansions. It's a complex manufacturing center where as the average person couldn't even begin to accelerate into the flawless depths of its sophistication. I speak of the mind rather than the brain, reason for such; For the brain is more readily identified as being functionary rather than in the causative sense, as the mind is considered. To establish a simple thought and to use it on any level is proof in itself, that the mind is a true and powerful source of energy, that in no way can be ignored; For, there are conditions that follow agreements. My comment for this is: The mind is a gift to us all, but only a few of us master this great gift.

13. A Prayer

What happen to me? I'm not happy! I drink from the cup of misery. What I see in the world distresses me! Am I all alone? Is this my fate forever? I'm I at a loss? Understanding eludes me! Why do arrogant people find security? Why do the proud shun the poor? O Most Holy One of Israel, guide me!

Make me an example of Your Love! O God, You Have Uprooted me from my childhood surroundings. You have pulled me from the depths of insanity; however, I still am bound! I still catch myself lusting after certain positions in life. Wanting to be prosperous in the devil's den. O God, it's a constant struggle to keep my thoughts on doing what is right and just! Show Your Will for me, O Most Holy One of Israel! Amen...

14. Usury

Everyone gets used. It doesn't make a difference if you are a cosmetic king, or a fool. The action is deeply rooted in reality; therefore, the act isn't a formality! When people discover they are being used in a negative form, they tarry about with the feelings of humiliation and scorn! At the beginning, the relationship used to be a scientific base ten; but now it has fallen into the isles of sin. The sin of usury, which is in the hearts of many men, has caused people to consider the life style of having no friends!

15. Confessions

O Most Holy One of Israel! I have harbored so much pain that it drove me insane! I am broken in so many ways and I have trouble remembering, there once were happy days. Nothing, or no person can ever fix me and pain and misery constantly confront me! We can't change our past, and I guess that's why I became so sad. There is no peace I can find, for my painful memories always seem to shine! If there is any future happiness for WB, it will come from the hands of The Most Holy!

16. A Holy Touch

Most Holy One of Israel, You are my only hope! Everything else in my life is meaningless to me. I find no pleasure in my work. I am a hired hand, accumulating profits for another man! I have no problem working with my hands; however, my heart tells me to devise a new plan. Each day I seek Your Advice in order to improve the quality of life. Life! That state of being only God Can Bestow – has truly shattered my ego! I will never be the same from this day henceforth, for The Most Holy One of Israel, has changed my life's course.

17. To The Most Holy One of Israel

Thank You Lord, for rescuing me! You pulled me from the depths of insanity. I praise You Lord God, for Rescuing me! If it weren't for Your Love, I don't know where I would be. O thank You Most Holy One, for blessing me! You've made my life worth living, and with Your Tender Mercy, you've Forgiven me all my sins. I was broke, alone, homeless, and scared, and nobody I knew cared! I'm on a mission now, Most Holy One, and I won't stop, even when the world has heard what You've done! I will use the pen; with all of my knowledge and insights, I will make it my life's work

18. The Lone Souls

Being on a level with no company in sight brings about thoughts of peace and long life. In the masses of humanity there are these individuals of a select few, who go through their lives with denounced feelings, yet they possess a positive point of view.

Dealing with the corruptness of society forwards an evil temptation that knows no end. For Individuals who venture into this liars den will forfeit all peace that is known to be in the soul within.

19. Being A Dope

Fifty here, seventy-five there, you're getting high and you don't care! Walking around town with no respect, killing your life with no regrets, what are you going to do when the rent is due, but look silly and like a fool? Stop giving your money to the dope-man! The dope-man!

Can't you see that you're not free? Your mind and body are locked up – gee! So take heed to this little rap, and get your life back on track. Just remember that you lost control, and leave the dope-man the hell alone!

20. A Step Towards Courage

Once again I am alone. However, this time the choice was mine to make. I carried out a decision, that I wouldn't normally take! No – I would hold on to misery, until it let go of me, but this time I trusted in The Most Holy One of Israel.

God Has Been So Gentile and Kind to me that I forgot the tensions of the world, and I dismissed the harmful things from my mind that have been building up through time. I find restraint in myself, where there used to be none! I take being alone in a positive way now, and I don't complain to God about what I've encountered. On The contrary, I thank Him for the guidelines He has set before me! How God, can I ever repay Your for Your Unconditional Love?

19. Metamorphous

I'm changing, I'm not the same person anymore! I feel alone among people. I don't strive for personal gain. I'm lonely, yet I need to be alone! Whenever I look towards The Most Holy One of Israel for guidance, something always seems to pressure me. It's even doing it now, as I write. This force doesn't want me to depend on God! I've noticed its patterns, through my decision to be alone, apart from a bad situation, the pressure has been even greater.

Now I know who, and what it is, and I stay on guard. Satan attacks my mind with mental projections, and he wants to continue to keep me in bondage. However, with each passing day now, I give more of my heart and soul to God, I belong to God. Worldly pleasures are beginning to diminish from my whole being! I can see a treasure that has no measure; However, I must obey The Most Holy One of Israel, through and through, no matter what!

20. Love Conquers All

My time is limited here on earth. O how I wasted time, valuable time. I am of Black and Indian ancestry, struggling in The United States of America, a country that is envied by the whole world, yet day-by-day I must face racial prejudice. On the job, in the streets, even at leisure! No more time will I waste. No more of myself will I waste. As of this day (8/23/98) I will abandon myself efforts to hate. Love conquers all. Oh thank you, Most Holy One of Israel, for reaching my mind- just to be able to see little sparrows play takes me away from the cruelties of other's actions. It's not my white brothers and sisters fault about how they were taught to think. Nor should it be the intent of people of color to hate them! Love conquers all. Abandon yourself to The Most Holy One of Israel and you will see and feel what I have. Don't waste your life and beauty on the hating of others. God is the beginning and the end. So please never forget this my friends. And even if you're not my friends, I will still hold out my hand in friendship. Nothing is more powerful than the love each and every person is capable of. O, thank you God! You, and only You God, Have Truly Set me free!

21. An Unconditional Sharing

There is no compromise left in my mind. My heart is closed to worldly things, material things always pass away, and my flesh is included on the list. However, my soul will live forever. We are all made in God's Image, and that part that we call the soul is the self, the immortal makeup! Yea we're going to exist forever, and while we live, we determine our fates! I will try not to be sad anymore, for Jesus Christ Said, "Take upon yourselves my yoke, and my burden is light". I write these things for the people who are left here after me! Oh I earnestly hope that people invest in The Most Holy One of Israel, opposed to worldly things! God will never disappoint you, however, The Prince of Darkness, will forever keep you in pain and distress, for God has already Judged his cruel heart, and Satan wants each and every one of us to be afflicted, right along with himself. Oh please, people of earth, my fellow brothers and sisters, turn your hearts to God, for He Loves us so much He Gave us His Only Begotten Son, so that we may live life more abundantly.

22. Innocence

There once was a young man who thought he had the master plan on how to live, and enjoy life! O, how quickly he was caused to stumble and fall! Over, and over again he would find himself to be a failure; However, he would pull himself together and start down a new path. One day he realized that he wasn't young anymore, and that his old ways of thinking never worked for him, no matter what path he took! So he became angry, and frustrated at God, for his own mistakes, and on the inside he never grew up! All his soft spots became hard, and all the people who knew him lost respect for him, but he didn't allow his heart to become hard, and that was his saving grace, though he knew it not. However, God uncovered his protected place! Pain was the order, for many months, but now the little boy inside has begun to grow up!

23. Bits and Pieces

There is a constant need to express myself, and I do it through my writings, expecting no fame, or glory! There are feelings that I've locked away inside of me, but now I want to write them down, and share them with my brothers and sisters, who live this life with me. Maybe one day, if I am allowed, I can put them all together, to form a book. But for right now, it feels good to rid my heart of this heavy weight!

I never know beforehand what I'm going to write about. I just open the doors to my heart, and it all starts to come out! I try to touch as many people as I can. That's my way of lending a helping hand! There are so many stories in the heart of WB, and I will do my best to express them, for all the world to see!

24. Realizing My Call

I see so much pain in the faces of my brothers and sisters who live this life with me that it has made me angry. However, I must not run from them. God has placed me in this situation for a reason, and I must use all of my abilities to help these people, who are me. Many of them don't even have a clue that they are in grave danger; however, I was given Spiritual Insights long ago from The Most Holy One of Israel. These Spiritual Insights I must now use! But before God Changed my heart, I didn't have a clue to why God gave me these Spiritual Insights. I couldn't use them even if I wanted to. O, how The Most Holy One of Israel works in mysterious ways! With each passing day now, God prepares me for this journey of helping others. I am His Servant, and He is my God, and there is no request I can deny Him! Whatever pleases God, makes me smile, and at the same time makes me cry. There is nothing in this life that has made me react in this way. I love You Most Holy One of Israel

25. Here Today, Gone Tomorrow

Happiness is a fleeting thing to me. It took a long time for me to accept this; however, happiness has its place. I don't discourage people in their search for happiness, but for me my search has ended. I pray for happiness for others, for they need it so desperately. When I look into their eyes it breaks my heart to see them so unhappy, so I pray to God and Jesus to send them some relief to their present unhappiness! But as for me, happiness is a fleeting thing, and trying to hold on to happiness always made me unhappy! So, I don't try and lock happiness up, and, if happiness comes to me - well that's a good thing, And if it doesn't, I'll try not to cry. Happiness is something that God Himself bestows, and whomever possesses happiness should consider themselves blessed.

26. Sending Help

We don't know how to live righteously. O Most Holy One of Israel, please God, change our hearts, cancel our selfish desires, for there is nothing You can't do! God, without Your Perfect Protection, Provisions, and Guidance, life is not worth living! I myself would rather have You take the breath of life from me; for I would have no good things to share with anyone. There it is... the key to living a righteous life. One must not think solely of one's self, but rather help as many people as possible find The Light, and That Light is The Most Holy One of Israel! I implore you, brothers and sisters, to put your trust in God, and leave it there! Have no doubt in the decision you've made, and in a very short time you will be amazed, on how your thinking has changed! You'll come to find yourself praying and depending on God for what you need in this life, rather than depending on people, places, and things. You'll receive what you ask for, as long as you doubt not, and let not evil stand in your path! I know this to be true, for God Has Sent me to tell you. May God keep, and bless you...

27. Searching and Finding

O most Holy One of Israel, I can never repay You for Your Unconditional Love; however, maybe I can make You smile by sharing with my brothers and sisters what You've Freely Given to me...no charge! I thought about how I could be of service to You, and You've Touched my thoughts with tears. You had me look at the poor condition of others, and I couldn't help but cry! Through the tears I found a smile, for I realized. Lord God, what You were revealing to me: "Give, as I Have Freely Given to you, and they will reap as you've reaped, depending upon the sincerity of their hearts".

28. Humbled Out!

I've been a fool, and I've been a fool for the majority of my life! I've put my trust in people, places, and things that possessed no power of goodness whatsoever! I sit here and write, yet I have an angry look upon my face, for I've come to realize that I've been a fool for a very long time, and I should have died, physically, a long time ago!

My life was wretched, and I am ashamed of myself, for I've wasted so many good things! I don't like to look at my past, but I must; for, it's a constant reminder to me, that I should be physically dead. However, God Has Shown Mercy to me, and now I live under His Grace. For the first time in my adult life, I am truly alive, with a wonderful spirit, and a sincere heart! All restored to me, by The Most Holy One of Israel.

29. Spirits on The Shelf

A walking dead man is what I used to be; for I filled my body with drugs and alcohol constantly! Thinking I was strong and popular amongst my peers, I kept right on drinking and using other drugs for many years. This drinking and using other drugs became my life, and each day became filled with stress and strife! I had no clue, to what drug and alcohol made me do! The constant use of drugs and alcohol blocked The Light of God's Spirit from me, and I wasn't conscious of it! I was on the road to destruction; however, The Most Holy One of Israel, put a detour sign on that road, and I took it! All I knew was that I was in pain, and my pain relievers weren't working anymore! All that I had done and all that I had become all hit me at once, and I was devastated! There was nowhere to go, but to God's Door! So I knocked, and God let me in, and He showed me all my faults, and I cried bitterly, and God Comforted me, yet (and) He showed me a way out of my pain. Ironically, it involved more pain; however, I began to see change, And some of my pain turned to gain, yet, I couldn't take the credit, though I wanted to. I realized through my recent humiliation, that, if I were to get cocky again, I would cancel out all my gains and joy.

30. Time That's Not Mine

Time is something that I don't worry about anymore. Why should I? What matters to me are my actions in Time! I am an example of God's Love, and to personally know this is truly wonderful! I stop, and I use time in the best way I know how, and that way is to listen to God! Time is God's to prolong, or to interrupt, so I don't waste the time God Is Allowing me! I wasn't always like this; I used to be an ungrateful person, sometimes appreciating what was given to me, but always wanting more! The Most Holy One of Israel is Truly Changing my heart, and I love God more than my own life! So why should I worry about time?

31. Off on a Tangent

"Monkey see, monkey do". That was truly me, for I hardly ever used the tools that God Had Given me. I always thought that something on the outside would fix my problems on the inside. O, how truly a monkey I really was! I went from "Monkey see, monkey do," to " Do monkey, do"! And one day I realized I didn't know what the hell I was doing, short of killing myself! It took eighteen years to reach this truth.

I was devastated, and in shock, for I realized I was inches away from death, and I would have no respect from my peers, or family members! I was a demoralized person, with only God to look to for help, and The Most Holy One of Israel, was the beginning of my recovery, from my "monkey see, monkey do" mentality.

32. On The Watch

I catch The Lord Winking at me more and more these days, and in my heart I know why! I've abandoned my old ways of livings, and I seek The Kingdom of God! The enemy, however, earnestly seeks to destroy my confidence and faith in The Most Holy One of Israel! Satan projects thoughts to my mind, in order to deter me from worshipping The Most Holy One of Israel! My Lord Has Set Before me the weapons I need, to protect myself, and I am not hesitant to use them today! I stand, and I watch, and I wait on You Most Holy One of Israel, and if You Call me from this world before You Return, Well, so be it.

33. Accepting Facts

We all want things to stay the same; however, they don't, and we don't, and many times it hurts so bad to face the fact that we must move on! The key is we're alive with soul, and we must experience things and then move on. O, Most Holy One of Israel, I Your Servant, can accept this today; however, for a very long time I couldn't. I couldn't even see the reality of it, let alone accept it!

As I write, tears are running down my face, for I remember some people, places, and things I wanted to hold on to, but I couldn't! I must have courage, and live this life sober and free of all mind altering drugs. O, Most Holy One of Israel, I owe it to You to experience the rest of my life sober, and free of all mind altering drugs. Whatever the outcome may be, so be it. God, You are my rock, and most happy place that I have connected to. Please God, never leave me.

34. A Miracle in The Making

As I look into people's faces today, I can see pain, I can see doubt, I can see confusion, and my dear brothers and sisters this is no illusion! O, how I wish I could cure everyone, including myself, but I can't. I'm just an ex- drunk fella who sincerely knocked on God's door, broken and crushed, and The Most Holy Spirit, sent me to a group of people, who helped to pick me up, and I kept drinking from their cup! Now I too play a part in helping people make a brand new start. O, God, You' re the real power, and I wish I could make more people see all the wonderful things, You've Done for me. Maybe one day I will get my wish, and then more people can enjoy Your Waiting Gifts.

35. Truth Being Revealed

God, I never knew what faith, or trust was, until I sincerely asked You, for help. O, sure, I knew what the dictionary stated about them, but I never found any evidence in people, places, or things, only an illusion thereof! O, God, You Have Made my decisions much easier today, and most of the time You Fill me with joy. I feel like a little boy again, and it's Christmas time! O, how my face just shines with a glow, and my soul is so happy to know that it's not an illusion. I've put my trust in You, and You've Delivered to me whatever I needed, at my point of need. Now I live by faith, in You, and not, by what I physically see! O, Most Holy One of Israel, You're Truly Changing my whole life – and now I can honestly say to people that there is a God, and He is Alive and Well, and I trust and love God, with all my heart, and all my soul, and all my strength, all of which God Himself, Has Restored to me without a blemish!

36. Trusting Your Faith in God

No one to share my life with yet, and I am sad and lonely. My mind is warped, and I must function in a world whose primary concerns are dollars and cents! I must stop, and adjust, and put to one side pleasures and lust! My faith in God, is what I must protect; for if I don't – again I will become like all the rest, swollen in ego, and damned, in all dealing. What tricky things, these powerful feelings! To those people out there who are like me, I must say this: We have two powerful friends. One is God, and the other is Jesus, and they made a vow, to never leave us! So consider Them the next time discomfort confronts you and pray to Them, and They Will Extract your pain from you. This is a promise.

37. Holy Business

The beauties I see are infinite, O, Most Holy One of Israel. Your Loving Kindness Amazes me, for You Continuously Provide for all of Your Living Creatures, and it ruptures my heart with joy! When I think of You, God, You Make me smile and cry, at the same time! Feelings of joy and concern enter my heart: Joy, for all of Your Wonderful Gifts; and concern for my brothers and sisters, who can't see, or feel what I do.

I want so badly for them to recognize and have a share in all of Your Beauties and Gifts; however, this miscommunication has been going on long before I was born, and probably will go on long after You Take the breath of life away from me.

Nevertheless, I must ask this: Please, God, Allow me to reach, at least some of them, by way of Your Power and Strength through me. I earnestly want to help; nothing would make me more happier, as far as I can see, than to accomplish this. Thank You, God, and Jesus, and Holy Ghost.

38. Looking Inward

I'm thirty-five years old; however, emotionally, I might be fifteen and it feels like a dream, but I'm not dreaming. You see, that's what drinking alcohol and using mind altering drugs actually did to me, not to forget to mention it almost killed me! Now here I stand, half of a man, trying most earnestly to grow up, and it's not an easy task; for each night my emotions drive me mad! I cry and I pray, and God Clears my heart, so that I can make it through another sober and drug free day. I know this is God's Gift to me, to live one day to the next sober and mind altering drug free! I never thought it possible, but here I am, building on becoming a complete and stable man. I don't regret the past, nor do I pry into the future. I just live one day at a time, with God as my Ruler!

39. A Further Grounding

With each passing day, O Most Holy of Israel, I'm learning tolerance and I'm experiencing a variety of life. The concept of live and let live enters my heart, and the thoughts of what's in it for me are becoming lesser, and lesser, on my part! How I respond to my brothers and sisters amazes even me, for I never thought I could venture into this peaceful state of being. Even when confronted with vile behavior, I think of God, and God, Gives me a new angle of tolerance that steers my mind away from hostile intent. The more I practice these principles, the more wise and peaceful I become. O, what a joy it is for me to experience life in this way now! All thanks to You, Most Holy One of Israel. Please never leave me God, I would rather die!

40. Putting on The Yoke of Jesus

O, Jesus, Your Love Amazes me, and when troubles come, You Make Things Clear for me to see! O, I am in limbo. I have left my former life behind, and new beginning I seek to find; however, You Remind me not to rush, but take my time! With each passing day I awake to Your Love, which never passes away. Lord Your Spirit Makes my heart shine, and I am learning from Your Teachings how to be friendly and kind. O, Most Holy One of Israel, I thank You, for Your Son Jesus Christ, Who Unselfishly Sacrificed His Life, so that we, Your Children, could live life more abundantly! So now, I live for Jesus Christ, Your Most Holy Son. I dedicate my life to be His Servant now, and in the everlasting life to come. So please help me God!

41. A New Gift

Joy, and more joy fills my life these days, and I am happy. Happiness, that fleeting thing that never used to stay put in my life, has now somehow become a member of my body! My face is seldom without a smile, for I enjoy these days, instead of trying to analyze them. I see love everywhere, and I go through my days without a care! I have a spiritual glow, one that only God can bestow. And in my nights there is no stress, or strife, only tiredness from my happy days. There are peaceful days now, all of which The Most Holy One of Israel Is Allowing me to enjoy. I praise God, all the day long, with sweet and meaningful songs... Songs of Praise. Praise be to God, for all my days and nights, happy, or not.

42. A New Experience

I was listening to silence, before the break of daylight, before the songs of birds, it brought me to a new level of consciousness. A place where I really felt peace for the first time, and silence was its partner. However, as the day progressed, the peace left, and silence was unheard of! Yes, the sounds of life were emerging once again, in a new day that God Is Allowing! And now I think to myself, what part must I play in this wondrous day? I didn't have to think long, for what pleasures me is to praise God, all the day long! I don't keep the love of God a secret, and in turn God Fills my heart with joy and hope. Hope that my brothers and sisters will ask me why I'm so joyous. And I'll get to tell them with a smile that it was, and is God, Who Has Changed and Turned my life around! Praise be to The Most Holy One of Israel - My best friend!

Volume - # 2

1. Thank You, Heavenly Father

Dear Most Holy One of Israel, Your Sweet Spirit, Which Has Descended, upon me, Has Caused me to Awaken to a brand new way of living and thinking. O, God, not a day goes by now, without my asking for Your Protection, Provisions and Guidance. Not a day goes by now, without my asking for strength, so I may be ready, to help my neighbors. Not a day goes, by now, without my seeking Your Face and Your Kingdom. O. God I thank You for Showing me my disease straight up and clear, for it is You God, Whom I fear. O, God, I thank You for my Most Holy Brother Jesus Christ, Who Unselfishly Sacrificed His Life, so that we Your Children, could continue to have life, and to live it more abundantly! O, God, may praise, peace and loyalty from Your Children who love You, be upon You...

2. The Father of Deception

God, Jesus, and The Holy Ghost, live in me today and the devil and none of his demons have power over what I do, or say! No alcohol and no street drugs of any kind enter into my holy temple, for my soul welcomes none of these evils! The Lord of All Creation, Has Saturated my soul with His Spirit, I am now filled with joy for all to see, feel, hear and enjoy! However, there are days when the devil and some of his demons stick right by my side and they try their best to temp me to backslide, and when they can't persuade me, they move into an unsuspecting soul, who in turn tries to upset me. Before God, Lived in me that tactic used to work, but now I understand how the devil and his demons use the unsuspecting man, or woman. Now I know why Jesus Christ, Said, " to love your enemies", for many men and woman are truly unaware of what is moving their souls. And when the damage has been done some realize they have been deceived, and the devil and his demons sit back, and laugh. So pitiful you are Satan, and all of your followers and I am not afraid to tell the people in the world! I know who Loves, Cares and Protects me.

3. An Observance

As I Your Servant God have life in Your Creation, I sit, and I watch Your Children, some tall, some short, some black, some white, all of whom are just the mere physical states that I've just described, but as Your Spirit Moves me, and I look closer, I can see a great many other detailed beauties; however, the immediate joy I find is in the littles ones O, God! When I look into their eyes, they make me smile so; for I see You God so clearly, and they see You, God, in me, with the exchanges in glances, and many of them smile back. However, I lose hope not in my neighbors, perhaps one day they will turn from their worldly concerns, and seek Your Face God, and Your Kingdom. O, God, it's You, Who Truly Turns the heart and Fills the soul, with everlasting joy! O, God, may You, continue to Protect and Guide Your Children who sincerely seek Your Face, and Your Kingdom! May peace, loyalty and thanks giving be upon The Holy God,...

4. A Prelude to Truth

Separation of Church and State has caused this country to

become a disease – infested place! Printed on our money you will find "In God, We Trust"; however, in many of our trusted officials' hearts lies evil intent and Satan's lusts! The spirit of the devil uses trickery to confuse our trusted officials and with assurance he works hard on the selfish man. Expansion of lies and mistrust is the vehicle Satan uses to disrupt and confuse God's Children on a worldwide scale! But don't worry, for all good and evil things will be brought out into The Light at the proper time, and God's Children, who have courage will expose and talk about Satan's deceit, without fear, of their lives; fore they have faith, that Jesus Christ, will protect them and give them everlasting life, no matter the outcome. Now the fun starts, for the truth will be told again, by way of the mouth and the pen. And I will truly be a part of this no fear expanse, coming to you from The Most Holy Spirit.

5. Undiscovered Truth

Here I sit in a shopping mall filled with thousands of Your Children, yet Most Holy One of Israel, I feel none of Your Spirit manifested, in them! As I observe, I see not even a spiritual glow, of You, and this upsets me! Tears of disappointment fill my eyes; however, Your Spirit feels to me that I shouldn't be at all surprised.

Nevertheless, this reality has captured my attention, yet I dare not wish to manufacture a resentment, but rather understand that this is the results of the self-orientated man! Now I must go out from here and realize that this self- orientation is bigger and vaster, than I ever imagined. O, God, I pray that You Make me More than just a beacon of light, for the darkness overshadows whatever light You Already Allow me to emit. O, God, I earnestly want my neighbors to receive Your Spirit; however, I must remember that piercing the mind, the heart, and eventually the soul is an ongoing process, so I myself must practice patience.

6. God's Glory

The Glory of God, is a splendor of excellence that God Himself, Has Allowed me to see. It dwells within my soul, and it accompanies my very sight! O, how I delight, when I see God's Light! Its rotating energy burns in my mind's eye, and never flickers out! In all of what I see, I am truly blessed, for The Most Holy One of Israel Has Granted me peace of mind, and spiritual rest. I have never received a gift which holds this much honor, and no man, or woman can ever match it! For the gift of life and spiritual insight no one can give except our God.

7. Reality up Close

What stops me from being continuously happy? People, places, or things always become obstacles, or irritants to me. I can never get enough of what I think I need to make me happy! O, what a sad reality this is for me! However, I was blessed by God to be able to acquire knowledge in order to release myself of these fears, one day at a time.

You see I'm an alcoholic; and I have the disease of alcoholism, It's an ongoing disease that has no physical cure, lest the constant dependence upon God. We must place God first in our lives, and turn our self will over to God's Care. This is the only peace of mind that I've found. I've noticed by me placing God's Will first in my life, I've become more stable in my life than alcoholics and drug addicts that don't.

For who is more powerful than God? Sometimes I become sad, and think to myself, this isn't fair, and then I start to despair; however, I then remember I am only what God Allows me to be anyway. Yet, that doesn't take away the reality of being different from other people.

8. The Intangible Help

May I lend a helping hand to my fellow man, with the words that I am about to write. We as alcoholics have a blind spot in our minds which comes to the surface when we entertain the thought of having a drink. The only defense for us is God: He Interrupts what we think with just the mere thought of His Being.

As a real alcoholic I know this to be true, for I've experienced insane thoughts. I am no expert, and I have no college degrees, but I can surely tell you that God Does Intervene. So the next time you contemplate on having a drink, just consider God's Goodness, and He will surely change the way you think!

9. A Joyful Note

God, You are my rock, and I am forever thankful to You for my present spot. May I never stray away, but always continue to meditate and pray. I never knew who, or what I was, until I got that nudge from the judge! O, how Mysterious Lord God You truly are, and I find this out the more I seek You and continue to meditate and pray. And when I pray, I can't stop the tears, for it is

You God Who Have Done Away with all of my fears. And now a smile shows up as the tears run, for in my heart I am having so much fun. However, there is a lot of sadness in my past, but today I don't care; for God Is The Past Cleaner, The Joy Giver, and The Mind Fixer. And guess what ? I don't have to drink liquor!

10. Being Grateful

To obey The Will of God, is this man's main concern, and on the inside I am so joyous and thankful, for what I've already learned! When God, awakens me to another day, the first thing I do is to hit my knees and pray. I thank God, for His Loving Kindness and Patience He Has Shown unto me; for I was so arrogant and noncaring in my personality! However, some of my defects still remain, but one thing is for sure: I am no longer insane. I don't know what the next day holds for me, but I will continue to pray, and thank God for the gift of sobriety.

11. Asking For Help to Help

O how can I help my Lord Jesus Christ today? Your Servant, eagerly seeks his position of service. O Jesus, I pray that I am ready on any given night, or day fore I never know what, or whom, You Will Send my way! I am forever grateful, for as I sit and search my heart, I can find in it no evil parts. And I am honestly thankful to know that You 've Given me my spiritual glow. May I continue to help my neighbors recognize and appreciate Your Loving Grace! Helping others seems to be always on my mind, and thinking like this isn't a waste of time! I feel comfortable when I think in this way, so please Jesus, continue to help me to help others find Your Peaceful and Joyful Ways.

12. The Goodness of God

I have nothing to say, lest it be to my alcoholic brothers and sisters that I might meet throughout the course of a day! I have nothing to give, lest it be of the story and glory of the new sober and mind altering drug free life that I now live. I have nothing to share, lest it be the message of God's Care! I have nothing to lose, fore it was God, Who Saved this fool! I have nothing but tears, which I've stored up over many years. And now God Has Shown me the beauty of life, and I don't want to die, so I will face my feelings, and continue to cry! I don't know how long this crying will go on, but through my tears I've become happy, joyous, and free, and all credit and thanks goes to God, Almighty.

13. Unwanted Yesterdays

For a very long time I lived with a twisted mind, and from day to day I possessed a broken heart, and on the inside there was a bottomless hole, that was my soul! I was in so much pain from my worldly dealings that I learned to use alcohol and mind altering drugs, to numb those bad feelings.

One day my pain relievers lost all their strength, and I could no longer escape from the realities of life, no matter how much I used mind altering drugs and alcohol to help me fight. At this I was confused, and demoralized, with no person around who cared, or loved me. I was a used- up broken person, whom no one had any use for! Yet The Most Holy One of Israel Didn't See It

My Way, and God Gave me some Comfort and Hope, and then The Most Holy Spirit Sent me to a fellowship of people who truly knew what was wrong with me. They loved me unconditionally unto this very day! "O how I now appreciate, and want more of these days!"

14. A Testament

Liberty, joy, and serenity for all is offered within the walls of God's Fellowship. Love, understanding and the absorption of loneliness and hate- these are our character traits. Our main endeavor is to obey God's Will forever! For its God, Who Grants us Liberty, Joy, and Serenity. We as recovering alcoholics and drug addicts are a strong force, when we walk God's Course; however, we are guaranteed pain, misery, and stress, if we don't practice God's Loving Steps. There are many of us, who are members in many groups, who can testify positively, that this statement is the truth.

15. What I See

May You please continue to help us Lord God. May You Help us to forget self. May You Show us how to concentrate our energies in regard to helping someone else. We are basically good people, at least we try to be. O please help us God, to be what You Made us to be. O there is so much pain, in Wayne as I try to write this, for I know the beauty and joy of Your Gifts! And on the inside I know this joy isn't just for me; it's available to all who put in the effort, to seek Thee!

16. Fuzzy Visions

Things to me are never as they seem, and facing reality is like trying to interpret a dream! In trying to formulate the meaning of things, I would always find myself in a mental ditch; however, now when I ask for God's Help, I receive my needed answers kind of quick! I can remember many times and many situations when I didn't ask for God's, or anyone's help, and I would get drunk and high, and later be confused about the way I felt.

I never really took the time to stop and discover I was destroying my life! But, on the contrary, I did get the chance, and I did discover I was destroying my God Given Life, and now I can honestly say that the use and abuse of alcohol and mind altering drugs has truly distorted my life, in many damaging ways!

17. The Subtle Enemy

Alcoholism is a thing- something I dare not forget; it's my foe, and I must stay conscious of its unsuspecting blows. It attacks all areas of my being with relentless pressure, and it never subsides, for alcoholism is out to get you! Alcoholism isn't prejudice in any way, it will attack the young, or the old, on any given night, or day. Alcoholism has my undivided attention, fore it has killed many members of my family, and now all I can do is miss them... Powerful this alcoholism is; however, God, Has More Power, and in me, God Lives! So now my main endeavor must be to practice The Attributes of God's Loving Spirit, and stay spiritually fit; for King Alcoholism patiently waits, for me to slip!

18. Faces to Face

There's no getting around my tears, when I sit and write about my drinking alcohol and mind altering drug use years! For now my conscious is free, and it's no longer numbed by my drinking alcohol and mind altering drug sprees. What I must face and accept breaks my heart; however, for any alcoholic, or drug addict, in recovery there is no skipping these tender parts! So onward we alcoholics and drug addicts must trudge, if we're to learn from God's Love! Unending faith in God must come from within, if we alcoholics and drug addicts are ever to accept not drinking alcohol, or using any mind altering drugs ever again. Soundness of our emotions, bodies, souls and minds will be our rewards; however, in order to maintain its strength we must continue to obey God's Will for our lives and to be of love and service to all people for the rest of our lives.

19. A Never- Ending Gift

Staying humble isn't a problem for me, for when I look back at my last year of drinking alcohol, and using mind altering drugs I am ashamed of what my mind reveals to me! Immediately the right-size sets in, and being ungrateful starts to leave my conscious thoughts. For many years this alcoholic, drug addict was very selfish; however, now in my sober mind I can't bear the thoughts of my past actions! O thank You God for Bringing me out of my selfish self, for I truly know that I couldn't have accomplished this without Your Help! Forever grateful this alcoholic will be, for each new twenty-four hours I have the chance to be sober and mind altering drug free.

20. Where to go From Here

O God, I Your Servant am confused, I feel so different from my neighbors, even my alcoholic and drug addict brothers and sisters of whom I am a part of. O God, please reveal to me what this feeling means. Just when I feel a part of, I get this strong feeling of separateness - not in being alcoholic, but separate in spirit-and I can see and feel the difference in me compared to them; however, I wish not to offend any of them. Please help me God how to be, and respond, for I don't know how! I wish never to hurt them! Your Will, not mine be done... So help me God!

21. The Truth Will Set You Free

There is no going back for me; the truth has been shown, and I am a respecter of the truth. I always was, and I always will be an alcoholic; however, the difference now is that I know it, whereas before The Lord God, Opened my eyes, there was nothing to know! Are you kidding me?

I was just like you. I loved to drink alcohol, and every weekend I partied, until at least one, or two. And I thanked God, what I could remember, for each new 24; however, I never knew I was an Alcoholic, in my inner core! Now finding out that I am an alcoholic, who in turn have a responsibility, not to drink any alcohol; for I can in danger myself, and others, has truly brought my life to a halt! By constantly practicing The Attributes of My Creator, I've come to find peace of mind, joy in in my soul, and no long periods of commotion in my emotions.

The best part is I've been blessed with an unselfish heart-all straight results from not picking up the first drink of alcohol, or any mind altering drug, coupled with practicing love and service to all people. These actions have released me from all of my previous burdens.

22. Another Admission

O God, may You continue to show me how to love, how to care, and how to give freely to others whatever is in my power to give. I have found true joy and happiness in these areas that I can't explain! Now here come the tears; there's no getting around them, no matter how hard I try not to cry! But it's okay, it's wonderful today, for the tears are tears of joy and happiness. O thank You, God, for these beautiful experiences-ones which I would have never discovered, if it had not been for the Love and Patience that You 've Shown to me! O God, my soul calls for more of this Love I've received, by practicing Your Character Traits, and I am eager to give away what is truly Yours! O God, Your Love Has Consumed me and now I am willingly Your Property, through all eternity.

23. A Noticed Change

O God, I thank You for releasing me from the bondage of self; however, now I must be really careful, not to point my finger at someone else. O God, may You continue to help me grow, for the more clean and sober time I accumulate, the more You Make me realize, how little about life I do know! I spent so much time trying not to confront life's ills, by using mind altering drugs, and drinking alcohol, that its effects have scrambled my emotions, and distorted my thinking. I'm still kind of mixed up; however, I'm not a total waste, and I receive new information, every time I seek God's Face! And when I use what You Provide, I am amazed and joyful, on the inside, and on the outside joy shows itself so much that people are beginning to ask me "What's up?"

24. Recycling The Gift

Holy Strength is what I need, in order to battle my alcoholic disease: Faith and trust in God, is my only psychological defense, against this mental monster. Alcoholism is on the attack each and every day, and I dare not sleep, and think that I am at any point okay! Alcoholism is a subtle foe, and it progresses with me as I continue to grow! However, I have a defender, who goes by the title, of being called God, and He Protects me, as long as I continue to seek Him, and trust Him. For me this is the easier, softer way, for without God's Plan, it would be just a short time before the disease of alcoholism would kill me! I now thank God, for each and every sober, and mind altering drug free day; for as God, Strengthens me, I get the chance to help others find the easier, softer way!

25. Back on Course

O God, may You, burn brightly in my life, with each passing day; may I experience Your Glory, in more fulfilling ways. I am now conscious of my holy duty, which took total surrender on my part. No more was I to depend on people, places, and things, and I must say, surrender wasn't an easy task. However, God, it was You, Who Changed the course of my life, and for the first time in my life, I was truly able to see what was standing in front of me.

What I saw angered me, for there was the real truth right in front of me. I lost the ability to control my alcohol consumption, and my mind altering drug use, and my life become a wreck because of it! Clear as day, God, Revealed the subtle truth to me, and now there was the big question in front of me, what to do about it? Although I was filled with anger, and seeing red, I kept on seeking God, and eventually God, Granted me serenity from my screwed up head! Now life is wonderful, and I am glad to be sober, and mind altering drug free, the way I believe God, wanted me to be.

26. The Constant Constancy

A chance to live a meaningful life has been laid out before me, and today and every day, I ask The Great Giver God, to please continue to help me! I've been given all the tools I need, to prosper, and succeed; however, I mustn't let these tools collect dust, or they soon will begin to rust like metal. I must kept them oiled, and in perfect working condition, always ready to handle any one of life's missions! A true gift I've received, and I thank God, every day for His Unselfish Generous Deeds! When I think about God, thoughts of helping others, enters my heart; for it's God, Who Dismisses my selfish thoughts!

27. From One to Many

May I send out this prayer to all those alcoholics and drug addicts, who are still in bondage, and are out there. If you are lonely and in fear, may God Whisper Sweet Recovery in your ears. My friends you have a spiritual malady that no one can fix; and how I received help, is when I sincerely asked God, to repair it. And if sincerity flows within your heart, you will experience a noticeable change, right from the start! O I do know what I am expressing here; for the disease of alcoholism and drug addiction has robbed me of my social respect, and nearly killed me many times, without a single doubt in my now joyful heart! So to all my neighbors who are still spiritual sick and come across this page, never forget that it's God Almighty, Who Has The Power to Save!

28. Things to Remember

Life is wonderful, life is a blessing, so be wise in heart, not to shun life's lessons. With every cause there is an effect, so observe the effect, and take notice of the results. Life is a process, life is a struggle; however, taking the fast track will produce heartaches and trouble.

Make heart determined decisions and always put forth your best, give freely of what you find and God Will Grant you spiritual rest! God Is The Observer of everything we do, so be wise, and know that God Is Watching You! Always be true to yourself, even if the truth hurts, for remember, in receiving pain, there is always the underlying gift of gain.

29. Lifting of The Fog

With the dawning of a new day, I am thankful and grateful, for I can truly say that I've been blessed again with the opportunity to live another day sober and free from any mind altering drug use! I've been granted freedom, from the compulsion to drink alcohol, or use any mind altering drugs. Now for the first time in my adult life I can clearly think. The obsessions of my mind still remain; however, by praying to God, every day He Grants me the power and courage to change! I've truly found my treasure trove and its beauties and benefits are endless! O my friends, it's God Who Have Performed these miracles in me; which will always be a part of me. So please take to heart the reality of God's Goodness, and apply this message to your soul, so that you may find your own treasure trove!

30. Treat Yourself

The Good Lord Gives, and The Good Lord Takes Away, and it's up to you my friends what The Good Lord Will Give, or Take Away from you today! God Has No Respect of person; for we are only men, just representing a small part of His Awesome Universe! Yes, I am one of His Servants, and I place God in His Rightful Position in my being! No spiritual being is more powerful than God Himself! So watch out for trickery and make way for fools; side step them both, and always practice for yourselves God's Laws and Rules! Treat yourself, don't defeat yourself!

31. A Remedy

Living life in the recovery process for alcoholics and drug addicts aren't easy roads for us to hoe. There are times when we feel like we haven't moved an inch! Self-pity takes over what we think, and if our spiritual progress is low we may contemplate drinking alcohol, or use other mind altering drugs. Obsessions of our minds are our major enemy, and this fact must be dealt with if we are to progress in God's Recovery Process. We Alcoholics and Drug

Addicts are different from our neighbors in many respects; however, we have a chance to lead fulfilling lives if we constantly seek out The Attributes from God Himself, and proceed to live by them. We must develop a willingness to believe there is an all-powerful God, and trust His Will for our lives, lest we'll perish from the disease of Alcoholism, and Drug Addiction!

32. What You See is Real

When You look into my eyes you may be startled by what you see! No, your eyes aren't playing tricks on you; for it was The Light of God that you did see! Go ahead - take another look, and you'll find that The Light still remains, for The Glory of God Has Taken the place of alcohol, cigarettes, marijuana, and cocaine! And with each moment of realized time I can feel God at Work, as He Continues to Heal my warped mind! One day maybe all you will see from me is God's Light, and if that happens I know God Will Take me from this life.

33. Battles to Fight – A War to Win

O Spirit of God, please descend upon Your Servant, and reveal to him what Your Desires are for his life! Order my steps, O Most Holy One of Israel, Heal me, Guide me. Father, I pray order my steps in Your Way! Jesus, joy does come in the morning; however, we have to hold on, and be strong, and make due with whatever The Most Holy One of Israel Provides us! O within each day I try my best to turn over to God my worldly lusts, for I find no lasting value in them now, for I live my life sober and free of any mind altering drugs. My soul longs to be with God; however, my warped mind tries desperately to intervene and destroy my hopes and spiritual dreams. But I am glad to say that my heart and soul are winning out over may warped mind with each passing day.

34. Documented Reality

The mind of a drunkard is an open wound that never begins the process of healing! The drunkard never realizes his malady, although he senses a keen difference, when he compares himself to the rest of the world. This may go on for years, with the drunkard suffering from countless forms of frustrations and fears! And the world pities the drunkard not, for others don't understand, or realize that it's a spiritual disease he's got! However, there is relief from his spiritual sickness, and the first step to recovery starts with God Almighty! From day one of recovery, and for the rest of the ex-drunkard's life, he will have to positively communicate with God daily, or risk the return to his former miserable life!

35. To Obey, and Serve...

As a child cries, God, You've been there to comfort me, as a boy wanted and never received, God, You've been there to console me, and as I continue at times to feel pain, God, You Still Have Plenty of Patients, for I Your Servant. Dear God, a billion thank-you's from me could never ever be enough to equal the Love and Generosity You've Shown unto me. God, You Gave me life-You're my Perfect Protector, Provider, and Guider, and I am Your Servant forever.

There's nothing in this life that's more important than to obey and serve You Lord God! God, You've Saved me, from physical death many times; however, I never knew it at those times; for I was so filled with the spirit of drunkenness, I couldn't see The Loving Kindness that You Provided for me! Lord God may You continue to bless me, and keep me all the rest of the days of my life, so that I may strive to be of excellent service to You Lord God, ...

36. Beware

O God, it's a constant struggle every day to be grateful for what You Lord God Provide for me within a day. For my mind tells me I should have more than what I already have: however, I've come to know how these thoughts come and go with the intent to inflate once again my ego! These thoughts are relentless and painful when they come into my mind; so I've learned to step into faith, and I pray to God, and believe God Is Preparing for me a really wonderful place! So I continue to hold on, and ask The Lord God to Make me more spiritually strong. I've come to know that this symptom of my disease will from time to time crop up and appear; however, having God, as my Perfect Protector I 've learned, to have no fear!

37. Something to Smile About

Today I have no fears; today I learn to live life without burdens and cares; I am in no rush, and for the first time in my adult life God Has Relieved me of my sexual lusts. I am so at peace on the inside that I burst with billions of bubbles of joy and happiness; for I am no longer a slave to that lustful spirit. God is more powerful than I imagined Him to be, and I love God more than my own appointed life! Today I get to experience love in its true form, without the physical stigma that the world so attaches to Love. I now know that in many cases, and especially in my own, on how it's just that evil spirit called lust, and with God's Help, it can be extracted from us.

38. Recovery - A Gift

Reality in its true form is a real joy killer, and most people become really depressed when they come face to face with life's ills! Many of us indulge in casual drinking of alcohol with the intention to express merriment, and to suppress the ill feelings sometimes reality confronts us with. However, in this form of addressing our joy, or ill feelings some of us have fallen into a habitual response to all of life's joys, or ill feelings. To begin to use alcohol habitually in this manner isn't natural, or normal. Alcohol, and mind altering drugs blinded me from God's Will for my life! Today I have no regrets for God Showed me a way to freedom and joy, and I am in The Recovery Process from God Himself. Living each day now sober and free from any mind altering drugs, God, Discloses more of Himself to me! What a Gift!

39. The Great Giver --- God

Today I have sobriety coupled with serenity-two wonderful gifts bestowed upon me from God Almighty. I am overjoyed you see, for God Has Provided a Place for me! I finally found my home, and now I am never alone, for The Spirit of God Lives in me, and with each and every sober and mind altering drug free day, I am happy and filled with joy. Some people may disagree, but guess what? They aren't me! God, bestowed upon me true happiness, and for this I pray to God to be forever loyal, for God Has Caused my life to begin to flourish, and not come to further spoil! God, when I think of You, You Give me New Breath, and in saying this, You are where my treasures lie. God, may You Always Burn Bright, in my life!

40. A Revelation

Change once again has shown itself to me; however, this time I am more eager to receive what God Is Allowing me. For I know it's God, Who Causes my eyes to see! There are times in my days when I will stop whatever I am doing and begin to pray; for The Spirit of God Moves me. I've come to know that prayer works, and God so far Has Handled All of Life's Ills that were irritating me. The Most Holy One of Israel has been so Good to me that I now depend on and trust Him for whatever I need, or want in this life, and I wait for whatever orders He has for me! God Loves me with an Unconditional Love, which has caused me to look deep within myself, and in doing so I've found a treasure beyond measure; however, there was at first a lot of pain that had to be expelled from my soul before I could freely flow into this newly uncovered spiritual vein. This source of power is what I had always wanted to possess; however, I've now found that the only way for a person to achieve it is to knock on God's Door, and sincerely ask!

41. Uncovering Truth

From dust I was formed, and to the dust I will return; however, I will be accountable, for what I 've done while I was, in the body! I've come, to learn in my precious life, that I own nothing, and I created nothing; however, the irony is, so ironic, in how I was given, so many things tangible, and intangible, and through time I took for granted, that these gifts were mine, from my own doing! Oh how selfish I became, and through the years how acute became my shame! Well, my shame drove me insane, and to this day I've, only myself to blame, for the insanity, that was self-inflicted; however The Most Holy One of Israel, The One, and True Living God, Has Changed my whole bring, and now I can give unconditional love, to my neighbors, without being ashamed, about the person I used to be. My efforts will forever stand, as a Glorification, unto The One, and Only Father God!

42. Love I Never Knew I Had

Every moment, of every day, God, You were there for me. Every moment, of every day, God, You Held Out Your Hand to me. However, in most of my days, I was either drunk, or high, or both, and I refused to obey anyone, for I loved to be drunk and high. Constantly living like that I became confused about the people, places, and things around me! But God, You Still Held Out Your Hand to me, and You called to me regardless of my contempt; however, I kept on getting drunk and high. One day I realized I was living a lie; and I had not the power to relieve myself from the grip of those evil spirits: I was trapped and insane. I constantly looked for something, or someone to blame! My life was a wreck, and I had lost what little self-respect I had accumulated. I had become a shell of a person with no dignity, or honor. I realized I had become a drunkard and a drug addict, and I couldn't stop drinking alcohol, or using mind altering drugs! With each passing day stress became more powerful, and I was never at rest! I was at the end of my rope, and my family members had already given up hope; to them I was already dead, and in actuality I was! However, one night I sincerely screamed out to The Most Holy One of Israel, and I pleaded to God, and Jesus Christ for Their Help, and it seemed as though They Instantly Relieved me from the bondage of myself. From that night until this very day, my life has been changing, in the most unexpected ways! All praise is due to God! God, Has Saved me, and with my obedience God Is Now Raising me! I love You God, with an endless love!

43. In The Image

To love is to give, and to endlessly love is to endlessly give. O God, You are the only reality of this previous statement: To realize this fact about Yourself makes me happy on the inside, for my warped mind can still contemplate one of Your Virtues, and in the pondering new light shines upon my being! O God, You give us human beings so much that many times we misuse, or take for granted Your Loving Kindness; however, You still continue to give. O God, may You please show me how to do like You! I want so very much to give, so that I can bring smiles to people's faces while I yet live!

44. My Duty

What I write isn't a journal, for my words of encouragements are eternal. Here they will stand, for my neighbors to read, a Gift from God, with the ability to plant a mental seed! Words of power, words that link, words of wisdom, which positively influence what you think. God, Has Stretched out His Hand upon me, and with His Power He Has Psychologically Changed me! With this noticeable change I am overjoyed, for God Has Changed Me into a man, and I am no longer a frightened boy! Holy, and acceptable to God I strive to become; however, I must always hold out my hand to all people, for God Will Send Them to me. Freely I must give, as was given to me, this is how I must perform my earthly duty.

45. The Road and Recovery

One step up, and two steps back, four steps up, and three steps back. It's not a wonder why we Alcoholics and Drug Addicts feel so confused and trapped once we begin to trudge the road of recovery! Yet we must face our past, without performing actions of old; we must ask God for courage, and move forward, and be bold. We will receive no rewards for being stagnant. There will be many times when we will want to lose faith and give up; however, we must hold on, and remember that God Himself is Guiding us! We Alcoholics and Drug Addicts have had many brothers and sisters who have come before us out of the darkest corners of this wretched disease, and who have told us, and shown us that there is a way to recover, and that way starts with God, and the programs of recovery He Has Established for us. God, and His Plan of Recovery Has Saved my life!

46. As I Sit and Reflect

May we make each moment positively count, for these moments will become the memories that will never be blotted out. Take advantage of your time, for God Is So Generous and Kind. My eyes become cloudy, my heart becomes faint, when I sit and ponder the unsuspecting Alcoholic, or Drug Addict's fate! God, may You please continue to have mercy on us Alcoholics and Drug Addicts: We have nothing but pain and misery; fore we have failed at the tasks God that You Have Given us to do in our lives! God Himself Has Given me The Opportunity, to reconstruct my life, and I am eternally grateful! Without God, there would be no life, or self-will to ruin life as I have done, by the abuse of alcohol and mind altering drugs!

MINISTER WAYNE BEVERETT

Volume - # 3

1. Pathway to Righteousness

It's a long and lonely road that I walk, for the pathway to the true and living God is rarely walked, let alone truly sought! My mind desperately tries to make me give in, for all it knows is that old lustful life of sex and sin! My mind is comfortable when it's numb; however, my heart and soul suffers from that illusion of fun! Living these days now without allowing my mind to make a decision is truly One of God's Holy Blessings. Today I have no regrets, and by keeping, in conscious contact with God, The More Love to Me God, Emits! Today, and henceforth I am a living miracle and with God's Help, I've come to notice and shun all evil!

2. Tricked, But Not Licked

There was never any joy, and there was never any fun; my former life was all an illusion passed on to me by the deceitful one. Neither prosperity nor peace was my mainstay, for drinking alcohol and using mind altering drugs became my forte! Yes I accelerated into insanity with steady flow, and before I realized it I had nowhere to go! I was alone and by myself-three thousand miles away from where I grew up! At least there I could get some kind of help from somewhere! However, help was right here in California just patiently waiting for me to ask. And with a sincere heart I asked for help, and from that night to the present time of this writing, God Himself Has Been my Help. If you ever get the opportunity to love and trust God, you'll find yourself never to be the same again.

3. A Sigh of Relief

In people, and in things I've learned never to invest all of my trust, for they are all fallible, just as the person who is pushing this pen! It's a healthy and valuable reminder to me to remember The One and Only God Who Has Created All that I can and can't see. A smile develops upon my face, for I know in my heart and soul Who is the Giver of All Grace! Prosperity is available for each and every man and woman; however, we must individually submit our souls to God's Holy Plan. God's Holy Plan has already been stated. It has taken years of frustrations for me to be able to realize this reality; however, I am forever grateful and I am free, and all praise is due to God Almighty.

4. The Work - Not All My Own

As I sit and reflect on my previous year, I can claim many improvements; however, I didn't accomplish them by myself, for God Almighty Was and Is my Help! My cup runneth over today with love, and I share love today with my neighbors; my cup runneth over today with hope, and I share my hope with my neighbors. All this love and hope was handed down to me from The Creator of All Things, and I am most honored to be chosen by God Himself to be entrusted with these Gifts, and today my soul is free and I am no longer hassled by the miseries of the world around me.

5. The Commitment

To consciously Pledge to be You Servant God makes my heart and soul so happy that tears of joy stream down my face, for I know within my heart many a day and night I deserved physical death! However, in actuality I was dead, and King Alcoholism was alive in me. Oh God, You Showed Mercy to me, and You Guided me to relief, and this is why I am now so grateful to be a living example of Your Loving Kindness, and nothing in this world is more important to me than to obey and serve You Lord God forever. Dear Lord God, may You please Reveal to Your Servant what it is he must do to make and keep Your Face Happy? Your Servant God, is always ready to serve.

6. Forever My Pleasure

Restless is my heart, restless is my soul. Oh I must stay focused, for there is so much more to be told! I've come a long way in a very short time; however, now The Message of God 's Love is Beginning to Sine! Wherever I go, I am an example of God's Love, and people who know me best know that I am empowered from above. I created nothing, and I own nothing, and that's fine with me, for I know within my heart and soul that everything belongs to God Almighty! God Provides me with whatever I need to live, and when I think about it I can never match what God Gives. So what can I do, but remain grateful and obey His Most Holy Words, and to stay forever faithful!

7. Praise - be God's

Dear God, I feel Your Most Holy Presence, and within my soul there is no resistance; my body shivers when I praise Your Most Holy Name, and thoughts of peace overtake my warped brain!

Thankful am I God for all of Your Spiritual Gifts, and my soul consciously knows that soon my whole presence You God Will Uplift: Dear Lord God, may You please let it be shown for all to see, that it be Your Hands that Has Saved, and is Raising me! I take no credit for what I have become; however, joy overwhelms me, in knowing I fit the mold of the prodigal son.

8. The Lord Provides

Nothing for me, but a hand filled with hurt. Nothing for me, but menial work, and more menial work! This is the present reality for myself; for I've wasted and destroyed so many good things that God Had Given to me as opportunities. And now all I do is cry, and continue to ask God why? Pain and disgust constantly appear upon my face; however, I blame God not for my uncomfortable place. On the contrary I step out on faith, and thank God for His Loving Grace! Not a day goes by in my recovery when I won't stop and ask God for guidance out of my self-made drudgery. And like birds, that soar through the air, God, always Gives me Something New, and beautiful to share.

9. Your Cake And You

Whatever the world offer me, I will reject; however., whatever God, Offers me, I will accept. In accepting God's Gifts, I can rejoice and be jolly; however, in accepting the worlds gifts, I can always expect impending folly! I speak the truth in whatever I write, and if false information is suggested to me, I will not dare to copywrite. You see that's the difference in me compared to a hack. I can't knowing mislead people, for such behavior would destroy all of my planted seeds, and eventually I would be destroyed by the snake, that venomous monster whose corrupt deeds I surely do hate! "You can't serve two masters: You'll either love the one, or you'll hate the other!" There are no two sides of the fence, when it comes to evaluating your character.

10. Insights With Sights

To sacrifice my wants, and restrain my desires is an attitude which makes my soul rejoice; however; it activates my warped mind to cry out in a revolting voice! Well that's just too bad for my warped mind, for God Almighty Is Blessing me with Spiritual Healing All The Time. I am truly joyous and fortunate, for I am responding positively to The Creator of All Things! My Treasure Runs Deeper and Wider than any measurement of measure that can be measured, and to me that's real Treasure! I created nothing, and I own nothing; however, I've been blessed with an ability to see objects which I've yet to hear anyone else in the world claim they can see, and within a dream God Himself Told me to always remember The Lights in the shapes of stars, beyond the containment of those objects that I can consciously see.

11. Forever Your Servant God

For over eighteen years, Lord God, I could see Your Light, yet in the majority of those years I squandered my Spiritual Insights . And in all of the days of my disease-infested life, God, Your Gracious Love Sustained my wretched life! How God, can I ever repay? In my heart God I know I can never repay; however, Your Unconditional Love I can practice throughout the rest of my allotted days. Unworthy of Your Gifts and downtrodden many a day in spirit, I must move forward and spread Your Holy Message! God, You Give me Strength, You Give me Good Health, and there's nothing I would rather do than to pass on Your Intangible Wealth. Please Lord God, make me an example for all the world to see what happens to a man when he completely surrenders to God Almighty!

12. A Short Stay

My main objective isn't to myself-my life isn't my own, and this world I live in is only a temporary home. A temporary home it truly is; however, I must enhance my follow brothers and sisters lives while I still yet live! To provide them with unconditional love, hope, and joy is the only reason why I am in God's Employ! This is the reason why my life isn't my own. However, I am honored and overjoyed with this job that God Has Chosen to Give me. I can never repay God for His Unconditional Love and Generosity. To see someone's life totally change right before your eyes is just one of the many miracles, God Does Provide. And having had one of God's Miracles Performed on me has strengthened my faith in The Invisible Lord, not by what I physically see.

13. God-The Only Power

"Not the same." "Different from the rest." "Never equal." "Always at unrest." These were the thoughts, and situations of a five-year-old, born into confusion! Remembering my distant past always makes me cry; however, I have a job to do, and I belong to

God, The Most High! Every day I pray for courage and I ask for spiritual zeal, in an effort to help me combat life's sometimes depressing ills. I step out on faith and I believe with all of my might that God Is Preparing me for Eternal Life. With this thought peace enters my mind, whereas in the recent past drinking alcohol and using mind altering drugs were my solution, or reward to any problems or triumphs I may have had. So you see this is why I worship God-Almighty, for God Has Done for me miracles that I could have never accomplished for myself!

14. My Sweet Creator

From my first memories as being a little boy, I remember being scared, always trembling with fear, as I lay in bed. Hollering, screaming, and shouts were always heard throughout our house! Yea I can still feel the pain of those long ago nights. Please God, grant me the courage to accept my childhood frights. Resentments I carried around for years of how I grew up so differently, from other little kids. Pain and confusion was my plight, and it would come back to haunt me on any given day or night. So alcohol and mind altering drugs I used for many years, for I could cover up, or stuff my haunting fears.

One day I noticed my alcohol and mind altering drugs no longer worked, and I was left alone, tired and filled with hurt! I had been beaten, by the sane things I used to call my friends. Oh how I thank you God, for You've Shown me that I don't ever have to depend on alcohol and mind altering drugs again, those on-going sins.

15. An Unknown Trait Revealed

Looks of anger appears upon my face, for another one of my subtle character defects has been identified to me, by way of God's, Wonderful Grace. I should be happy and present my face with a smile; however, I can't at the moment, for I now realize how my disobedience through the years was so distasteful and so vile to so many people. I boil with anger, and I mustn't construct a resentment on how my disobedience spoiled commitment after commitment. Onward I go, to and fro, traveling on the road of recovery and along the way as I pray, I find more pain and drudgery. I guess this is the price we Alcoholics and Drug Addicts must pay, if we're ever to become free of our old destructive ways!

16. Life...More Than Just What You See

To give something of value to another without charge is truly the essence of love. Oh God, may we Alcoholics, and Drug Addicts practice more of Your Generous Character Traits without generating jealousy, and or hate! All who have life are precious in Your Sight Lord God, and may You Bless Us to Grow in favor of Your Most Holy Will as we experience life. So many of us view life as having no value, and we abuse each other without a care. God, may You Reveal more of Your Spiritual Insights to us so that we may know that Satan is real, and that he is consciously here! People have each other, and we are all born from Your Holy Grace God, and may You Bless us to become steadfastly conscious of the reality concerning Eternity, once we leave this place called earth.

17. Today's Grace

Today I am a tool, yesterday I was a fool, and tomorrow has yet to come, Tomorrow for me is how I live today , and today I enjoy life, and I constantly continue to pray! Today I pray on how to carry out God's Will for my life within my day, and by doing so I don't become trapped and possess the feelings, of ease and comfort no matter where I'm at. I thank God with all of my heart, and with all of my soul, and with all of my strength and mind; and God Returns my thank yous by keeping me sober and mind altering drug free within the present time. So you see, I have no wants for tomorrow; for I'm content with the present day.

18. My Wonderful Place

Today all I want to do is pray; today I don't lust after things I see; today I give thanks to God Almighty. Today I don't desire what my neighbors possess, and in my heart I wish them all the best. Today all I want to do is pray, and thank God, for Allowing me His Grace to experience this day. Today I've Been Blessed by God with the sudden reality of leading a brand new life, and within it there aren't any expectations of grandeur. Today a smile appears upon my face, for I have faith that God Is Preparing for me a truly wonderful place. And in my heart joy is mine, a gift from God that always shines!

19. My Soul's Desire

Responding to God's Holy Business is my main endeavor; to make and keep The Face of God happy is what I want to do forever!

God, Has Done So Much Good for me that I don't concern myself so much about the material things around me! Meaningless are material things, for they never could, nor will they ever keep my heart singing! To those who have sought to please God, and still seek You are the only people who will truly understand the words I write. To give something of value without any charge is the true Essence of God's Love! If it be in the form of the material, well so be it; however, I've come to realize that it's the intangible gifts that fortifies our God Given Souls...

20. The Most Holy Touch

Please touch my mind God, if You will, please touch my mind God, so that I may carry out Your Holy Will for my life. Please touch my heart God, if You will, please touch my heart God, so that I won't be afraid to feel.

Please touch my soul God, if you will, please touch my soul God, so that I may continue to heal. Please saturate my whole being God, if You will, please saturate my whole being God, so that whomever I come into contact with may be healed. Dear God, there is nothing You can't do, and this is why I ask with confidence, for these intangible things from You! Within each moment of realized time, I've become wiser, for I've placed You God, in the forefront of my mind.

21. A Lifetime Membership

I am not by myself today, and that's truly a blessing to know. I've been guided to a fellowship of men and women who are just like me. We are identifiable by our mental thoughts patterns; peace of mind for us can in no way be bought! The threads of our past lives are despised by many of our neighbors; however, God, Continues to Reveal His Love for us, and many of us have become reconstructed people, through time by way of God's Love and Protection.

Many of us have truly found no other way to recover from Alcoholism and Drug Addiction. We must constantly continue to ask God what is His Will for our lives, on a day to day basis? If not, we surely experience the disease of Alcoholism and Drug Addiction once again without delay by way of our conscious thoughts. This is a proven fact by way of some of our members who have relapsed. They thought they were cured... No way... The way of our fellowship has been designed especially for us Alcoholics and Drug Addicts by God Himself! And it must be lived out the way it was laid out.

22. God, My Only Guide

Dear Lord God, may You please guide my precious life-that intangible gift which I so many times have almost lost by way of my own self-will! Personal desires I continue to try my best to sacrifice; for carrying out Your Holy Will God must come first in my life! God, You're The Creator of All Life, and I must never forget this fact. May I always Praise Your Most Holy Name, no matter where I'm at.

Lonely am I among humankind, for there aren't many people who truly seek You God in their hearts, souls, and minds. So my associations with many people are short, for they soon come to realize that I am Godly taught; however many people desire what they see in me, and that's Your Most Holy Spirit which, thanks to You God, Has Descended upon me.

23. Saved by God

May The Glory of Your Presence God become manifest within me! May Your Light God of Everlasting Life become available for all to see! Through the years alcohol and mind altering drug use blocked Your Most Holy Spirit from me, and I was always unsure of what I was striving to be. Darkness started to impose itself upon my life with regularity, and rationality began to become foreign to me. At present my head hurts to write, for my former self hates to be revealed. Fortunately, I learned from God to face my pain, and not look to the world for my salvation. The Most Holy One of Israel is my Guiding Light, and He is my pain reliever; Who is available to me on any given day or night! Today I am an honest man who regularly insists on helping his neighbors.

24. Corrupt - But not to the Core

Strong and powerful I am, I'm strong and powerful, even though I'm just one single man! Pure energy flows through me; however, I won't abuse The Power that God Allows me! I now strive to be like my Creator in every possible way; whereas before God got my attention I corrupted whatever happened to be in my path! I was hurt, I was alone, I was sad, and I didn't care about what the next man may have had. I just knew that I was dissatisfied with what I had, and with each passing day with the use of alcohol and mind altering drugs I was steadily going mad! Not a day went by without my obsessing, on how to get drunk and, or high. This was the way my life turned out to be. I corrupted myself by my own hands and evil influences; until one day I sincerely sought out and cried out to God and Jesus Christ, and They Directed me from the road that leads to destruction.

25. Forever Loyal

I'm all alone, I'm all by myself; however, I'm not sad, for God is my help: God, Has Rescued me from the devil's lot, "He Is My Only Best Friend, and no one touches my heart like God can". I can't help but cry, for His Love, and Protection you can't buy. I'm by myself, and today that's okay, but I'm not going to disappoint The Lord God anymore with my old selfish ways! He's all I truly have, and I won't disrespect Him in order to possess material things. God Is Transforming my being; He Has Granted me Peace of Mind, and I won't turn my back on Him now, or at any other time.

26. Confronting Disease

I put forth my best efforts into not being depressed; however, reality has its way of catching up with me. I can't sincerely write without addressing the pain of my former life! Unpleasant memories bombard me with regularity, and to drink alcohol and use mind altering drugs was always the solution for me. However, today I've been blessed by God to be able to confront reality with a rational and sane mentality. I am a living miracle who is constantly changing, and as I make an attempt to improve my life, God Helps me with the rearranging. I can see improvements and most of time I am okay; however, what really brings joy to my heart is the fact that I have The Most Holy One of Israel to thank for each and every sober and mind altering drug free day!

27. Revelations to a Rebel

In the calm of the morning I can feel You God, and as the day progresses I constantly thank You for my Most Holy Job. By Your Grace Lord God, You Have Revealed to me the fact that I am an Alcoholic, and that I always will be an Alcoholic.

My job isn't easy and I must always pray for Your Guidance God, to perform my best. Pain is my constant, and I am seldom at rest. We all have our crosses to carry, and the disease of Alcoholism just so happens to be mine; however, there is joy in the accepting, for I am blessed with the ability to make others people's lives shine. I live and work for God, He is my Heavenly Father. He Has Rescued me from shame and total disaster.

28. Service in Time

As the day grows old, may I not contemplate on how a flower grows. But rather appreciate its beauty, and smell its fragrance, for one day, it will be no more: One day God, everything that I've ever seen will become a memory and everything that I've ever felt, or touched will be gone, and then what will become of me? I am not afraid of what will become of me, for I trust in The Most Holy One of Israel to receive and redirect my Eternal Energy that is me! God Created me, so I will do my best to not ever hurt, or offend anyone ever again; fore in the Sight of God that behavior isn't acceptable. To enhance and support life, is what draws me closer to my Eternal Brother Jesus Christ.

29. Recognizing Corruption

In the mist of all evil, God, I seek Your Face. In the mist of all evil, God, You still can transmit Your Loving Grace! O Most Holy One of Israel may You continue to dissolve the remaining inclinations of evil that is a residue in my mind. At certain times I can feel evil's presents, trying its best to influence me, and it disturbs me. However, I must continue to pray, and maintain my faith that someday God You'll Totally Expel the remaining evil traits from me! It's War God, and I fully understand that it's Your Fight; however, I'm Your Servant standing ready for a battle on any given day, or night! The thought of a fight intrigues me, and this serves as proof that evil still lurks within me.

30. Blessings in Disguise

I am blessed today; even though, I am an emotional wreck, I am blessed today, for God Keeps me in check. Every day I live sober and mind altering drug free, God Reveals to me important facts about my character that I should see! I find myself being overwhelmed by character defects that are very subtle to me; however, they are probably glaring to other people.

The uncovering and discovering, of these faults shuffles my emotions. Life situations that involve insecurity draws me closer to God, I am grateful for the trails; fore without them I would be less spiritually stable! Life is definitely not a bowl of cherries, and this I am sure about; however, to be blessed to live life sober and mind altering drug free are Gifts from God, and I won't ever take God's Gifts for granted!

31. Reality, Unsettling Truth

Blessed today I truly am! I'm blessed today for I live the life of a sober and mind altering drug free man. No alcohol, or street drugs enter into my Holy Temple, for my soul abhors those corrupting evils. Those spirits have ruled and corrupted me for over eighteen years, and I would be a fool, to invite them back into my life again! Alcoholism and Drug Addiction are evil things, and I must never allow myself to forget that. These evils have destroyed many members of my family, and now all I can do is miss them.

As I write, hatred envelops my heart; for I am fully aware of how this Alcoholism and Drug Addiction can rip lives apart! Justifiable anger registers within my thoughts; however, I must remember that God Will Handle all evil, that constantly marauds.

32. Evil Spirits

Many things in my life are unstable, and for many years this fact I just couldn't see, for the diseases of Alcoholism and Drug Addiction mentally blinded me: I found myself insane, broken hearted, and an emotional wreck... a man with no dignity, bankrupt, with no self-respect! I lost everything of value to me at a very high price.

The evils of Alcoholism and Drug Addiction had a contract out on me to claim my life. However, I knew enough to sincerely call, upon God and Jesus Christ, and The Most Holy One of Israel Provided me with Relief. Thus I now live a sober and mind altering drug free life.

33. The Gentlest Gentleman

All praise is due to God, for God Is Always on the job. He's more than willing to be anyone's friend; however, individuals must invite Him in. His Deeds of generosity boggles my mind, and whenever I am in pain God Provides me with relief every time. The remainder of my life is dedicated to God, and I will constantly pray that He Will Guide my heart away from further sin! I am God's Property, and the reality of this acceptance makes me pleased, even though I've been restricted with this Alcoholism Disease. My main objective is to make and keep God's Face Happy, by way of my own conscious decisions. A billion thank-yous would never ever equal The Generosity God Has Shown me and millions of people like me! "Thank You Lord God"!

34. Thanks- To my Only Best Friend

My life is wonderful today, for I've come to realize The Many Priceless Gifts God Has So Generously Bestowed Unto me. My whole being overflows with joy, for I am no longer a frightened little boy. On the contrary I'm a happy one, for I've come to truly believe that I am God's Son: I have no fear of where I am, nor do I worry about what I am to become.

I am just starting to enjoy this wonderful life, and I am learning how to have fun! When I look at people today I smile instead of frown. Oh thank You God, for this one hundred and eighty degree turn around! Now there is nothing in this world that I am in a rush to get; I'm just truly grateful to You Lord God for rescuing me, Your Son.

35. Never- Ending Praise

I have all I need today, and my mind searches no more. I have all I need today, for God Has Allowed me to walk through Eternity's Door. It's really Super Terrific in what God Allows me to see, and He Would Do the same for anyone - all you have to do is believe! I belong, to God, and He belongs to me and this is the reason why God Allows me to see the things I can see. With each passing day I feel more safe, for my heart and soul tell my mind that God Is Present, in every place: He is The Creator of all life, He is The Gentlest of Gentlemen, He's The Giver and Sustainer of life, and He shall always be My Only Best Friend...

36. The Reason Why

Today is another day that I am alone; however, this is nothing new! Today is another day and I am alone; however, there is progress, and I am not sad, or blue! Today I am alone; however, I don't drink alcohol, or use any mind altering drugs. Today I am alone, and I worship God, The Most High. God, is my Only Best Friend, and I am conscious that He Has Saved my life many times.

Today I am alone, and I am God's Living Miracle. God Is my Maker and Teacher; however, for many years I ducked His Teachings, and this is the reason why these days I am alone. God Transmits His Glory from His Throne. God's Holy Will, will be carried out, and I am a witness to this. Through people, places, and things, God, Constantly Teaches His Son and Servant that is I....

37. No Veil for Me

No one can touch me, lest they be my own kind; no one can negatively influence me; fore God Is On Guard within my mind! Worldly matters I turn over to my Loving God, for I am powerless over such things. I have a responsibility not to drink alcohol, or use any mind altering drugs, and this is a blessing from God's Love! I stand out among people; however, I don't stand alone and God Strengthens His Children as they seek His Eternal Throne! So I will not compromise God's Will for my old self seeking ways. My former life is dead, never to be born again. I pray to God My Father to take my life before I ever fall back into Satan's Den! Anger registers upon my face, for I've experienced the evil that's in the four corners of this earth!

38. Unshakeable Truth

Teach me God Your Loving Ways. Teach me God over and over again, so that I may always serve You and obey. My soul longs to be in Your Most Holy Presents; however, I must acquire Your Character Traits while I am yet a part of this physical residence, and in turn live by them. With each day now lived sober and mind altering drug free, I seek out The Kingdom of God, and in my efforts I am not disappointed by what I find! In this very short time God, You've returned me to sanity. You've Taken Away the compulsion to drink alcohol and use any mind altering drugs, and with these miracles I am living proof of Your Unconditional Love. And now I can confidently say to people that God Is Real, and His Love is True. All you have to do is seek Him, and He'll Perform Miracles for You too!

39. Priority One

The intangible has been made visible to me, a Gift from God that He Allows me to see. I've no conceit in my heart and only God Knows why I was chosen to possess this ability. It really sets me apart from most people, and I've learned to keep the knowledge of this ability to myself! There are spiritual axioms that will always be, but to the wayward they will stand out as mysteries. I am blessed, and I know it, I am an example of God's Unconditional Love, and I am not ashamed to show it. God's Blessings are evident whether I'm conscious of them, or not, for God Himself Is The Director of my heart. I am a man who has grown to think less and less of himself. I've learned to seek out for myself God's Will for my life, and in the process I've come to believe that there is nothing more important for me in this life, than to obey The Will of Father God, no matter what!

40. The Intangible Touch

No distractions – No – Not for me- No distractions; for God Almighty is Teaching me... Within in each day now lived sober and mind altering drug free, I am beginning to see more of the straight and narrow path that God Has Laid Out before me. My old behaviors one by one are beginning to become unacceptable to me; for I'm starting to seek The Guidance from my Maker. Materialism was never a big issue in my life to begin with, and now that I seek The Kingdom of God it matters to me even less. The power of the intangible forces is where God Draws me to study, and in the studying I've received Gifts beyond Gifts, and Riches beyond Riches. At this point in my life I am truly amazed and overwhelmed concerning The Endless Power and Beauty that

Surrounds us all, at all times. "He Told Moses to Tell Pharaoh, I am Sent me!" But most people call Him by His Title- God!

41. Nothing for Granted

There's pain, in me today, and this is nothing new, there's pain in me today, pain I must patiently work through. God, is my help, and in Him I can depend. God Is my Help, and He's my Only Best Friend. Tears are being manufactured from my face, and I am not ashamed even though I'm in a public place. My feelings I no longer hide; for they would hurt me more if I were to keep them locked away inside! I've been truly blessed to have learned to freely vent my feelings, whereas for years I drank alcohol and used mind altering drugs, and those evils were progressively killing me! Today, and for all times I owe my whole being, to God, for without Him, there would be no life. I will never ever take another moment of realized time, or unrealized time for granted! I mean this with all my soul, and all my soul is all I have that is valuable, and God Gave it to me to experience life now, and for Eternity!

MINISTER WAYNE BEVERETT

Volume - # 4.

1. Recognizing The Real Treasure

Within each moment, of realized time, and within each moment of unrealized time - God, may You please bless me with the alertness to identify the remaining evils which still remain within my character? God, the removal of these evils must be by Your Power and Strength; for I possess not the ability.

These evil intangible forces are the reality of Your Very Own Creation Lord God; however, their actions You Abhor!... No one knows Your Most Holy Plan - Oh Most Holy One of Israel, and I as Your Servant trust You God, and I decline to ponder Your Will for this world. God Himself is the only constant.... His Kingdom Is The Real Treasure...

2. To Watch and Wait

It's War God, and I thank You for Your Insights which You So Lovingly Continue to Bestow upon me. It's War God, and I as Your Servant stand ready for Your Orders without no regards of becoming a casualty! I am Your Property Lord God, I belong to You, so may You please continue to touch my heart and direct me in what Your Will Is for me to do.

As I write anger and resentments develop within my mind, for I contemplate on how Your Enemies plot to destroy Your Subjects all the time! In my own mind I want to repay; however, I quickly remember that this is Your War Lord God, and You Yourself Said, "Vengeance is Mine, and I Will Repay!" Nevertheless, loyal to You

Lord God I am, and I will stand on watch, and I will wait...

3. A service That's a Pleasure

I am a living miracle, for I am sane, sober, and mind altering drug free, and I shouldn't be! I am an example of God's Love, and every day I continue to ask The Lord God to work on me! We all have our crosses to bear; however, the disease of Alcoholism is a subtle foe, and its evil influences always continues to grow. It's an evil thing and its mental aggressions are relentless; for its intangible make up centers within the sufferer's mind and it launches its deadly attacks all the time! We alcoholics are identifiable by extremes within our characters, and our extremes maybe directed towards various functions within our daily lives. This disease is a destroyer of God Given Life, brought on ourselves by our lack of obeying God's Decrees concerning intoxication from generation, to generation. Now, The Good Lord God Has Blessed me with The Truth and The Solution concerning the disease of Alcoholism. I must always be of service to those who are ignorant of this killer, who is always trying to kill us.

4. Nothing Worldly for Me

Time matters to me not now, power and prestige amongst men matters to me not now, fame and glory matters to me not now; for all that matters to me is to obey The Will of God for my life. Worldly desires fall from my heart, and what takes its place are God's Character Traits. God Constantly Continues to Deliver Spiritual Insights and Strengths to me in the mist of much evil, and Satan is aware of my newly formed connection with God Himself.

Satan, desperately wants to destroy me; fore I am a treat to him concerning the souls of many people; however, God, Protects me! I don't know what the future holds for me and I don't worry to care, for God Is my life, and wherever I am turned to go I know within my heart and soul that God Will be there! I belong to God, and He won't abandon me. I live by faith, not by sight...

5. An Indispensable Account

My former lifestyle I don't miss; however, within each day of my recovery from Alcoholism and mind altering drug use, at some point within the day, or night I become sad and lonely. I guess these feelings are the aftereffects of living on the edge of death for so many years. I have Alcoholism, and my character traits are bent on extremes – And it's OK today; for I am aware by God's Grace most of the time concerning my mental delusional schemes! God, Stands in the gap of my sick warped mind, and all credit and thanks are due to Him for all of my sober and mind altering drug free time that has been accumulated! When old haunting feelings invade and stir my insides, virtues from God are my only weapons to counteract their destructive drives!... I am blessed with a new way of living my life; for I recognize and depend upon The Creator of all things...

6. A Little Reminder

This goes out to all of my fellow Alcoholic and Drug Addict Brothers and Sisters – Keep your heads up, and don't let this evil disease make you afraid – Never lose, or throw away your faith; for I am writing this to let my neighbors know that God Has The

Power to save by way of His Holy Grace. This is War, and our God Calls us in this way to serve, and let the enemy know that we stand by God's Most Holy Words. God doesn't need us at all; however, He is so Generous and Kind; fore He Allows us to make our own mistakes even though we were born with these warped minds!...Always remember that everyone who has breath has a cross to bear —And for us Alcoholism and Drug Addiction is our cross. We have a responsibility not to drink alcohol, or use any mind altering drugs that causes us to fit in, or escape from reality. God, Is our Strength and our Life, He Will Continue to Reveal to us how to live righteous lives, provided we continuously sincerely seek His Will for our lives. God Is our Only Defense against the evil that constantly marauds within our minds.

7. Care That Never Ends

In striving to serve God, I am forceful by tongue In striving to be of maximum good, I am constantly bombarded by old memories of false fun; however, I quickly remember what God Once Told me never to forget, and instantly the ponderous memories of what I use to do suddenly leave my conscious mind. Within each moment of realized time, I become more convinced of the evil intent concerning Alcoholism.

Alcoholism's relentless mental attacks are devastating, to say the least, and to say the most, if left untreated, Alcoholism will kill its human hosts! Alcoholics are of a separate kind, for our subtle evil offender dwells within our minds! There is no physical cure for us; however, there is a remedy to help us overcome our intangible enemy: God Is His Title and Being Here for all Is His Glory!

8. Singleness of Purpose is my Code

I must practice singleness of purpose every day, on and on... I must practice singleness of purpose, until I am dead and gone... For over eighteen years my life was a living hell, and I was very unhappy within my physical shell! Evil Spirits dominated the majority of my thoughts, and my heart and soul were powerless over the darkness I unconsciously sought! One night I bitterly cried out to God, and Jesus Christ for Their Help, and They Showed Up. They Took Away hopelessness – That night marked the beginning, of the end of my former lifestyle. I truly believe a drive of some kind was placed within me that would eventually change my whole life. God, Is Here and His Words are True, and to carry out His Will for my life is the singleness of purpose, I now live to do!...

9. A Priceless Awareness

It's a lonely business of love that I am in; however, the thank yous of appreciation from friends and well-wishers are starting to roll in! Living life sober and free from any mind altering drugs is a daily challenge, and I must always ask God for His Protection, Provisions ,and Guidance, in all of my worldly affairs! I am an Alcoholic – and I am the possessor of a deadly killer disease, which stops at nothing when it comes to inflecting torment and misery. This is a fact which for many years I couldn't see! Alcoholism is an evil entity, and it's a patient killer, so within each and every day I ask God to reveal more of its character traits to me. As I sit and write this intangible evil contemplates on how to destroy my life. I shall never, ever be complacent again; for I am consciously aware of the evil that lurks within...

10. No Dollars and No Cents...

I am a rich person now and forever; for The Most Holy One of Israel Is my Treasure! In God I wholly depend, for I've abandoned my faith and trust that I once tried to establish in men. My dependence upon them was soul crushing, and physical death was knocking at my existence; however, God, answered my soul's call for help. God's Faithful Response Has Caused me to turn to Him for everything else. Now I look towards my neighbors with no expectations of support. However, my damaged mind still sometimes tries to hold on to its old habitual thought process, but God's Healing Process Has Been Activated within me. God's Healing Process Vanquishes my mind's old destructive ways, which used to dominate me in any positive venture I would undertake! Within each moment of realized and unrealized time, I thank God in my heart for what He Has Done and Is Still Doing for me – My Precious Treasure, that has no measure!

11. The Transformation

My mind is the center of all my troubles, my mind was the creator of all my past delusions of grandeur! No decisions now do I allow my mind to make, of its own accord ; and for me that's a miracle! Before God's Holy Spirit Descended upon me I was a time bomb, just waiting for the right switch to be flicked; however, now I am a new person in every way as far as character goes.

I'm not the same person anymore, at this point I can no longer write, fatigue warps itself around me with a progressive grip. The energy of my mind fades into unconsciousness; however, God Gives me new breath, and He Delivers to me new strength. Oh thank you God, for always supplying my every need!

Alcoholism, Drug addiction, and sexual lusts are my three enemies, which God Has Brought to my attention! Thank you God, for saving me, and now with each moment of realized time and within each moment of unrealized time I consciously ask You God to raise me – Oh how I want the whole world to see the results of the new lifestyle, of a sober and mind altering drug free man. God's Very Own Handy Work, His New and Positively Constantly Changing Son! A transformation that only God Himself Has Done.

12. My Ongoing

Evil is my adversary now and forever; for I am an agent of good – Evil tried to destroy me many a day as I consciously walked through my old neighborhood! I was unaware of its deadly influences through the people around me and myself as well! However, God, Has Uncovered its presence from within me. Evil is around us all, The Most Holy One of Israel Protects us all, to a certain point. If there is no effort on our part to rid ourselves of the marauding evil, then we ourselves become agents of evil! The truth is the truth and a lie is a lie, and I've been so Blessed by God Himself, to have been Shown The Truth. The only fulfillment in life for me is to help my neighbors connect themselves to The Creator of all things. "I am" is His name and "God" is His Title!

13. Following Orders

To give freely of what was freely given to me is how I profess to be! I hold nothing for myself, for God, Is my Unending Wealth! Everything I feel, hear, smell, taste, and see belongs to God

Almighty! So there is nothing I can put a label on and claim it is mine. For it is not, for everything that has existence is God's Lot! These facts keep me healthy and free from my known Alcoholic Disease! I'm blessed with many   gifts, and they were appointed to me as God, Saw Fit. Now I must constantly continue to give them all away, this is God's Holy Will Instructed to me within my allotted days.

14. Disease Mine

Always there, always present, and beyond a shadow of a doubt it's evil. This is the reality of Alcoholism my subtle and deadly foe! Alcoholism shall always be a part of me, no matter how much I may physically, spiritually, mentally, or emotionally grow. Alcoholism attacks every part of my being, and it's relentless on how it constantly launches its deadly attacks; however, by surrendering to God each and every day, I am blessed with restraints, and I am learning how not to react! I was born with this spiritual malady, and I must always stay aware of my faulty mentally! I shall always try and do my best; for God Has Reached Out to me, and in Him is where I find peace of mind and spiritual rest!

15. A Living Miracle

"O God"- Your Servant watches and he waits for Your Most Holy Orders to descend upon him from Your Throne. However, until that time I will constantly continue to thank You for restoring me to my rightful mind. I am a possessor of an evil deadly disease called Alcoholism, and in my heart there is no doubt; the only known solution for people like me is the constant dependence upon God – day in and day out! To what I am, and to what I've received, there has grown a loyalty to God, that makes it impossible for anyone to ever make me disbelieve in His Power and Greatness! I possess the disease of Alcoholism and it's incurable; however, by seeking daily for God's Will for my life, I don't obsess about drinking alcohol anymore, and I don't drink it! This is God's Great Gift, Given to me, I am a living miracle; I couldn't stop drinking alcohol, and stay stopped!

16. Essence of Love

No expectations do I expect from my neighbors – I've been set apart and put to one side, yet many people are attracted to me – I don't know the reason for this; however, The Will of God, shall be done! In my new life that I live sober and mind altering drug free, I spend much of my time seeking the counsel from The Creator of All Things! And in the process I receive wisdom, that is not my own. The evil that still remains within my mind constantly tries to destroy The Gifts and Lessons that God Is Transmitting to me; however, my heart and soul are too overbearing for my disease at this point in my life – And this is what I claim as being A Blessing, from The Lord God! All Praise is Due To The Most Holy One Of Israel...

17. The Hunt for Knowledge

To suffer and to see my fellows suffer is a daily reality for me - You see I possess the disease of Alcoholism, and it's my incurable enemy! Alcoholism is alive, and it's an evil intangible thing, it's a downright killer, and I've seen firsthand the destruction it brings! Its identity may go undetected for many years; however, even if detected, the sufferers may be unable to confront their fears! And in the process, the sufferers may live in denial for even more years. This is a real complex and intriguing evil, and I constantly pray to God, for Him to reveal more of its character to me – So that I may in turn divulge more of its subtle characteristics to my fellows.

18. What's Not Mine

Fame I want no part of, and glory I pray never to come knocking at my door – My soul's desire is to obey and serve God, forevermore! Life is an order from The Will of God, and responsibility of power I must intake; however, fame and glory for me would be a huge mistake! Fame and glory are appointments I reserve for God, alone; I as God's Servant will with every opportunity pass fame and glory over to The Lord God, its rightful owner. No matter where I am, or no matter what The Spirit of God may call me to do, I will always praise God's Holy Name, through and through! I love God more than my own appointed life, and I state this with gladness in my heart and I wear a smile upon my face; for all fame and glory belongs to God, our Most Holy Grace!

19. Standing Strong

At first no one will love you, no one will care about you practicing God's Virtues and Restraints in all of your affairs. You will feel left out and alone; however, if you persist in your work and faith, God

Will Strengthen you from His Most Holy Throne! The enemies of God will constantly seek you out – But you must keep your faith and believe with conviction that God's Will, will work out! So stand strong and have no doubts in what you are standing for, and always remember that God Has Made the enemies, which seek to cancel your life out!

20. Instructions to Save Life

In the mist of much life, I The Servant of God, constantly continues to write, and the work isn't my own, but rather a communication, from God, to me, from His Most Holy Throne! God, Constantly Transmits to me spiritual insights about Alcoholism's evil destructive characteristics! Alcoholism affects the human host in so many ways that self-will is incompatible to remedy its constant relentless mental attacks. I've discovered God Himself, to be the only defense against the marauding evil of Alcoholism! Dependence upon God, for the alcoholic must become for him, or her their way of life, anything to the contrary will surely erode what is left of their already damaged lives! This King Alcoholism will go around and around, and it will take the unprotected sufferers with it, for they aren't Godly Bound!

21. Expectations - The Setup

In lessons there is always a measure of pain. This is what I've found to be necessary in order to commence any change! There is never a feeling of bliss, when a person is confronted with contrary expectations. To expect something and not receive it, causes a person to feel as though he or she has been deceived!

However, in reality the deception may be an illusion, brought on by wishing on a hope ! So expectations, from people, places, and things will always present a chance for disappointment; for none of those things are sure things! God Himself, Is The Only Constant!

22. Room for All

A design for living is what I have today, and to continue to grow within the design is why I constantly continue to pray! My life is destructive without the continual guidance from God Himself. I've come to realize that it is from God, that I 've acquired the ability to demonstrate unconditional love! No matter what the situation, I've come to realize that there was and always is an underlying explanation In God's Universe, there is always a code of order; however, where there is anarchy – there without a question, you will find God's Enemies! Their greed has caused and still causes them great misery, and God, Sets this as an example, for all to see! So be not afraid and seek The Most Holy One of Israel's Most Holy Face, so that you may forever secure for yourself a space, in God's Most Holy Place!

23. Property Known

God – as I continue to seek Your Kingdom – worldly desires constantly fade from my heart! Within each new lesson You Bring – I am in awe about how it makes my soul sing! Most times in the beginning there is much pain; however, in the meaning I become overwhelmed with freedom the answers bring! "O God" I am so happy most of the time that many of my fellows don't understand how You Have Changed me form a once lonely and domed man! Convictions from Your Existence God, burst from all of my pores, and I constantly state to everyone I meet that I am Yours. Yes I am God's Property, Sent by God Himself, to help the people I was called to help!

24. Seeking a Spot

I must be patient, I must stay alert, I must step to one side and let God do His Most Holy Work! Within each passing day I find myself consciously making an honest effort to accept people, places, and things just the way they are, and to consciously accept the fact that I don't possess the power to fix them! It's not my job; however, I may play a part in God's Will, to perform whatever task that may be on His Schedule.

All of what I am is meaningless when I let self-will get in the way! I pray to stay humble and low key, and know in my heart that God's Will Allows The Action of All Things! I am just a creation out of God's Creative Hand, sincerely seeking a spot in God's Holy Plan!

25. What Is? - And What Must Be Done?

Living on self-will is like playing Russian Roulette with my life! I have the incurable disease of Alcoholism, and I must always wholly depend upon God for everything! No person, place, or thing can ever fix me, or make me whole! God Is my life, and the consumption of alcohol and mind altering drugs is my death! This reality for me is pretty simple; however, drifting into self-will makes the simple become downright mental! The unaided will for the alcoholic is his ongoing malady; for there the intangible enemy launches his attacks! This evil intriguing disease has many parts; however, this alcoholic in recovery constantly prays to God for His Guidance into this disease's true heart! And while I wait, my top objective in life will remain the same, and that is to obey and serve The Most Holy One of Israel!...

26. My Best Foot Forward

I've heard it said many times in my life from all types of people, surely there must be truth in this cliché - "Make the best out of what you've got": Well I've got Alcoholism and I am an ex-drunkard, and there are so many evil aspects of this incurable disease that the mere thought of them sends me into a funk! However, I must not stay in the anger long, for I may miss what God Is Transmitting to me, and with His Kindness, He Would just Make me go through it again! I'm trying earnestly to learn not to emotionally beat myself up but rather accept my situations, and for the first time in my life painfully grow up! Self-will isn't an easy thing for this alcoholic to give up; however, I sincerely try my best with God's Help to be honest with myself and to be straight up!

27. Unconditional Trust

My heart and soul must always stay alert; I must constantly seek out, for myself The Most Holy One of Israel's, Assigned Work. The disease of Alcoholism is alive, and its evil intentions are relentless and cruel, and God Is my only defense against this disease's mental moves! I've been mentally deceived and manipulated, by this evil disease for many years; however, one night I asked God, for help and He Has Delivered me from paranoia and many delusional fears. Coming to realize God's Power and Compassion, has caused me to trust God with everything I own- and that consists of my life and my self will. I place them in God's Care daily, and He Hasn't Yet Failed me.

28. Lessons I Had to Learn – The Hard Way

Life is a gift from God; however, for many years of my life I never knew it: There was always pain, there was always trouble, and throughout it all, there was never a place where I did fit! I was always too fast, or too slow, I tried with all of my street skills for people to like me; however, many starts would end up in disappointment, after disappointment, with no clue that my drinking alcohol and using mind altering drugs had anything to do with it!

I became withdrawn, and I had no close family members, or friends, and within each passing day the disease of alcoholism and drug addiction was closing in on me! Oh what a blessing in disguise; for I had come to realize that I had accomplished nothing in my life! My biggest fear was death, with no respect from all of the people that I had come to know in life. It drove me to my knees and I sincerely asked The Creator of All Things and Jesus Christ for help.

Starting from that night until the day of this writing that prayer is still being fulfilled by way of Their Loving Kindness.

29. A way of Life - Long Overdue

Patient is truly a virtue, and the more I practice it, the stronger my connection becomes with The Spirit that Is God! Now that I live my life sober and mind altering drug free, I pray that it's not too late to start my life over. Here I stand almost a middle-aged man who for a long time never discovered a clue that living life without The Guidance from God, was long overdue! God, is my Perfect, Protector, Provider, and Guider, now I'm learning to make no moves without God's Approve! The Lord God Has Given me back my sanity, and with it I possess the power to choose, and I've chosen to be God's Servant forever, and I consciously refuse to live my life any other way! God Is my never-ending treasure that has no measure, and I am His Created Being, who stands, watches, and waits, on The Lord God-without any regard whatsoever, for this earthly place!

30. Fear – Nonexistence

God – May You please keep me focused, may You please keep me on Your Spiritual Track? May I not judge my neighbors and forever condemn them for their unfavorable acts! You God, Alone Are The Only Judge, and You Sit in the judgement seat concerning our Eternal Souls! God, I pray that You Grant me The Wisdom to always submit my wrongs to You – at the base of Your Feet! I've been a drunkard and used mind altering drugs for many years, and that was my lot in life until one night I sincerely asked You and Jesus Christ for help, and ever since then – The Help Has Been Nonstop! God Is where my treasures lie, and I have no fear, or worries to care about when, or where I am to die! Ha, ha, ha...

31. A Promise - I Will Keep...

If I don't have a suggestion to improve my neighbors, I am learning it's best to say nothing at all! Their feelings and healthy welfare are important to me; however, when I was drinking alcohol and using mind altering drugs, I didn't care about my neighbors well-being, or their emotional status in most situations. God, Has Shown me How to Love my neighbors unconditionally, and in return most of them show me a decent degree of respectability. I am the doer of none of this, It's The Spirit of God that's Uncovering from within me, old and valuable gifts! I am in awe upon the discovery of all these old assets which I have totally neglected for years! I truly thank The Lord God for Rescuing me from the hands of the evil one – and for that I never can repay; however, my allegiance to God will run past my dying day; for my soul is Eternal.

32. No Resistance

I am a Servant of The Lord God, and Lessons from God I must undertake; however, many times during the lessons I begin to lose sight of the objectives, by way of jealousy, anger, or hate! These three feelings have always been a hindrance to me; however, just by being conscious of them has been a huge improvement for me! I am still dysfunctional in many ways but I pray for patience, and I work on what is in my life at its present stage. The main objective in my life is to become holy and acceptable to The Most Hole One of Israel Life is The Will of God, and life is a treat; however, I must always remember that there is bitter mixed in with the sweet!

33. The Life of an Ex Fool

Becoming an alcoholic is a step up from being a drunk; for when I was a drunk, I was a punk; for I couldn't face life on life's terms, so I drank to fit in and not feel, and for a long time this is how I handled all of life's joys and ills! I became a recluse, and a slave to alcohol and mind altering drugs, and in reality I was ignorant of what I had become! This went on for many more years, and I was clueless on how to manage my life, and I was dominated by many forms of fear! Many nights I could have died; however, having no sight of this I kept right on getting drunk and high, thinking I could handle it. Now after being given The Gift of Sobriety from God Himself, I would rather die than to ever become drunk, or high again!

34. Designed for Me

Living life on life's terms is a tall order to fulfill, for us all or nothing alcoholics; however, we must earnestly try, or our never ending - enemy will frustrate us into relapse, and in reality some of us die! I said it be for and I'll keep on saying it over and over again; about how Alcoholism is alive and evil, and if given the chance it will continue to kill over and over again! This is a reality realness in which every day granted we alcoholics must face, or we run the risk of neglecting, or taking for granted God's Many Generous Gifts! This disease is a certified killer, and it knows how to kill! But as for me there was and is The Grace of God – God Is my Prefect Protector, Provider, and Guider, and this design for living is how I live my life!

35. Reaching Above The Tangible

I am an alcoholic, and not a drunkard! And in reality that's a huge step up, for this ex-drunkard! I am a drug addict, and not a drug user, and that's a huge step up, for this ex- drug user! I take responsibility not to put alcohol, or any mind altering drugs into my body. I seek Guidance, from The Most Holy One of Israel, day and night; for its God Who Is Changing my life. Self can't change self, The Most Holy One of Israel Is The Creator of All Things, and to His Spirit I give my total allegiance! I created nothing and I own nothing, I merely possess, and that's only by God's Generous Will and Loving Kindness! I could never repay God for what He Has Done and Is Still Doing for me! The facts from God's Actions, turns my being towards a never-ending search for God's Most Holy Kingdom-without any breaks in the seeking!

36. Fate Revealed

The enemies of God are all around, and I pray never to forget-The enemies of God are subtle, and I underestimate not their evil intents! They are wicked and corrupt beings who got caught in a plot to rid themselves of The Creator of all Things. Now by God's Love their time burns short, and I am blessed by God Himself, to divulge this spiritual report! Nothing of this world will ever be a benefit to me; for my life and will is guided by God Almighty, and by God I am free from the bondage of the enemies of this world. And by my constantly seeking The Kingdom of God - God Rewards me with spiritual insights - insights which can't be obtained at any earthly price! For this I am grateful and loyal to The Most Holy One of Israel...

37. My Soul's Goal

There's nothing virtuous about me, I'm just an ex-drunkard and mind altering drug user who is responding positively to what The Most Holy One of Israel is putting in front of me! I am a living miracle; for I could have died on many occasions; however, God Is So Kind and Merciful; fore He Spared my life. Now I live to promote and exalt God 's Most Holy Being! God Has Delivered me from self-destruction, from the scrap heap of lives gone corrupt. He Has Restored me to sanity; for I was insane for many years, and there's no one on this planet, or elsewhere that can prove to me that God Doesn't Care! I am His Property, and He is my Creator, and my soul longs to dwell with God in His Most Holy Presents!

38. The Gift of Love

God Has Given unto me no woman to love, and though my heart is troubled, I have enough faith in God to say it's OK! However, God Has Given me The Gift of Sobriety, and by The Grace of God I haven't had to drink alcohol, or use any mind altering drugs for many days! Life has new meaning to me, and I've never felt these feelings of gratitude ever before; for I was always drunk and high, and with an obsession of how to obtain more alcohol and more mind altering substances. As I write these words my everlasting soul thanks The Most Holy One of Israel, for His Patience with me, and for rescuing me from the bondage of Alcoholism; however, I must give away what The Lord God Has Freely Given unto me, so as to fortify my own sanity. I am the possessor of an evil killer disease that stops at nothing to destroy me!

39. Guilt – Slow Poison

God, Your Servant is ashamed of himself! I deserve not Your Grace; yet God You Constantly Continue to sustain my life, and Your Actions mystify me! There's one true thing God Has Revealed to me, and that is I possess the disease of Alcoholism and Drug Addiction, I'm truly mentally and bodily different from most men and women. Newly sober and mind altering drug free, I've noticed how I was experiencing much shame and guilt, so I constantly sought out God to help me live in the present with a past I was ashamed of and couldn't change! Through time, God Has Shown me I must never allow my old egotistical self to ever reappear in my personality.

40. God's Will – My Benefit

As I grew within my mother's womb – God, You knew that in many days I would face confusion, disillusionment, and impending doom; however, God, You also prepared for me a way to peace and happiness, a way to live life so that I would never look back and regret! And I am grateful to say that through much pain and misery I became willing to sincerely seek Your Help God! The Lord God Has Provided for me a design for living which I could have never accomplished on my own! God Has Truly Shown me what I was, and the reality of it angered me; however, I've made a decision to trust The Lord God unconditionally for the first time in my life. And up to this day that I write, I've not been let down, or misdirected while under The Lord God's Direction! I constantly pray to God to remain teachable and loyal to The Trinity only...

41. Please Love Don't Ever End

Oh God, may You please continue to show us all how to live and relax? God Is The Guiding Way from all of the enemy's hidden traps! I was born with the disease of Alcoholism, and till death I shall always possess its negativity; however, The Lord God Has Provided for me and people like myself a way to compensate Alcoholism's deadly attacks! I can never repay God for His Unconditional Love that goes on and on, and to be a witness to this fact fills my heart with joy, not to mention hope – hope that The Lord God Will Not Turn to Destroy! Dear God, may You please continue to have and show mercy to all of our souls, despite our learned ungratefulness and shortsightedness! May You please God Continue to Help.

42. Relief Upon The Call

Now that I am sober and mind altering drug free, I've been Blessed by God to realize many undesirable things, and these things are a part of me, and they bring hurt to my feelings upon their recognition! However, these things I must face; for they are a part of my recovery, and their presence must be identified and nullified in order to achieve unshakeable serenity: Now there is nothing a drink of alcohol, or any mind altering substance can ever do for me; for God Has Given me The Gift of Sobriety.

There have been days and nights where my killer disease has pressured me with all of its might; however, I remembered God, and I stepped out on faith, and The Most Holy One of Israel Has Granted me Relief from my disease's relentless destructive pace; however, God didn't destroy the disease itself, but rather turned down the heat, and I am forever grateful for the relief! And now this is what I do each and every time my killer disease launches its deadly attacks within my damaged mind!

43. Holy Business Assigned

Every day I deal with death, every day I receive no rest; It's a constant awareness I must undertake, for Satan lies in wait – and my soul Satan wants to take! However, by The Grace of The Most Holy One of Israel I am constantly aware of this marauding Satan and company who are everywhere on this planet called earth! There is no rest for me, and for this I stand in honor for God Has Chosen me to carry out His Will, so I must walk through pain and hurt! Satan has many forms and for many years I've been mentally deceived by these mischievous beings who thrive on seeing others misguided from The Many Gifts from God.

44. A Goal of My Soul

I am finally where I belong, and within each day I receive from God Increased Peace. My soul is overjoyed by how God Cares about me! As I ponder on my life, and as I constantly reflect I came to realized how God Always Cared for me. This caring is in no way limited to just myself, but rather directed towards all! "God, I am Your Property, and there is nothing in this world that will ever fully satisfy me!" Everything here is temporary and has no lasting value, so I choose not to set my soul up for disappointments. God Himself, Has Taught me this! However, I must be a living example to those who search for the true treasure. And the only true treasure is God Himself, and I constantly pray to dwell with God...

45. The Only I AM

I Am In No Rush – I Am The Only I AM – there is no other I AM Like Me! There are images of me; however, I Am complete, I Am Whole, I Am The Creator of All Things, and All Things I Own! I Am In-Comprehensible, My Beginning of Existence no man, or woman can ever bring their imagination to sanely seek; for I Am The Only I AM Who Vastly Surpasses the word unique!... So constantly ponder I, and one day the thought will come to your mind – that I Am The Only Real Satisfaction that you could never seem to find! I Am The Only I AM – and there shall never be another I AM Like Me!...

46. Life- It's Not a Game

Restless, irritable, and discontent was the true nature of my life as far back as I can remember. Happiness was a fleeting thing, and unconditional love was an illusion! It emotionally hurts me to look back on my past life; however, I must; for I must demonstrate unconditional love to my neighbors – just as God Has Shown and Still Shows Unconditional Love to me! "God, Is The Only I AM, and I as His Servant always start to cry whenever I ponder The Unconditional Love that God Has Shown Unto me". As I, God's Servant writes these words I am crying, and I am in a public place and I have no shame; fore The Only I AM Has Shown me that life is not a game!

47. No Comparison

Oh God, may You Provide me with more ways to identify. For I am no I AM – You God Are The Only I AM and I, as Your Servant wish to remove this false identification from my conscious and subconscious thoughts. Oh God, may You Continue to Burn Brightly in my life, standing as the solution, to all of my problems. God Himself, Is The Only Constant, all things that have existence are by His Allowance Only! I've learned to willing turn my life over to God's Care. Nothing in this life will ever fully satisfy me, lest it be to obey and serve God Himself! To make and keep the face of God happy is my heart and soul's # 1 desire! This is the only way I can ever repay God, for All of His Unconditional Love He Has Shown Unto me. There is no comparison to God's Generosity...

48. Prayers From a Servant

God – May Your Lessons of Correct Behavior Continue. May Your Unconditional Love Continue to Flow, I Your Son was very sick, for a very long time; however, now it's by Your Power Father God, that I now start to mature and grow! We alcoholics and drug addicts live day to day, with an incurable disease and the only relief we truly receive without being destroyed by alcohol and other mind altering substances is by constantly seeking Your Wil God, for our lives. God's Spiritual Insights Enable us alcoholics and drug addicts to live and function without having to ingest alcohol, or any other mind altering substances! From those of us who know You Lord God, there is no end to our loyalty to You! However, what of those souls who still suffer from this marauding evil God? Dear God, may You please use me, Your Son and Servant, to become an instrument of information, to reveal nothing but the facts concerning this evil disease of Alcoholism and Drug Addiction; for the pure sake of those who have no clue of the pain and misery they cause to themselves and others!

49. The Promise Keeper

Change is the reality for all men and women, no matter whether they choose to seek God, or stay enslaved to their own inherited sin! The conditions of my life were not of my own choosing; however, I must make good of what The Only I AM Has Given unto me, and be glad about The Gift of Life God Is Allowing me! I have a chance to live forever according to The Promise of The Only I AM! If only I believe and live by the words of God, this promise of Eternal Life will be granted to me. God, Does Not Lie – as a matter of fact God Abhors Liars!... The Only Most Merciful and Faithful Father God Wouldn't Lead His Creation Astray! Why would God Give so much to His Children, only to destroy them ? It doesn't match His Character – For God, Is Love, not Hate...

50. The Must That Must Be

Today I am content, today this alcoholic drug addict is free, today this servant thanks The Lord God, Almighty. This alcoholic drug addict takes responsibility not to induce any substances into his body that would alter the conscious state of his being. By The Grace and Generosity of The Only I AM – His Son and Servant is no longer a slave, to The Evil Forces that be! And to keep it that way and grow, I must be willing to turn my self will and life over to the care of God, each and every day, for the rest of my allotted days, in order to stay sober and mind altering drug free!

51. God's Grace

For the joy of the gift of sobriety, this alcoholic drug addict truly thanks The Lord God with an endless-ness to the thanks! God Has Spared my life, and He Has Presented me with the opportunity to spread and share the joy of a new way to live life with my neighbors without drinking alcohol and ingesting other mind altering substances into my body! My cup runneth over with gratefulness and joy, and these feelings overwhelm me. I've asked myself why has God Chosen me out of so many others who are more worthy than I to receive The Gift of Sobriety, and to carry The Message of God's Good News? Before this alcoholic drug addict could get out the word news, his face has become wet, maybe that's the answer within itself! This alcoholic drug addict loves God more than his own appointed life, and this pleases me to no end...

52. The Only Solution

My disease lives, and it shall always be a part of me; however, by seeking The Kingdom of God, day and night The Most Holy One of Israel Pardons me! In order to be able to keep my disease under arrest this alcoholic drug addict must always continue to seek God's Will for himself.

God Is The Solution to all of my problems and God's Blessings are Processes, not just one time events: So bitter must be taken with the sweet, joy with pain, hot with cold, and through the experiences come to know that God Is The Creator of this Spectacle we human being call life! For what this world has to offer – This alcoholic drug addict prays to lose his longings!

53. May the Process of Love Continue

The Alcoholic, and The Drug Addict – We were very sick people; however, now we live meaningful lives in recovery. The Drunkard and The Dope User are very sick people who live not in recovery, but rather in misery, who constantly suffer with their incurable malady! Oh God, may You Continue to Help us and them who are one and the same. The only difference in being is that one group has accepted You Lord God, and live by Your Words, while the other group lives in denial against what they have heard! This alcoholic drug addict's heart goes out to them; even though, I know it's only God, Who Has The Power to heal them, and by Your Rules Lord God, the choice is theirs! So this alcoholic - drug addict continues to pray, that You Lord God Will Continue to Make me a Blessing to my neighbors each and every day!

54. An Invite to a New Meaningful Life

Recovery for the alcoholic – drug addict is a never ending process; for the symptoms of our condition are forever present within us! Hopeless as it appears, it is not! God Offers a way out, and the out isn't a one-time event! Alcoholics and drug addicts are a separate society of people, who are from birth set aside for a specific reason, and that reason lies only in The Mind of God! This alcoholic – drug addict is over-joyed to be chosen to relate this message to the world, and most importantly to the fellow sufferers of this evil wretched disease, for which there is no physical cure! However, like earlier stated, God, offers a way out. The beginning of the end of a living hell begins with ten sincere words from the heart and soul - "God, please help me, I can't live like this anymore"!

55. Healing – The Touch of God

The process of healing is oh such a wonderful thing; for we alcoholics and drug addicts become conscious of All The Goodness that God Brings! God's Goodness Has Been Here All The Time; however, the bondage of our disease has blocked the reality of God's Goodness from our minds! This alcoholic – drug addict is a living miracle of God's Healing Power and Presents. Circumstances and situations of the world with each passing day concerns me less and less; for it's God's Holy Business which attracts my interests. This alcoholic – drug addict is like a firefly attracted to the light with the purpose of seeking fulfillment, through love and service to God, and my neighbors.

56. In Your Midst

Treat everyone with respect; however, ask the world for nothing, but if the world asks of you give whole-heartedly; for your giving shall be a blessing to them; for I, The Lord God, Have Blessed you!

Hold for yourselves nothing, give freely of what you have, never turn your neighbors away empty of hand! Life, I The Lord God Have Given as a Gift, and All Things therein. Learn to ponder my Goodness and you will soon turn your paths from all forms of sin! Study the face of a child, and you will soon see Me – ponder on how their behavior is guiltless and care free! When you look into the face of a child you are looking at Me – The Lord God Almighty. This is just one of the many gifts, I The Lord God Have Placed within your midst!

57. What Only Matters

The Moves Are of The Spirit, and The Spirit of God Is of Great Abundant Love. Oh, there are no mistakes on how God Directs His Will! The Spirit of God Moves not only in mysterious ways, but rather in ways that are as plain as sight. God Loves All of His Children, and He Awaits their sincere call for help on any given day, or night. The Creator of All Things is Abundant in Unconditional Love – The Creator of All Things Loves His Children Unconditionally! God Himself, Is All we human beings have got, and God Himself is all that there is. May You Lord God Always Continue to Love us, and Show us how to let go of our earthly lot.

Volume - # 5.

1. True Blessings

An alcoholic- drug addict in the recovery process from God is what I pray to always be; for this is the true business of my life that God Has Given Unto me. This alcoholic – drug addict can never become a success at anything else unless he always makes a practice of taking an honest self-inventory, and always ask God to help him improve himself. My soul has begun the process to prosper in this existence, for The Lord God Has Blessed me, by Showing me what I truly am, now I can carry the message of recovery from Alcoholism and Drug Addiction! Nothing worldly matters to me anymore, for God Has Opened Up Freedom's Door! This alcoholic – drug addict no longer tries to fit in, or escape from the realities of this world, and these are true blessings!

2. Nothing of My Own

God, You Show me how not to be selfish, You Show me how to care. Oh God, You Teach me many things, and Your Son and Servant is forever grateful; for You are always there! When my lifestyle broke me, God, You didn't laugh at me, and turn me away; however, You Showed Up and Comforted me, and now Your Son and Servant is new and different in many ways.

My life has a positive purpose, all possible by listening to and obeying Your Holy Words Lord God! This alcoholic – drug addict takes no credit for what he has become; for I know in my heart that it was God Himself, Who Has Redirected my path! Now I

Your Son and Servant will live by Your Holy Words Lord God, and I pray to leave this world by them.

3. Reality Realness

The disease of Alcoholism and Drug Addiction, this alcoholic - drug addict shall always possess; however, I, as God's Son and Servant constantly pray to stay in recovery from this evil unrest! My soul knows without a shadow of doubt about how this evil manifestation constantly plots on how to take me out! Out of all The Goodness God Himself, Has Placed before me to perform; even with the conscious knowledge of possessing this incurable disease, we alcoholics and drug addicts are still given the opportunities to live productive lives by way from the Will of God Himself. Living to obey and serve You Lord God, and my neighbors. Your Son and Servant.

4. Act of Providence

Alcoholism to my left – Drug Addiction to my right – and it really doesn't make any difference where they stand; for these evils shall accompany me for the rest of my life! Responsibility to the reality of these evils is my business. This alcoholic – drug addict has been Blessed by God to have had the compulsion to drink alcohol, or use any mind altering drugs lifted from my conscious and subconscious thoughts; however, the many symptoms of my diseases still remain intact. Nevertheless, this alcoholic – drug addict has been Blessed! Not to drink alcohol, or use any mind altering drugs are Gifts from The Creator of All Things – by which I have failed to accomplish on my own will power, and that to me is a miracle. This is an act of Providence, which This Son and Servant prays never to forget! Always I must remember that Father God Himself, Is The Solution to All of my shortcomings.

5. More Than Hoped For

One of the hardest tasks to perform daily for this alcoholic – drug addict is to unlearn what I've learned over many dysfunctional years! Not to have the compulsion to drink alcohol, or use any mind altering drugs were much needed Gifts that God Gave me! However, confronting myself and continuing to face my surroundings caused me daily to continue to seek God's Kingdom and Counsel in an effort to solve ,or subdue my remaining inferiorities. I, as God's Son and Servant, live my life in obedience to God's Gifts. My life constantly changes for the better as this alcoholic – drug addict continues to respond to The Holy Blessings that Have Been Bestowed Upon me from God! In this responding, worldly things constantly dissolves from my heart, and are replaced with childlike joy and happiness, only granted from the Lord God Himself.

6. Not Always Happy

The road of recovery for this alcoholic – drug addict at times becomes very lonely and sad; however,

those stretches of road can't be skipped , or avoided. It's essential to confront one's past and present conditions, in an effort to develop a measuring stick of productivity, or progress. This alcoholic – drug addict must continue to confront his shortcomings, as well as his assets; despite the feelings of self-pity, or sadness. This is what I as God's Son and Servant must do in order to find the core of why I drank alcohol and used mind altering drugs! It's not an easy, or welcomed exercise for me; however, in searching my feelings in this way, this alcoholic- drug addict becomes more free and pleased with himself, opposed to being enslaved and powerless over my known diseases! All possible by The Generosity and Unconditional Love from God Himself.

7. Giving is Receiving

Being of service to others has been one of the best gifts this alcoholic – drug addict has given to himself, for it's the giving that truly relieves me from the bondage of my selfish self. To see people benefit from my contributions confirms to my soul that I live in God's Healing Solution. To see hope restored to them encourages me to repeat the giving over and over again! To help fellow drunkards and dope users achieve sobriety is a Gift from God Almighty! I as God's Son and Servant constantly thank Him for this loving unconditional job! There is nothing else in this world that this alcoholic – drug addict would rather do, than to direct more of his neighbors to God Himself.

8. Blue in the Face Truth

The responsibilities of an alcoholic – drug addict are tough, and God Doesn't Perform any Special Favors for us! We must bear our crosses just like any other man or woman; however, there is one big difference. The majority of people in the world don't understand, or care about to understand the alcoholic – drug addict woman or man! We alcoholic -drug addicts are mentally and physically different people; however, God, Loves us not less. Our priorities are explicit, and we must keep them to always be; lest we return to drinking alcohol and using mind altering drugs, thus giving up our precious sobriety! In pondering, we come to realize we have lost so much more than sobriety, but rather many other gifts, like our conscious contact with The Creator of All Things to which our disease will lie to us, will tell us we never really had a disease! I pray that The Lord God Allow these words to stand as the truth and bear witness against the evil makeups of Alcoholism and Drug Addiction for all times, for the sake of God's Children.

9. Fruits From Observation

Practicing self – forgetting has become a joyful exercise for me; for the joy of giving to others is becoming a permanent part of me. Giving something of value to others is the real meaning of love! And with no expectations for anything in return is what is called unconditional love. These statements are true and relative; God Himself, Constantly Continues to Unconditionally Give! In observing God's Actions, this Son and Servant of God is beginning to abandon the idea of self – satisfaction; and the wisdom isn't his own!

10. The Intangible Killer

Denial, isolation, and periods of constant unhappiness are just a few negative symptoms of the diseases of Alcoholism and Drug

Addiction. Just these three states of being alone cause the sufferers so much pain and confusion. As this Son and Servant of God writes, I can remember my daily plights – Plights of an Evil Obsession that had and still have plans to kill me! The diseases of Alcoholism and Drug Addiction are alive, and they're evil temptations that know no end –They lie to their human host telling them they can drink alcohol and use mind altering drugs without any threat of a problem! They are killers and have killed for thousands of years; however, this alcoholic – drug addict has been given a Gift, and on a daily basis I face my fears. God Is The Key! Seek God, as I His Son and Servant does, and you too can be freed! Please continue to help the sufferers God.

11. Ask? And You Will Receive!

Up until the age of thirty-three, I the floundering Son of God had no identity: I was a walking dead man with physical death, and no respect from my peers close at hand; however, I received a moment of clarity and I screamed out to God and Jesus Christ for Their Help, and They Showed Up with a plan of recovery for the broken person I had become.

I pray never to forget that night; for that night marked the beginning of the end of bondage evil had upon me! There was no instant permanent gratification that night; however, God Himself Placed a Drive within me that night which remains perfectly intact, all the way up to the day of this writing. My life now stands as a testament to the title of this passage – Ask? And you will receive.

12. Willing to Face Evil

The evil inclinations of my heart must be faced. This Son and Servant of God The Father, must become its master! The infectious influences of its nature must be filtered out from my whole being.

Evil must not be allowed to corrupt me any further; there for this alcoholic – drug addict must seek out God's will and Perfect Guidance concerning every aspect of his life, for the rest of his life. God Has Removed the veil of ignorance from my eyes, and now God's Holy Spirit Sits within my damaged mind's eye, and this alcoholic – drug addict lives his life to do the work The Lord God Places Before him.

13. Treasure That Has No Measure

Each day lived in recovery for the alcoholic – drug addict is like a new found discovery! In earnestly seeking each and every day The Will of The Creator of All Things we become overwhelmed by the spiritual insights God brings! Little by little God's Spirit Engulfs us, and we become less interested in the business of the material world around us! We truly come to comprehend the meaning of what Jesus

Christ said "He who is in Me is stronger and greater, than he who is in the world"! Desires in our hearts for worldly things begin to diminish; we become truly aware of God's Words when He Said, "Love and Treat your neighbors, as you would Treat yourself". The alcoholic – drug addict in recovery truly begins to live life by God's Words – with no exceptions!

14. The Contract

To drink alcohol or to use any mind altering drugs for me is to die; as a matter of fact, this Son and Servant of God, has asked God to do just that: To take my life – for me it's a desired request, one which this alcoholic –drug addict could eternally respect! What was freely given to me is more than an opportunity; for not only has this Gift saved my life, God, Has Made It Possible for me to give away what He Has Freely Given to me! This wisdom has placed me in the state of constant wonderment! This alcoholic – drug addict sees Father God at work daily within my neighbors who possess the same evil diseases as myself! There is no more question in my mind Lord, whether You Love some people and You Hate others – God, You Love All.

15. The Seeking

With full conviction from my being I, Your Son and Servant seek Your Holy Kingdom Lord God! May You find favor in my efforts to serve You. One by one my fellow alcoholic – drug addict brothers and sisters make an effort to seek out my counsel; however, it's Your Gifts to me God that they seek! And this God, You've Blessed me to know is of no power of my own! They seek advice from me constantly – Yet my worldly status is low. In each case I, Your Son and Servant send them to seek out Your Holy Kingdom. For in You God Is where we all find peace of mind from The Evil Forces that be! All of what You Give Me Lord God Is what I, Your Son and Servant give to them. Always with a sincere hope from my being that my words may lead them from their lives of bondage, fear, and sin! - You God Are our Only Salvation.

16. Nothing of This World

Blessed be this alcoholic -drug addict; fore he knows that ninety-nine point nine tenths of everything that exists is none of his business; however, the remaining one tenth is his business, and that reality is plain he possesses the diseases of Alcoholism and Drug Addiction, and that and only that is his business!   Blessed by God Is he or she who is Allowed to truly see The Evil Forces that be! This alcoholic – drug addict has truly experienced the fact that nothing in this world is ever truly stable; for evil is present, and it constantly turns the tables. So having God, Place this wisdom within my conscious and subconscious thoughts has caused this alcoholic – drug Addict to abandon everything that he once sought!

17. The Enlightenment

God, this alcoholic – drug addict prays to never forget all the pain and madness evils transmit! Evils are obsessed to the extreme by trying to destroy all of what You Bring God! This alcoholic – drug addict knows firsthand how evils have frustrated many a man.

The hoarding of material things and power are the tools it uses to block mankind from seeing what God The Father Wants men to see! God Has Truly Blessed me to see these marauding evils that be. Now this alcoholic – drug addict constantly prays to God to be able to pass this valuable information on...   In an effort to help those who suffer from these marauding evils! Blessed are those who constantly seek out The One and Only Living God!

18. The Reality That Is...

For the alcoholic – drug addict to make a decision not to drink alcohol, or use any mind altering drugs is a very difficult commitment for many of us to keep. However, God Is the key; we must constantly seek God's Will for ourselves, or we lose our way to The Evil Forces that be! We alcoholic – drug addicts are the possessors of an evil incurable makeup within our minds and bodies, we have no defense against alcohol, or any other mind altering substance once ingested into our bodies! One drink, or one puff of marijuana starts the evil cycle of dependence which we can't by ourselves stop! God Is our only defense and our only offense against The Evil Forces that be!

19. A Sought After Desire From the Heart and Soul

God, I as Your Son and Servant sincerely pray to You Lord God for the constant ability to stay deep in thought, represented by the color purple. I need Your Teachings Lord God in an effort to stay humble and of very, very low stature in my heart and soul as I live out the remainder of my life! My mind seeks constantly to wander and stray away from the inner beauties that You Lord God Make Available to us all!

The fact that I possess the diseases of Alcoholism and Drug Addiction warrants me no excuse to ever again abuse myself. For You Lord God Have Provided for me a way out of bondage from The Evil Forces that be! God, may You Always Continue to Make me an example of Your Unconditional Love.

20. Reality – Hard Line

There is no one to my left, there is no one to my right, there isn't even anyone by my side, as this alcoholic – drug addict lives these early years of the clean and sober life! This alcoholic – drug addict lives by faith and trust in God's Words as he lives in recovery from the bondage of his former life! Living in recovery for the alcoholic – drug addict at times is a very lonely business; however, the Rewards and the Gifts we receive are priceless and endless! So forward this alcoholic – drug addict will march; even though, little by little from this world he must depart! For us comes an end to the double life; for now we are called to walk by faith, not by sight! God, may we all come to the realization to know that nothing belongs to us. All are Gifts from You Lord God!

21. Back to Love

God, as this alcoholic – drug addict travels the road that leads to You, he becomes overwhelmed and amazed at the work You do! The things You Show me Lord God Cause me to ponder and reflect about

the worthlessness of most of my past acts. God You Continue to Show me the foolishness of my former master. For years Alcoholism and Drug Addiction ruled my life; however, constant frustrations and disappointments finally brought me to a moment of clarity to where sanity sank in for a brief period, and Your Created cried out for help! And God You Showed Up! God You Caused me to finally realize the inevitable force of change! The illusion of being complacent was the constant for me, and it pushed me further and deeper into insanity! God You've Showed me that my life isn't my own; it never was and it shall never be!

Life is a Gift, and this wisdom God You've Placed before me!

22. Bondage That Is No More

All by myself and each man shall be judged alone, all by myself; however, this alcoholic – drug addict is not alone! The diseases of Alcoholism and Drug Addiction are evil wretched entities, and they will never relinquish their grip once they have the human host within their midst! However, there is a way to relief, from the pain and suffering these evils release; I AM Is His Name, and being there for all Is His Fame.

My heart and my soul still feels the pain of the many years of bondage I experienced when evil in my mind reigned! My eyes burn with disapproval; for this soul personally knows what evil can do to you! God may You Continue to Make us alcoholic - drug addicts examples of Your Unconditional Love and Tolerance.

23. Freedom or Slavery

My mind the machine versus my soul the eternal being , and my body is the playground! Oh, how real this analogy is for the alcoholic – drug Addict. Day in and day out we alcoholic – drug addicts are attacked by negative thoughts; thoughts that cover every aspect of our lives past and present, and project to the future with the intent to once again place us in the vicious cycle of active Alcoholism and Drug Addiction! God Is our Only Defense and Offence. We must constantly override these negative thoughts with virtues from God Himself; and through seeking God, we'll come to find these virtues where buried within our hearts all the time! The heart is the orator of all emotions; therefore the heart of the alcoholic-drug addict must be inventoried frequently, in an effort to properly respond to The Evil Forces that be! May Your Spirit Dwell within us alcoholic – drug addicts forever God.

24. A Grain of Salt

Situations that occur in life are by no means mistakes; they are designed for human beings to benefit through God's Loving Grace! So when evil events form and take shape, vent not anger, but rather take the opportunity to present unconditional love coupled with an undying faith! So trust in The Creator of All Things that the evil events taking place are what must be! For surely it's no mistake! Remember unconditional love conquers all hate! Men and women who constantly seek God learn how to restrain themselves from the evils of take, take, take; moreover, they learn how to patiently wait on God to distribute their fortunes from their deeds of unconditional love, coupled with an undying faith! "You will reap what you have sown".

25. Valleys That Must Be Walked Through

This life itself is a very irritating experience, not to mention frustrating; however, what would we have if we didn't have life? God, Your Infinite Wisdom devastates my thinking process, and without hesitation my soul yearns for more of Your Infinite Thought Process; even though my known diseases of Alcoholism and Drug Addiction totally disapproves Your Help! God, You Have Blessed Your Son and Servant to identify the subtle enemy with regularity! This conviction is nothing short of a Gift that You Yourself God Have Given Unto me by way of constantly seeking Your Counsel Lord God, no matter what situations were placed before me! For this Your Son and Servant frequently experiences a state of being overwhelmed by Your Grace.

26. Salvation – God

This alcoholic – drug addict has no luxury of having a day off; for every moment of consciousness must be realized as being an opportunity to seek God's Will for my life! God is everything; however, I am not! So how can this sinful being afford luxuries! My soul knows much misery, opposed to experiencing long periods of joy and happiness! Only children and people who live by every word that proceeds from The Mouth of God have these Gifts! All who are in the middle of this reality are in the power of The Evil Forces that be! There are no mistakes about this reality realness which this alcoholic – drug addict has been Allowed to experience. The truth hurts, yet it can also heal! Thank You God for the truth, and the reality of those who lie. Satan is a liar!

27. The Center of Recovery

Undying faith in God must be laid in the alcoholic – drug addict's heart coupled with humility, which will reveal to the alcoholic – drug addict that it was not by his, or her power that they now enjoy the Gifts of being sober and free from any mind altering drug use! To stay sober and mind altering drug free we alcoholic – drug addicts must constantly seek God's Will for our lives, and there are no ifs, ands, or buts about maintaining our sobriety and growing to prosper in all levels of our being! God is our strength and salvation, and there is no other form of relief to our condition. So the heart of the alcoholic – drug addict must be inventoried frequently in an effort to promote positive motives, while at the same time asking God for the relief from the bondage of the negative ones. For the heart is the orator of all emotions!

28. Inside – Out!

What's in my heart many cannot comprehend, and my Immortal Soul is overjoyed with laughter; for it has finally recognized the wages of sin! God – The Only I AM – Has Answered my conscious and subconscious prayers! This alcoholic – drug addict is overjoyed with his conscious contact with The Creator of All Things. Obedience to God's Will has changed my whole life, and the changes are endless. The more this alcoholic – drug addict seeks God's Will, the less fearful he becomes, and more freedom is possible for him! The Evil Forces that be are clearer to my sights the more I, as God's Son and Servant seek God's Undying Light!

29. Forever Present...

To be loved, to fit in, to be a part of something is what we Drunkards and Dope Users search for within our lives; however, the more we drink alcohol and the more we use mind altering drugs the less this becomes a reality. When we practice these evils we cut ourselves off from God! We become stigmatized and demoralized, and no one shows us love, and we soon become outcasts within our daily surroundings; people shun us and call us hurtful things, and in desperation we look for oblivion, for at least there we don't have to feel! In reality we are walking dead people, existing without any positive purpose, yet God Still Loves us while everyone else abandons us – Oh God, Hallowed Be Thy Name....

30. Predestined

There have been many days and nights this alcoholic – drug addict has been alone. However, God's Plan for me was Designed just in that way. This man in recovery has come to accept Your Plan! It's not to punish me, but rather to show me that it's You, God, Who Are my salvation, and for me not to put my total trust and allegiance in no person, place, or thing, so consequently this alcoholic – drug addict had to be placed by himself to realize this! One of my brothers called me a lone wolf, and in all actuality he is correct. As this alcoholic – drug addict in recovery lives, he constantly seeks God's Will for himself in an effort to obey every word that proceeds out of The Mouth of God, so that life may go well for himself and countless others who are just like him.

31. Everywhere

Everywhere you will find Me, and everywhere you will seek; however, I AM not of this world, but I Have Created everything with and without of your reach! So don't trouble yourselves with the physical search; however, always remember I AM Forever Present and Always at Work! Look beyond this world and there I shall be, look within yourselves and inside you too, you will discover Me! Wherever you may come to be, I will be there in the midst; for I AM God Almighty! So fear not my children and present smiles upon your faces, and always know in your heart that your Creator Resides in all places!

32. Without a Doubt

God, You Are All that Is, and without You none can live: Without You life would be impossible, and that is why You Sent Your Only Begotten Son Jesus Christ to Teach The Gospel: I Your Son and Servant God am weak; this alcoholic – drug addict earnestly seeks to live by every word God that You May Speak! However, in my heart this alcoholic – drug addict knows he will come up short; nevertheless, trusting in the words that You Have Spoken Lord God has brought me more comfort than anything worldly taught! So forward Your Son and Servant shall march, forever keeping Your Words God constant and fresh within my heart!

33. Change to Change

Endless are my lessons – this alcoholic – drug addict welcomes change; however, this attitude took a long time to develop the acceptance of constant change! Spiritual progress is hard earned; for my aim is to be obedient to God's Will, and it always takes genuine effort from my whole being to get results. For The Evil Forces that be are here to temp me, and distract me on any given day, or night! So acceptance of their presence must become a part of me, for it's all a part of what God Wants me to see! This alcoholic – drug addict truly is on another level with no company in sight; however, I must always continue to seek out Father God for even more Spiritual Insights. For The Evil Diseases of

Alcoholism and Drug Addiction constantly seeks to take my life!

34. Spiritual Essence

Happiness, Joy, and peace are mental states of being; they aren't fleeting things! Only God Can Give and Maintain for us these things! All are Intangible, and all are Eternal! Nothing of this world can give and maintain these feelings! Material things have their place; however, the immaterial is above and beyond this physical place! Totally Eternal are their makeups which have no tangible matter! God Indeed Works and Continues to Work in Mysterious Ways! God Has Truly Chosen me to bring this message to the world! Through the soul of an alcoholic – drug addict, God Performs His Work! I, God's Son and Servant Am His Tool, and nothing from myself is revealed here! Always at Your Service Lord God...

35. Left to God

The Diseases of Alcoholism and Drug Addiction have bedeviled mankind ever since the first form of civilization came about: These Evil Entities have killed for thousands of years, and they have no plans of dying out! However, The Most Holy One of Israel Has Provided a way out of the burning house!

The burning house for the alcoholic – drug addict centers within their minds! The medical profession has no physical cure for these diseases. All they can offer is absolute abstinence for our conditions! However, there are deep subtle symptoms of these two known diseases; and total abstinence is only half the solution.

Ours must be of a total psychological change, and no pill can do that! Total dependence upon God Himself is our only chance to live an alcohol and mind altering drug free life. Countless numbers of people have turned away, or never sincerely sought out The Spirit of God, and trusted in Him as being The Solution!

36. Reality for the Alcoholic – Drug Addict

From birth the alcoholic – drug addict is spiritually sick! We are disappointments soon to become a reality: Nevertheless, God, Loves us all! We all have our crosses to bear: Ours just so happens to be Alcoholism and Drug Addiction! However, fear not; for God Has provided a way out of this damnation which wasn't of our doing! Alcoholics and drug addicts in the recovery process from God Himself must always seek God's Guidance, lest they lose their cover and return to becoming slaves to The Evil Forces that be! This is the great fact of reality for us! From our curse we have found salvation, and that salvation is God Himself! God Is The Only I AM and The Only Constant that ever was and that shall forever always be!

37. In Recovery

There comes a time during recovery when the alcoholic – drug addict's concerns for selfish gains become undesirable, and The Will of God for them becomes top priority in the mainframe of their thoughts. In God's Recovery Process, we truly become conscious that this recovery process is not of our power! Gratitude fills our hearts, and we experience joy that we can.t verbally explain! These intangible things no person, place, or thing can ever give us! We know from within our hearts that these are Gifts from The Creator of All Things – A. K. A. God! The self becomes secondary, and The Will of God for us becomes primary; for loyalty to God's Will has begun to set in, and worldly desires constantly continue to diminish from our hearts! This is an undeniable truth to those who have and are being recovered by God Himself!

38. Liberty or Death

We who have experienced Alcoholism and Drug Addiction are a troubled people! Mental obsessions are our character traits, and in everything we do, we try to fit in, or escape from reality! Many of us die from our spiritual illness not even knowing that we were sick people! Many of us have done great damage to ourselves over many years; by constantly drinking alcohol and using mind altering drugs coupled with insane thoughts that our usage would fix us! When we took that first drink of Alcohol, or ingested for the first time any mind altering drug, we cut ourselves off from God's Spiritual Cover!

Everyone needs God's Spiritual Guidance; it makes no difference whether you have the diseases of Alcoholism and Drug Addiction, or not! However, for the alcoholic - drug addict, God's Guidance must become top priority in our lives lest we perish! Death with no dignity, or respect is the condition The Evil Forces that be would desire from our God – Given Lives! God, may You please Continue to Strengthen all those who constantly continue to seek for themselves Your Kingdom.

39. No Ending

We who possess the diseases of Alcoholism and Drug Addiction are people who are subject to constant mental attacks which drive us insane! There is no known physical cure for us! These Evil Forces are so powerful that the idea to kill ourselves sounds like a real good solution for us, rather than go on living this life of mental and emotional torture: People who don't possess our diseases can't even slightly come to know our spiritual sickness! These mental attacks are relentless and evil, with one intention, and that is to kill us! We are truly cursed; however, God Provides, for us an opportunity, to live our lives usefully! Oh God, may You Please Continue to Help us, for we are a troubled people from birth.

40. Exposure

Every day Allowed this alcoholic – drug addict must surrender and pray! Surrender from the delusion of control, and pray for God's Perfect Guidance which Is Infallible! The Evil Forces that be are present and real, and their main objective is to kill! This alcoholic – drug addict is powerless to destroy them; however, God Constantly Gives me spiritual principles to live by plus intuitive thoughts, in an effort to subdue the relentless mental attacks from The Evil Forces that be! There would be no spiritual principles to live by, or no intuitive thoughts needed if The Perfect Guidance from God were constantly sought! Dependence upon Father God must become a way of life for us alcoholics– drug addicts, lest we perish and soon die.

from the relentless mental attack produced by The Evil Forces that be! Always remember God's Unconditional Love!

41. Objective Constant

To Stay Spiritually Centered – we alcoholic – drug addicts must constantly seek out God's Will for our-elves if we're going to be successful at staying sober, and mind altering drug free! "God's Will Must Always Come First, No Matter What!" Alcoholism and Drug Addiction takes no days off, and these evil wretched entities stops at nothing in an effort to kill their human hosts! Obeying and trusting God's Guidance must become a working part of us, lest we fall powerless from The Evil Forces that be! So we alcoholic - drug addicts must always seek God's Kingdom in an effort to stay Spiritually Centered! Without God's Care and Protection we have no chance of living productive sane lives! Our enemy centers within our

minds; there for we alcoholics – drug addicts must have God's Spirit Residing in our hearts and souls at all times!

42. Intervention: A Must

Repetition of prayer and action must become a regular working part of us alcoholic – drug addicts. For many of us, probably for the first time in our lives, we must learn how to trust our innermost gut feelings! This is a practice many of us don't know how to do. And that's no surprise, nor should it be something to be ashamed of. We are alcoholic – drug addicts in The Recovery Process from God Himself, and our m/o "Most Often" was not being able to comprehend our feelings successfully; without altering ourselves by drinking alcohol, or using mind altering drugs! Years of such behavior leaves us bankrupt in every area of our lives; not to forget to mention a wrecked life, and damages done to people whom we have had relationships with! How can we fix the damages and change ourselves by ourselves? We can't – we must have God's Intervention, in order to psychologically change ourselves; and as a result we can come to a position where we can to some degree fix some of the damages done, by our previous behaviors! Self cannot positively change self. We all need The Divine's Help!

43. A Vital Part

Forever changing we alcoholic – drug addicts must forever be, forever adjusting our attitudes as we move closer towards God Almighty! We must keep a close knit consciousness of God's Presents at all times, and place a mark within our hearts to know that it was and is God, Who Has Restored us to soundness of mind! For many of us, obedience to God's Will for us is a very difficult action for us to practice and keep; however, this practice is vital to the life of our sobriety and dignity; for the diseases of Alcoholism and Drug Addiction are alive in us and steadily on the creep and sneak! So we must always seek and keep The Perfect Guidance that The Most Holy One of Israel Has for us! This must become our way of life

44. High Risk

Life for us alcoholic – drug addicts who are in The Recovery Process from God Himself, is no easy cakewalk experience! We have obstacles to overcome just as all people do; however, we can never afford not to seek God's Perfect Guidance, for if we do, we leave ourselves open to mental attacks from The Evil Forces that be, which live within us all! We people of the world who possess the diseases of Alcoholism and Drug Addiction have no defense against our thoughts; they proceed straight to our hearts, and the thoughts influence our feelings, and our emotions cause us to act hastily, whereas most people wouldn't act hastily at all given the same thoughts. Our emotions overwhelm us, and we drink alcohol to fit in situations, or we use mind altering drugs to escape from situations! This process becomes our solution to all of our problems; however, in reality it's an illusion which pushes us further into insanity. We are very sick people from birth, so we must constantly seek God's Perfect Guidance in order to be truly happy while we live out our lives here on earth!

45. Pondering The Only One

The alcoholic – drug addict who is in The Recovery Process from God, Has Been Blessed with many gifts! And all who have breath also have their opportunity to be blessed by God with many gifts! It is by searching out God's Kingdom when we are profoundly overjoyed by The Awesome Power and Loving Kindness of The Creator of All Things, which makes all other desires and longings lose their power from within our hearts!

We who possess the diseases of Alcoholism and Drug Addiction, and are in The Recovery Process from God – At some point find ourselves loyal to God, even over our own lives! God's Will for us becomes first in our hearts, and worldly desires and longings steadily diminish from our hearts! We become agents of God's Unconditional Love and Tolerance. This is the result of constantly seeking God's Kingdom.

46. A Ticket to Freedom

We alcoholic – drug addicts in recovery by God, must constantly continue to inventory our hearts. We must constantly be honest with ourselves, on how we really feel! This practice will outweigh evil thoughts of returning to drinking alcohol, or using mind altering drugs that will come across our inhibited minds; by inventorying our hearts, we find gratitude for being sober and mind altering drug free. We will forever carry the cross of Alcoholism and Drug Addiction; however, by seeking God's Counsel and living by God's Instructions, we alcoholic -drug addicts keep our evil diseases under arrest! God becomes our disease's jailer and our eternal souls are granted freedom while we possess our physical bodies. Only The Most Holy One of Israel Has Granted me the knowledge that this alcoholic – drug addict is privileged to write. Please, my fellow brothers and sisters who possess The Spiritual Sickness of Alcoholism and Drug Addiction, give yourselves the chance to live a fulfilling life by the way of The Only I AM.

47. The Destroyer

Anger is as a thief; it robs people of all serenity and peace! Disrespect for all people, places and things is its command, and its purpose is to destroy and hate everything it can! Sorry to say, anger is a real and present force, whose purpose is to destroy by means of poisonous thoughts: For the drunkard – dope user, or alcoholic – drug addict who are in The Recovery Process from God, this emotion identified as anger is a deadly reality for us! We can't make rational decisions while under its influence; it's a total liability to us; we are vulnerable and confused when under its mental attacks! So neighbors beware of the emotion called anger; its harmful to all who are attacked by it; however, don't worry, for God Is Always Here Watching and Handling with Care!

48. Maladies

The diseases of Alcoholism and Drug Addiction are deficiencies within the makeups of the sufferers' bodies and minds; we have inherit maladies! All appearances on the outside are normal; however, on the inside these deficiencies are real and present; they stem from within our minds and bodies! These character traits are very subtle, only recognizable by fellow sufferers who are in The Recovery Process From God – or by those who are professionally trained in the field of Alcoholism and Drug Addiction!

There is no physical cure for our deficiencies ! The medical profession can only prescribe total abstinence from the usage of mind altering substances! For us alcoholic – drug addicts this is only half the solution to our problem; it's directed at the physical side of our maladies, wherein God must be constantly sought in order to psychologically change our thought patterns, and eventually change our emotional makeups as well! This is the other half of the solution that will solidify total abstinence for us.

49. The path to Salvation

In regard to the possession of the diseases of Alcoholism and Drug Addiction: Your Created, God, wholeheartedly admits and accepts these deficiencies. However, God – As You Allow Your

Created to move closer to You; he has come to realize that these deficiencies are blessings from You! Upon receiving relief from Alcoholism and Drug Addiction's destructive symptoms; the results caused me to continue to seek Your Perfect Guidance for every aspect connecting to my life!

My life is a gift from You Lord God, and by constantly seeking Your Will for my life God, You are Blessing me with wisdom that isn't my own. People seek me out for my advice to their situations, and my being overflows with joy; for Your Created knows that it is Your Character Traits that are becoming a part of me, those by which they seek.

50. Internal Conviction

Faith without works is dead, and to be dead is to be void of soul, and to be void of soul is true nothingness! God, be my witness; for God Is Forever Present. I have lived for many years a worthless life.

However, by being whipped thoroughly by The Evil Diseases of Alcoholism and Drug Addiction; I sincerely cried out to God, and Jesus Christ, for Their Help! From that night to the present day of this writing, my life has slowly progressed from being truly worthless! God and Jesus Christ Have Touched me in ways this soul has never been touched be for and all the work in my life has been accomplished by having faith in Them!

All of my accomplishments belong to God and Jesus Christ – The Father and The Only Begotten Son: There is no greater power in all existence – Save Father God!

51. Our Salvation

Recovery for the alcoholic – drug addict is for all times and must be constantly worked on in every way; for without such practice, God Will Not Grant us peace within our days and nights: What is freely Given to us must be freely given to our neighbors who are suffering as we used to suffer: Father God Is our Only Salvation, and we must become forever loyal and grateful to Him! The I and the me must be abandoned and turned into we. There is no such thing as recovering on our own individual power! That's fantasy for the alcoholic – drug addict throughout the ages! God Is our Power and Strength; It Is God Who Relieves us from the compulsion to drink alcohol, or use any other mind altering substances. All Praise is due to Father God ...

52. Gifts Received and Used

Alcoholism and Drug Addiction are two realities of what my soul possesses. To have had God Show me straight up what my maladies are has been the greatest gift to me in my whole life, except my life! No one or nothing do I totally trust – Save "Father God"! Becoming One with The Creator of All Things is this soul's # 1 Desire! All other desires and longings fall short; for my soul has come to learn that they are all short term and meaningless! True satisfaction and salvation is only found in "Father God!" And everything else is meaningless! So The Diseases of Alcoholism and Drug Addiction has become a very great gift given to my soul! Only people possessing these maladies and are in The Recovery Process from God Himself will be able to comprehend what has been expressed!

53. Real Power

Having The Diseases of Alcoholism and Drug Addiction Arrested from within me are Gifts from God! God Has Become my diseases' Jailer. By regularly seeking God's Will for myself, God Has Granted me Peace of mind, Stability in my emotions, Renewed physical strengths, and Progress in spiritual growth! All of which are accomplished by blind faith in a power which is invisible to me! However, trusting that power has resulted in accomplishments that this soul could never have accomplished while drinking alcohol and using other mind altering drugs! God Has Truly Done for me what this soul could never have done for himself! So now with every day granted – this soul gives thanks to The Creator of All Things! My life is dedicated to The Will of God! No desires mustn't come before God's Will! This soul belongs to God, and by the self-will which God Has Given unto me, I, His Son freely turn my will to God's Bidding!

54. Against the Wind

It's one a.m., and we desperately await the dawn; it's one a.m., and we constantly seek God for the strength and courage to just hold on! Joy comes with the dawn; and life is a new; we must hold on and live life as God Has Instructed us to do! We alcoholic –drug addicts must hold on and not pick up a drink of alcohol, or any other mind altering drugs no matter what happens in our daily lives! We must constantly always remember that God Cares and Unconditionally loves us! So let's let our holding on not just be for our selfish selves, but let's let our suffering stand as obedience to God's Most Holy Will!

55. Marked in Eternity

Selfless behavior is how I strive to be; selfless throughout eternity; however, at the moment my being is subject to the confinements of space and time! Here is where God Calls me to sacrifice worldly desires that have manifested themselves within me! Possessing The Diseases of Alcoholism and Drug Addiction turned out to be a giant plus; for my malady has caused me to continue to seek The Creator of All Things in an effort to find answers to relieve my daily pains. And in my seeking God Introduced me to the quality of selfless service to others! This character trait has not only relieved me of my depressing feelings, it has filled my life with joy, by consciously knowing that I am constantly helping others without any expectations of anything in return, and that's true unconditional love.

56. Code for Prosperity

For the alcoholic -drug addict in recovery by God, the daily prescription must read work! - work! And more work! We must ask God what that work should be; for every person's situation is different; however, work awaits us. This isn't a favorite task for any alcoholic – drug addict, simply because for many years we have lived very selfish and self-centered lives, and the only work we have accomplished was for our own selfish desires!

Living sober and clean is a very real and tough challenge for us, and it's even tougher when we don't have God to rely upon! We who possess the diseases of Alcoholism and Drug Addiction must come to a point of understanding that we can't live this life without God's Guidance, Protection, and Provisions. Prosperity will not be granted us! We are laymen and must be taught how to live life quietly and walk humbly under the Obedience of God's Decrees!

57. Subtle Killers

The extremes are the main character traits of the alcoholic – drug addict ; there is no middle ground for us: It's all the way, or no way! This is how we live our lives; we are complicated people with an insecurity about us that constantly suggests to us that we are not good enough, so we must work harder to be "better than"! We are very sick people, and many of our character traits go unnoticed for years. Many people are unaware of our maladies, including us! Untreated Alcoholism and Drug Addiction is deadly! Not only do we kill ourselves, but many innocent people are killed, or injured by us daily! The Diseases of Alcoholism and Drug Addiction are evil wretched entities that are alive and real. They stage relentless mental attacks, with intentions to kill their human hosts! I've come to learn that God Himself Is our Only Hope to arrest their deadly influences.

58. The Keys to Our Lives

Recovery for The Alcoholic – Drug Addict is for the rest of his or her life! We are never cured of Alcoholism and Drug Addiction; however, God Provides us with a safe haven while we live out our lives in our bodies; provided we make a practice of seeking God's Perfect Guidance for our lives! God must become our Perfect Protector, Provider, and Guider; there are no exceptions! If we desire to never be enslaved by These Evil Wretched Diseases ever again, we must walk by faith in God, not by our own sight! This is what God Has Shown me by various examples! This alcoholic – drug addict in the recovery process from God, questions not the recovery process! I have been Blessed by God to see and bear witness on how the enemy of God uses our thoughts to deceive us. So are thoughts are tainted with deception; there for our thoughts are worthless and deadly! What do we do? We develop an undying faith in The Creator of All Things and we learn to make decisions from our feelings; our feelings never lie!

59. The Reality of What Is

Living with an incurable disease from one day to the next is oh so frustrating. And for alcoholic – drug addicts in the recovery process from God, there are no exceptions; however, our lives are much better than they ever were. Now we live by The Guidance from God. We walk through our daily pains without picking up a drink of alcohol, or any other mind altering substances no matter what; and through the passing of time we gain dignity and an unshakeable faith in The Creator of All Things. For God Has Given us Insights to know that the path we now walk, is the path that He Has Made Straight for us! We alcoholic – drug addicts who are in the recovery process from God Himself are Blessed with Gifts beyond Gifts and Riches beyond Riches! For what we possess no thief can rob from us and no moth can destroy through the passing of time! We live our lives by God's Will for us... Nothing comes before God's Will. There are no exceptions!...

60. A Common Deception

I'm so tired! - Where do I go from here? I'm so tired of being ruled by so many forms of fear! Nowhere am I safe. There is no peace within; I'm a slave to alcohol and other mind altering drugs, and I'm afraid this is how my life will end! What a shame to be ruined like this. In the process I will forfeit God's Many Bountiful Gifts! Yes, a fool I would truly be, in not seeking God's Spirit to help me! All power and forces are from God! So fear not your present situation, and believe in God's Healing Spirit and that it will wash away your sins! Now this doesn't happen overnight; you must constantly surrender over to God your self-will! This isn't an easy task to practice, especially when you're used to doing what you want to do! However, doing what you wanted to do brought you to your knees, and your life became unbearable filled with much pain and ongoing agonies! God is our life and our salvation; remember this truth and it will guide you through any given situation!

61. A Different Breed

It's always tough, and the it is life! Living life with all of its unseen forces working upon people who have life is a very difficult task to master! Now in the case of the alcoholic – drug addict, the effects of these unseen forces influence us to where we withdraw from people in general, and way before we picked up a drink of alcohol, or used any other mind altering substances we were deemed different by our peers, and many of us knew we were different people! The way we react to these unseen forces causes us to try very hard to be like people that are around us. We never took opportunities to explore our own selves to find out who or what we are, or were! This is no fault of our own; we are just simply made to carry the burden of these ills! Alcoholism and Drug Addiction are Evil Wretched Diseases! I've come to learn that

God's Spirit Holds The Solution, to our maladies!

62. The Succession

Unconditional Love, coupled with an undying faith in God is what we alcoholic – drug addicts must constantly seek to practice so that we may become useful tools for God to use, and in turn God overwhelms us with joy and happiness; which pushes us further away from our old selfish thinking! To experience joy and happiness in this manner is an appointment from God Himself! We alcoholic drug addicts are in constant need of attention and acceptance – but who isn't? It's just so acutely demanded by us! However, seeking God's Will for ourselves we learn how to demonstrate unconditional love and tolerance in every situation that may confront us while we live on Earth. Unconditional Love, coupled with an undying faith in God makes our actions stand as everlasting marks of goodwill to all people, places, and things we may come into contact with!

63. Facts of Reality

No group of people knows what it is to be unloved like the alcoholic – drug addict in the recovery process from God, (or not)! We know what "Living Hell" truly means! All who possess these Evil Wretched Diseases can truly identify with being separate and unloved by family members and peers. Unaware of our diseases we try so desperately to fit in, or isolate from events that occur in our daily lives. We are seriously ill people, and society can't fix us! Only God Can Save us, and God Has Done just that for many of us who were cursed from birth with these Spiritual Maladies!

However, we as individuals had to be thoroughly beaten up by Alcoholism and Drug Addiction to arrive at the point of total defeat, and in desperation we knocked on God's Door and sincerely from our hearts asked for His Help! Then and only then did we receive relief from the death grip of Alcoholism and Drug Addiction. There is no other help for us! And that's the cold stone reality for people who possess the diseases of Alcoholism and Drug Addiction. We must constantly seek God's Guidance for our lives, or we are doomed to die by the way of Alcoholism and Drug Addiction – known facts of this world!

64. The Infallible

Expect nothing from people; for they are all fallible, and in no expectations you'll save yourself from their weaknesses. You yourself are weak; there for why damage yourself further? Ask only from God, and expect nothing but great things! God will never let you down, or misguide! This comes from a person who is truly Blessed by God Himself! Alcoholic – drug addicts who aren't in the recovery process from God are always dependent upon people, places and things, which always fail them, and they become heavily distraught! Even in the recovery process from God Himself, we sometimes get caught up in this dependence; however, according to our spiritual condition we may or may not be seriously injured; for we quickly remember that our salvation isn't in people, places, or things! Our salvation is delivered from Our Precious Father God – Our Maker!

Volume - # 6.

1. Not of Our Minds

Incomprehensible is the only way to comprehend life! Who amongst the breathing holds the true purpose for the reason for life?

Only God knows the answer to the previous question! Maybe after this soul is removed from his physical body the answer from God may be revealed to me! However, until then this alcoholic – drug addict, who is in the recovery process from God Himself, must live in the effort to be of maximum service to God and to all who have the gift of life as I do! No more questions to why life is! Now is the time to live! From a living hell to the preparation to the ascension to Heaven.

2. The Stand

There is nothing that God can't do!... He has all power; however, God is no bully; neither is He a doormat! In a short time God Has Done for me what I could have never done for myself! God Relieved me from the death grip of Alcoholism and Drug Addiction and this soul will always be grateful and loyal to The Most Holy One of Israel forever! I stand for God, and if be God's Will I will die for God! This soul that is me will one day return to The Creator of All Things, so why not return to Him with loyalty, by upholding and honoring all of His Decrees, and above all no regrets?

3. The Road to relief

For alcoholic – drug addicts, change from their alcoholic – drug addict thinking is a must! A psychological change must occur from within them, if they are going to stay in God's Recovery Process! No pill can do that! They must experience an intervention from God! God Is the Only Power that can produce the change! This alcoholic – drug addict is a living example of this fact! And from all times this has been the end result from all who have received relief. They would tell you that they truly asked God for His Help! - That they could no longer live the way they were living anymore! And the asking was from their souls, not their minds!

4. Hard Yet Freeing

The mind of the alcoholic – drug addict is totally different from others. We are mentally different from birth! This fact isn't easy for many of us to accept! For years many of us may live in a state of denial and soon to follow total isolation! Lonely, hurt, confused, and in constant fear is the basic description of the alcoholic – drug addict who is not in the recovery process Provided by God Himself. Depending upon our personalities and how much damage we have done to ourselves, these character defects may persist for a long time, even while in the recovery process from God Himself! However, we must stay diligent and keep in our hearts the conviction that God Loves us and surely knows of our malady. We are never cured of Alcoholism and Drug Addiction; so we must never entertain the thoughts of having a drink of alcohol or the use of any mind altering substances, thinking they will make our lives better!

5. No Exceptions

Complacency for the alcoholic – drug addict in or out of the recovery process formulates misery! In either case self-centeredness is being promoted! This is a very dangerous posture for the alcoholic – drug addict, whether he or she is in the recovery process or not! We must rid ourselves of self-centeredness or eventually the effects will kill us, or push us into having thoughts of killing ourselves! The condition of the alcoholic – drug addict is very complicated in many ways. This is way we wholly trust infinite God, rather than our finite selves! The alcoholic –drug addict who functions with an unaided will is surely doomed to die an alcoholic – drug addict death! This statement comes from the heart and soul of an alcoholic – drug addict who is in the recovery process Laid Out by God Himself! There are no exceptions!

6. Under Grace

No cure, only temporary restraints are the realities for all alcoholic – drug addicts. Life is a process and relief from our ongoing diseases holds no exceptions! Our diseases centers from within our minds, and there is no physical cure! However, God isn't heartless and He Has Provided for us a way to live meaningful lives, and that way is through His Spirit. We are all called by God to live our lives in a certain way, and when we who have Alcoholism and Drug Addiction start to live by God's Guidance, we receive relief from the mania of Alcoholism and Drug Addiction. There are no exceptions for our society of people! We are mentally and physically different from birth! Our symptoms are very subtle; only blessed people can recognize the symptoms in an individual! Alcoholism and Drug Addiction has been untreatable for many years. Relief from these deadly diseases is only able to be interrupted by God Himself!

7. Numbered Days

Alcoholic – drug addicts are very sad people, for we experience loneliness over and over again. For us this turns out to be a living insanity! We constantly seek the alcohol and other mind altering drugs; for it provides us with temporary relief from the terrible loneliness that gravitates our souls! However, it's a cheat, for it pushes us closer to physical death! To observe the lives of practicing alcoholic drug addicts is truly a heartbreaking experience, especially for those who are close to us! When our diseases are in control of us the viewing of our behavior in the eyes of the world is one of astonishment! Only God Can Save our souls, or else we destroy ourselves! A reality realness that is oh so real for us!

8. Shades of Eternity

This work that is being done the fire cannot consume; for this work is handed to me from God with intentions of helping my neighbors sidestep impending doom! Alcoholism and Drug Addiction are intangible prisons that are oh so real! This evil constantly continuously attacks the sufferers, and God is our only shield! With each breath I take, the diseases take also. It will always be a part of me, and this part God calls me to master and rule; for this evil is intangible, and my soul it wants to consume! The Father of life I diligently seek; for God is my only defense against this evil that is always on the sneak and creep! So there it is The Theme of my life. The choices of God and goodness, or death and bondage. The realities of The After Life...

9. Alive and Present

Alcoholism and Drug Addiction are two very deadly diseases; they are intangible forces that are oh so real! They constantly continuously attack the thought process of the bearers! There is no known physical cure from their attacks; however, God Has Provided a way of release from their death grip! It's a way to live which God Has Graciously Provided for us. We must live this way in order to live productive lives. Else we are engulfed by the devastating attacks this evil attacks our mind with!

This evil is alive yet unseen; however, it is there! This is the awesome gift that God Has Allowed me to mentally, physically, and spiritually see! I am a bearer of this evil , and it is a part of me; nevertheless, God's Power Is Always Available to me!... This evil will never cease in trying to consume my soul! This is why God Has Provided a certain way in which we alcoholic – drug addicts must live! Any variations from His Orders will place us in the powerlines of evil. There are no exceptions!

10. No Greater Gift

To uplift God is the only thing that makes me constantly pleased. Nothing else comes close, except The Only Begotten Son! Deep runs my loyalty to Them Both! The Father of Life and The Only Begotten Son were the only two beings who cared for me – when the rest of the people who knew me counted me out! They simply gave up hope for me, or they just didn't care! No hard feelings do I harbor; for God and The Only Begotten Son Show me how to unconditionally forgive and love all who breathe the breath of life! Sometimes though, I get caught up in self, and I lose sight; however, The Ways of The Father and The Only Begotten Son Quickly Remind me of my duty! Their Ways Are Becoming Sealed in my heart! There is no greater gift than this!

11. Beyond Man

An open wound no man or woman can ever fix, Only God Can Fix, and slow and painful is the process! This wound the eyes can't see, nor can the hand touch – it's intangible and it hurt very much! This wound is called Alcoholism and Drug Addiction, and it constantly torments the sufferers' souls! God's Instructions are the only relief for the sufferers' souls, and we must obey them lest we perish from The Diseases of Alcoholism and Drug Addiction! Worry and self- pity must be abandoned; for this state of mental

being only adds to the problem. For years alcohol and other mind altering drugs were used as pain relievers; however, they turned out to be chief deceivers! When my drug activities finally broke me, all alone this child of God stood, with an intangible open wound that no man or woman could fix! In desperation I called to God and The Only Begotten Son, for Their Help! They were and are my only help.

12. Of Self

We must learn to master the realities of what we truly are in an effort to become useful tools for God to Use. External things have their place; however, it is of the intangible forces that we must address constantly! Rigorously we Alcoholic – Drug Addicts must confront these forces – there is no complacency for us! The self must be sacrificed – for the benefit and well-being of others!

This is essential for our recovery and personal well-being. This practice must become a part of us, just one more addition to the way we must live our lives! We must strive to demonstrate unconditional love and tolerance towards all we come in contact with, with no exceptions! For this is how Father God Treats All of His Created Beings!

13. A Circle Within a Circle

From deep within my soul these words are spawned with an intention to captivate the alcoholic – drug addict's heart and soul! We are bonded together beyond any other bond, we share the same brain circuitry pattern, and we are different from the rest of humanity. However, from God's Grace, He Has Given us each other, and we possess many gifts; I am reaching out to my neighbors by way of these words with the intention to uplift those who are still suffering from Alcoholism and Drug Addiction! God's Power, Protection, and Care Are Available to all who seek Him! But for The Grace of God, there go I who is no greater or lesser than any man or woman who breathes the breath of life!

14. The Eternal Trench

Warped are my thoughts, yet how does this soul continue to live his life without drinking alcohol or ingesting any other mind altering drugs? Scrambled are my emotions, yet how does this soul make decisions that are beneficial to himself and others without the aid of mind-altering substances? Down trodden is my soul, yet how does this soul manage to survive the many heartbreaking mistakes that have already been made? There is only one answer to all of the pervious questions, and that answer is practicing faith and trust in God's Power, Protection, Guidance and Care no matter what the situation! A constant surrender to God's Will for my life is the driving force I, as an alcoholic – drug addict must always practice! I will not prosper without God's Perfect Protection and Care; this is a reality realness that has been made available to me through God's Grace.

15. All We Need

Alcoholic – drug addicts who are in the recovery process from God's Grace must always stay deep in thought with the intentions and direct asking of God what it is they must do in their allotted time to help the people who are still sick! We trade in our old lifestyles of drinking and using other mind altering drugs for the life God Wants us to live! God becomes our new found Power and Strength, and with His Protection and Guidance we alcoholic – drug addicts come to find we can face any life-given situation, with dignity and respect for ourselves and our neighbors who once knew us as drunkards and dope users! We come to learn we don't need drugs or alcohol as a crutch or coping mechanism to face life! For the alcoholic – drug addict who is still sick, or for those in the recovery process from God's Grace, there stands but one simple truth – God Is All We Got and all we need to become useful tools for God to use. This comes from one who has been greatly blessed from God.

16. Thoughts and Process

Alcoholics and drug addicts are mentally different people: Our mindsets are obsessive; we can possess a positive or negative thought and run it through our minds over and over again, without any intentions of stopping, or even being conscious of what is taking place. Truly creative or destructive we can be; this is the reality of those who possess this mindset! Trusting in God to guide our thoughts and actions is our only hope to live productive lives. The alcoholic – drug addict functioning with the unaided will is like an accident just waiting to happen! In the light of our obsessive minds, so many unsuspecting people are harmed by us that it is hurtful to the thought! Recovery for the alcoholic – drug addict is slow and painful; however, we must face the reality of what we truly are! Everyone who breathes the breath of life has problems, and all roads are from God, and all roads lead right back to Him! So, may we all find the joy of God's Grace as we travel.

17. From Darkness Into Light

In the soul of every alcoholic – drug addict there is a pressing feeling of being different. Before the first drink of alcohol or any other mind altering drug was ingested into the body, there were pressing feelings of not being like the rest of the people we happened to be around. The heart knew of the difference; however, it could not display the information to the soul with explicit conformation! Our unaided thoughts constantly ran information to the contrary! This kept us in the dark about ourselves for years, and for many unfortunate countless souls to their deaths! For many years this soul knew it was something wrong with himself, but what? But there for The Grace of God go I; newly sober and free from any mind altering drugs of an addictive nature! As he writes these realities about himself and many who are just like him, he praises God! Whoever possess these diseases will identify with everything that has been written: If so, now is the never-ending task of seeking God's Will for yourselves to end your deadly obsessions!

18. No Questions

No identity and marked with a future of futility is the best description of the alcoholic – drug addict who is unaware of his or her condition! For many years this description fit me to a "T". As time passed my condition worsened; physical death was close at hand many a night; however, Father God Protected me!

Now as this soul lives the life of being sober and free from any other mind altering drug use, my life belongs to Father God, I am His Property; for it was and is God, Who Keeps me free from my obsessive mind. God's Will for my life is my number one concern! This soul stands for The Lord, and this soul will die for God, with no questions asked! This is the reality realness of my life!

19. Set Free

As this soul ponders his past, anguish registers upon his face! The reality of what happened must be confronted for the sake of those who are just like me! The diseases of Alcoholism and Drug Addiction ruled my life! It was my master for years! However, God Has Saved me, and now this soul is allowed the opportunity to divulge the message of recovery! It's not easy to face the reality of what you truly are, especially if it points to negativity! When this is done, then and only then can the process of recovery begin. My life today is Protected by The Creator of All Things. It is God Who Relieves me from the bondage of evil! From one of many who is being blessed by God.

20. Standing Alone

This soul stands alone, and it's O.K. This soul stands for God Almighty, and He's my Bread each and every day! This soul's number one desire is to do The Will of God! In this life there are many temptations to draw souls away from turning to God, and this is as it should be; for it is the will of Satan! So alone this soul will stand for God, and it's O.K.; for God Has Given me life, and this soul belong to Him The Only I AM! Nothing of this world is for me and that O.K; for God Almighty Is The Master of all my days!

21. Steadfast Reality

Precious, Precious, Precious, Precious, Precious Father God, You are all we've got! Without Your Perfect Guidance Father God, we alcoholic – drug addicts perish by way of our unaided wills! All people need You Lord God; however, we alcoholic – drug addicts are extremely vulnerable to our thoughts! Only Your Power Lord God, Can Shield us from our unaided obsessive thoughts! I am an alcoholic – drug addict, and that's a reality realness that shall always be! Nevertheless, God's Power and Strength are available to all who sincerely ask for His Help! We alcoholic – drug addicts in the recovery process from God must always seek out God's Perfect Guidance for our lives, lest we fall subject once again to our unaided wills. The falling could register a relapse, which may delay the beauty of freedom, Set Forth from within us by God Himself!

22. Mental Marks

The thoughts of alcoholic – drug addicts are repetitive, they run over and over again. This function resembles a broken record, which constantly repeats itself! Pain registers upon my face, as I remember my early childhood. The repeating thoughts, telling a joke and saying it over and over again, to the point of aggravating others! These mental marks are signatures of an alcoholic – drug addict! We must learn to face the reality of what we truly are and sincerely ask God, for His Help! This must become a regular practice for us, lest we fall victim to the obsession of our thoughts, and thus drink alcohol and use other mind altering drugs to the death! A reality realness that is oh so real for people who possess the diseases of Alcoholism and Drug Addiction!

23. Nothing Else

Everything that is – Is by Your Will Lord God! It's by Your

Allowance and by Your Allowance only that everything exists! So as for myself, there is no rush to do anything. Nothing is mine; everything including me belongs to You Lord God! If it be Your Will Lord God, may You Continue to Allow me to seek You? You are the only stability that there is; everything else is meaningless or temporary! I trust You and only You, Lord God, totally! Nothing else gets my total loyalty... People, including myself are beginning to bore me! But You Lord God, are to the extreme contrary!

24. The Never-Ending Search

As I look deep within myself there is much pain; however, the searching must be done, for the benefit of those who possess the diseases of Alcoholism and Drug Addiction like myself! Information about this evil must be exposed! What good is there in drinking alcohol or using other mind altering drugs to one's own death? Only the constant dependence upon God can break this evil cycle! This is a fact, not a theory; for I am living proof of God's Handy Work! God Almighty relieves me daily from the obsessive thoughts of my mind to drink alcohol – or use any other mind altering substances. This is a gift that no person, place, or thing can ever take away from me! God is a Shield of protection and a Perfect Guide to right living; His Assistance is available to all who constantly seek Him!

25. A Forum of God's Grace

Life for the alcoholic – drug addict who is a part of the recovery process Laid Out by God Himself has a very rocky time of it at first! Once the drinking of alcohol and other forms of mind altering substances have been abandoned, and God Living is attempted to be lived, we alcoholic – drug addicts need constant contact with our brothers and sisters who have come before us. We are granted the opportunity of living a second life. All of our old ideas and ways of living must be abandoned, even if only a little at time, and generally that is the basic transformation that we all go through. A total psychological change must happen from within us. God, and only God Can Perform this act! There but for The Grace of God, go we alcoholic – drug addicts, who have been blessed by God Himself, to have not the obsessive thoughts constantly to drink alcohol, or use any other mind altering substances. Only Granted by God Himself!

26. Leave End-in God's Hands

Undying faith in The Creator of All Things, we alcoholic – drug addicts must constantly have burning within our hearts, souls, and minds at all times, with no exceptions, if we are to stay sober and free from all forms of mind altering drugs! God calls us to worship Him in all areas of our lives! For it is You, God, who art our Perfect Protector, Provider, and Guider, and we alcoholic – drug addicts who have been blessed with the gift of sobriety and freedom from all mind altering drugs must always remember this fact, or we are sure to drink alcohol and use mind altering drugs again, and we may die from our known diseases! It's just that simple for us! The Lord God Truly Loves us, and He Has Prepared a place for us. So my fellow alcoholics – drug addicts, never lose faith in The Creator of All Things, and bear whatever situation with unswerving confidence in God's Decision.

27. All We've Got

The Creator of All Things Is the alcoholic – drug addicts only defense against the wretched mental attacks we are prone to at any time! As I write about the reality of my condition, my soul becomes troubled. I am an alcoholic – drug addict, and I shall always be an alcoholic – drug addict, whether I am a part of the recovery process Laid Out by God Himself, or not! This is the fact of my existence – not a theory! I am subject to mental attacks from the enemies of God, with no form of relief, but by way of alcohol, or other mind altering substances. God and His Spiritual Way of Life is my only defense against the ruthless enemies. There is no complacency for people like myself; we must be forever diligent in regards to adding our wills to God's Will and to trust and obey His Perfect Guidance no matter what. This strict obedience takes practice, and The Creator of All Things knows this, and He Graces us according to our willingness to become willing to allow Him to Guide our hearts and actions!

28. Life or Death

It's tough for the alcoholic – drug addict to live life on life's terms whether in or out of the recovery process Laid Out by God Himself! In the recovery process we have hope, and if we're honestly consistent in seeking God's Will for our lives, we soon discover that His Way of Living is the best way of living

life we have ever come to know. We learn to live by principles, not by our own wills! Living by self-knowledge we are handicapped, confused , and frustrated, we are drunk and high constantly, we are unstable individuals who are never at peace, we are always at war with the world, we are a doomed people!

The Spiritual Way of Life is our only hope to have a useful life. We are at peace when we constantly seek God's Kingdom, we're able to have healthy relationships with the people about us, and we're no longer enslaved by physical substances – God Is our Newfound Power and Strength forever! We have finally come home at last!

29. On Point

No rest, yet there was plenty of stress – no joy, yet there was much pain! This was a constant reality for my young life; I was unaware of possessing The Diseases of Alcoholism and Drug Addiction! I don't want to write about this, but I must; for The Almighty God Has Relieved my soul from much of this terrible stuff! It hurts to remember; however, I am called by God to never forget the evils of Alcoholism and Drug Addiction, and that it will always remain for me a constant threat! It lies and waits for me to forget the downward path that it constantly projects! But God is my newfound strength and power, and I seek His Kingdom "Himself", hour after hour. No words can describe the joy and fulfillment God Supplies; however, I can show a part of it with a smile through my own God – Given eyes.

30. Fact – Not a Theory

Alcoholism and Drug Addiction shall always be a part of me, as I breathe the breath of life: God Has Shown me there are no ifs, ands, or buts about this fact of my makeup! My mind undergoes constant attacks, even while not drinking any alcohol or not using any other mind altering substances. This is a fact, not a theory. This malady is deadly if it is not treated. It has killed for thousands of years and it's not going to stop! It's evil in nature and its intentions are to destroy all it can. God Has Blessed me by Giving me a Daily Reprieve, one day at a time, to be relieved of the deadly obsession to drink alcohol or use any other drugs that will alter my mind. Alcoholism is intangible; however, it's oh so real! God is intangible, yet He is oh so real also! The sufferers will be driven to the point to choose one over the other, and this a fact, not a theory!

31. Life's Terms

Everything in life is based on how we as individuals feel. No one who has the breath of life is exempt! These feelings all have an opposite, they influence mankind greatly! Now for The Alcoholic – Drug Addict, these feelings or emotions are our handicaps. We cannot accept them as they truly are! So we use alcohol and other mind altering drugs as a solution to the emotions: Many of us do this for long periods of time, and the end result is that we have become immature in regard to accepting life on life's terms! Many of us become remorseful because of it. We feel there is no way out; some of us contemplate suicide as a solution, when the drugs reach the point of being non-effective! Oh what a real problem for these type of people! Only God Can Save – For God Has Saved me.

32. It's Alive

At any given place, at any given time, The Diseases of Alcoholism and Drug Addiction can attack me through my thoughts! It will use any method it can to deceive me. What we call Alcoholism and Drug Addiction are alive! Yet it's intangible and oh so real! Its number one concern is to kill as many people as it possible can! It has no respect of person; there is no mercy in its house. It's a ruthless killer! Alcoholism and Drug Addiction are very powerful; however, God Has All Power, and seeking God for relief from these evil diseases is what I've found to be my only defense against the relentless mental attacks form Alcoholism and Drug Addiction. May the words I have written be beneficial to all who can hear! I've said it once and I will say it again: Alcoholism and Drug Addiction are evil and it's alive. Those who suffer not, cannot even imagine the pain we constantly go through!

33. Always There

The disease that centers from within my mind is evil! It longs to destroy the soul that is me! It torments me even to this day that I write; it's a sure killer of human life! However, I turn to God, for direction and salvation from this intangible killer, who has killed countless souls like myself, over many years! Alcoholism and Drug Addiction are very tricky and sneaky; its main purpose is to kill the individuals who are susceptible to its persuasions. I've learned to turn my will and my life over to God's Care, for God would never harm me. God Loves me, and His Power, Protection, and Guidance are available to me at all times.

All I have to do is ask God and have faith, and I have learned that God surely does for me what I can't do for myself; however, God won't do for me what I can do for myself! So work must be included along with my faith in God, to enact His Loving Power that is always there.

34. Enemy Constant

The enemy pressures me most of the time; the enemy centers from with my mind! So what am I to do with this evil that is intangible and oh so real? How can I live a productive life with this evil constantly plotting to destroy and kill? There is only one solution to this ongoing evil, and that is to live by spiritual principles. The only support of the universe is God Himself! When I seek out God, the enemy in my mind takes cover; however, its standing by waiting for another opportunity to frustrate, confuse, and manipulate me! Its mission is to take me and all people it can from the many gifts of this life that God Has Given us all! I am so grateful to The Lord God, He Has Made me aware of the enemy! The enemy hates God's Compassionate ways! This revelation to me is a gift beyond gifts and a treasure beyond treasures.

35. Without a Cause

Defiant, defensive, aggressive, ready to attack was the way I lived my life for many years before I surrender to God and His Plan of Recovery! My former lifestyle brought me closer to physical death. Nothing positive did I ever accomplish that was a benefit to others or myself. I was really warped mentally and emotionally, when I asked God, and Jesus Christ for help. I was at my last tiresome end.

I ran out of ideas to make life work for myself, I was truly beaten up by The Diseases of Alcoholism and Drug Addiction! I had drawn up the white flag, but to what at the time I didn't know, but what I did know was that I couldn't live my life the way I was living it anymore, or I would surely lose my mind-or my life-because of my acts! Now I live by faith not by sight!

36. A Clear Picture

The Grace from God that is upon the whole world will one day be experienced by each person that has the gift of life. To be conscious of God's Grace must become manifest in the mind of The Alcoholic – Drug Addict who is in the recovery process from God. Total surrender to God's Care must become an ongoing practice in the lives of people who possess these incurable deadly diseases of Alcoholism and Drug Addiction. This will formulate true sobriety for these types of people. Anything short of total surrender to God's Care will cause a gap, between sanity and ego buildup! This attitude for these types of people will sooner or later formulate the idea to start drinking alcohol again or the usage of other mind altering substances; this a fact not a theory! God's Way of Living must become the apex of our lives, or destruction from our known diseases will become reality.

37. The Formula

For The Alcoholic – Drug Addict to stay sober and free from any mind altering drug use, the following formula must be obeyed at all times, if we are to stay happy, joyous, and free one day to the next! The Heart, The Mind, The Body, and The Soul must be relinquished to God's Control! This is what I've found to be the truth for people like myself: Any holding back in any one of the four areas cause us to be off balance; and therefore troubled in some way. God must be in full control, lest we stagnate our growth! Only The Spirit that is God, Can Change us for the better;

according to our willingness and faith in His Spirit Does God Come into us to Change and Rearrange our thoughts and actions! We Alcoholic – Drug Addicts are incapable of changing ourselves for the better without God's Help!

38. Carrying God's Message

The Spirit that is God is oh so foreign to so many who possess The Diseases of Alcoholism and Drug Addiction. When I share my experience with my follows about how I had to build a positive relationship with The Spirit that is God, oh Lord God, by way of Your Power I can feel how so many of them fall faint within themselves; however, Your Spirit Strengthens them by way of my experiences that I share with them. I can feel the hope come from some, in the sense like maybe, just maybe, this can happen for me also! And in turn that strengthens my faith in God's Spirit! I must constantly remember that what I have been given is a gift and I must use this gift to uplift; no matter what the situation, place, or conditions be!

39. The Focus

How to live life without drinking alcohol or using other mind altering substances is the main objective for alcoholic – drug addicts who are in the recovery process Laid Out by God Himself! There is a spiritual way of life which we are led to live by. We alcoholic – drug addicts must stay forever diligent in our search for God's Will for our daily opportunity to live life! Our inability to live life on life's terms centers from within our minds; there for we must develop a faith in a power greater than ourselves to solve all of our problems! For this alcoholic – drug addict that power is The Spirit that most people in this world call God! I've never seen God; however, I've felt a presence more than once in my lifetime that totally made me feel safe and protected, even though circumstances were to the contrary!

40. The Real Me

I am an Alcoholic – Drug Addict, and that's the true identity of what I am! However, from a drunkard, and dope user did God, Miraculously Change this man! As I write, my mind and heart are under reconstruction from the ongoing Diseases of Alcoholism and Drug Addiction's realm of total destruction! Only God Gives me much – needed strength to neutralize the relentless mental attacks from these evil wretched diseases that has no physical cure. My conscious contact with God is the greatest possession I have! Without God's Guidance and Help I could not stay sober and mind altering drug free; that has been my experience. I need not go back and test the waters ever again. And practicing a spiritual way of life has proved to me to be the best way to a useful and happy existence that I have ever come to know.

41. The Uncovering

The Insidious Diseases of Alcoholism and Drug Addiction are always there; It waits for the sufferers to drink alcohol and or use other mind altering substances, so as to increase the deadly cycle of its impending doom! These forces of Alcoholism and Drug Addiction are intangible, yet oh so real! They are evil negative forces that are alive; God Has Blessed me with the ability to actually see these negative forces at work from within myself and others! It's a destroyer of God- Given Life, it's totally the enemy of God! These forces are at work constantly; only God's Power Can Overcome their influences! We who have The Diseases of Alcoholism and Drug Addiction must constantly seek out " The Glory" if we are to live productive, useful lives – there are no exceptions!

42. The Ticker That Ticks

The mind of the alcoholic – drug addict is circular by birth; our thoughts are repeating by nature. There is nothing bad about that; however, it does explain the obsession part of our diseases. Those of us who possess the diseases of Alcoholism and Drug Addiction must come to know certain facts about our makeup, if we are to become successful in getting to know how we think and act! We all have certain patterns in the way we think and act that are identical to each other! We relate on many different episodes out of our past lives. Being unaware of these circular thoughts and engraved patterns of actions that produce negative outcomes is dangerous ground for these types of people – myself included! God Saves us by our reaching out to Him. We have become devastated by our own continual patterns of failure after failure by drinking alcohol and using other mind altering substances, without any insights of a solution. This is the stark reality for us!

43. That Which Is Real

The Spirit that is God Is Always Here – God Waits for His People to sincerely seek Him! We who are alcoholic – drug addicts must sincerely build a positive relationship with God, if we are to ever gain freedom from the negativity that is Alcoholism and Drug Addiction! This force is alive and evil and desires to claim our souls! This is the knowledge that I have obtained from my experience of being in the grip of this Evil Force for more than twenty years! My wisdom comes from divulging the knowledge I have received by way of God's Grace concerning these Evil Wretched Diseases that has already claimed countless souls! I am truly blessed by "The Most Holy One of Israel – The Everlasting Glory that is God!"

44. The Killers Elite

We alcoholic – drug addicts must seek God constantly with a sincere heart in the effort to receive from Him relief from The Evil Forces that be. These Evil Negative Forces seek to acquire our souls; worldly things must be abandoned or ignored, for the true gifts of living life are peace of mind, self-worth, and the love of God, and the people about us! However, the evils of Alcoholism and Drug Addiction cause the sufferers to act in negative ways against God; and the majority of people they may come into contact with, while at the same time they have disharmony within their minds!

The Evil Forces of Alcoholism and Drug Addiction pushes the sufferers to self-destruction in subtle ways! It's subtle to them, for in most cases the sufferers are unaware of what is happening to them, and has benn happening to them for years! Many people become so subdued by The Evil Forces that be, and they lose their lives because of it!

45. Ongoing Confrontations

For those who are like myself, who possess The Diseases of Alcoholism and Drug Addiction as I do, I find that when I speak about the nature of the malady of how it's evil in essence, I see the many of my fellow sufferers hesitate to relate; for the evil is in them! Many of us are at different levels of deterioration when it comes to the blessings of recovery! "Only God Can Bless." Many cannot or will not see the evil for what it truly is! However, I will continue to confront this Evil Enemy every chance The Lord God will permit me to do so! I will use my blessings to the fullest; even if it means my physical death! For even in that, many will be helped by the unselfish sacrifice of my soul!

46. What Works

My willingness plus my weaknesses plus God's Will plus God's Supernatural Power = my recovery. This is the equation which brings me relief from my ongoing Alcoholism and Drug Addiction. It really works, and I don't screw around with it! Many times my mind tends to wander or manufacture some wants out of my past to take me away from my present state of being. These were the patterns I used to dwell on, any many of them were sad occasions. I would drink to numb the feelings, or use other drugs to blot out

the mental pictures my mind would project! Oh what a mess my past life used to be, and this was happening while I was in the present! I am truly grateful that my present state of being is progressing for the positive good! Only possible by The Supernatural Power that is from God's Grace, that which imposed a total psychic change upon me!

47. On and On

We alcoholic – drug addicts must constantly confront the evil and negative aspects of ourselves if we are to become successful at never ever drinking alcohol or using any mind altering drugs ever again! This is a moment-by-moment operation that never has a finish! It's tiring for us; for we are partly flesh and therefore weak in many areas. However, this is where our intangible will must be practiced to seek God's Will and Supernatural Power to give us direction and strength! Again without our seeking God's Will and His Supernatural Power, there would be no protection from the intangible forces of The Evils that be! This simple equation renders life and prosperity for the alcoholic – drug addict who is in and will stay in God's Recovery Process. I have experienced no better way to live my life; living by God's Spiritual Principles has positively changed me for the betterment of my Eternal Soul.

48. Reality Upfront

The Evil of Alcoholism and Drug Addiction is a very strong force; however, God is even stronger! We alcoholic – drug addicts who have entrusted our very lives to an unseen power which many of us call God, have undergone what many in the medical profession call a total psychic change! There is a new way in regard to the way we think and act! Things that used to excite us don't excite us anymore. We come to associate with a whole new group of people; spiritual principles have taken the place of our own destructive egos! No pill can do that! This psychic change is only performed by God Himself; it's only by God's Grace that we are granted these gifts! And gifts are what they truly are! May You please continue to save us Lord God from The Evil Forces that be.

49. God's Love

Deep runs this evil that is Alcoholism and Drug Addiction, and harsh is the acceptance of it! However, those who have been granted a solution to its constant agitation must come to find within themselves to show a smile. For God Has Given them the pathway to a useful life that truly is worthwhile! So many times I found myself cursing The Evils that be, only to come to a halt in my heart; for I quickly remember Who has all things in His Hands, God Almighty Is The Reality. At once compassion takes the place of anger. Oh thank You God, for Your Abundance of Love that has over spilled upon and through my heart! For without love, I too would become an agent for evil! Nothing pleases me more than to constantly confront these evil forces, and by way of Your Power God, continuously deny their temptations!

50. The Intangible Tool

Having identity and knowing what I am doesn't make the recovery process from Alcoholism and Drug Addiction any easier! On the contrary it calls for me to become more diligent in seeking God's Guidance for my life. These incurable diseases progresses as I continue to live! Complacency for the alcoholic - drug addict formulates problems for us. We must constantly strive to become selfless. Constantly being selfish is a behavior which is truly dangerous for us! We can't live productive useful lives with the ingredient of selfishness within us ! Practicing (spiritual principles) to rid ourselves of selfishness has worked for many who possess The Diseases of Alcoholism and Drug Addiction. So our work is ongoing and never has an ending! There for by practicing (spiritual principles) to rid ourselves from selfishness we have also been relieved from the mania of Alcoholism and Drug Addiction, so long as we wholly continue to trust God, our intangible tool!

51. Insights From the Inside

To ignore the many thoughts of the mind, to banish countless views from our sights, to muffle the many things that we hear, to discern the many emotions from our hearts, is nearly impossible for alcoholic - drug addicts who are still unaware of the intangible enemy who is forever agitating our physical death! This evil that resides within us is relentless; it will never stop trying to destroy us! This is a reality realness that is oh so real! I can state this as being a fact; for I can feel its negativity as I write! Only a close conscious contact with God, keeps me focused on the intentions of my known Evil Enemy. I can live a useful sane life today and forevermore, so long as I continue to seek God, and to wait and listen for The Creator to instruct me in every aspect of my life. Then and only then do I acquire a constant peace!

52. Self – Survey – A Must

We alcoholic – drug addicts must self – survey ourselves routinely; for we possess incurable deadly diseases, which if left unattended would eventually kill us or others! This is a stark reality for us! I don't want to sound like doom and gloom; however, the truth is the truth, and it shall never wane from the same results! My Alcoholism and Drug Addiction is alive in me, and it shall be so – until the day I die! This truth is oh so difficult for many of us to accept, and as a result (the denial) destroys us and many innocent people. I can't live comfortably from one day to the next day without facing These Evil Wretched Diseases that live within me, and I am grateful to God, for God Has Provided The Solution to our discomfort; however, it's up to us to routinely self – survey ourselves in order to grow to encounter our incurable, deadly diseases.

53. Tunnel Vision

Deadly is the enemy, deadly is its touch, oh how The Evil Forces that be constantly desires to consume us! It's always at work, it's always plotting new wicked plans to claim the souls of all the people it can! We who are alcoholic – drug addicts are very vulnerable to The Evil Forces that be; in fact, without the constant reliance upon God for Protection, Strength, and Guidance, we eventually become defeated by The Evil Forces that be! However, by living the way we believe God's Wants us to live, This Evil Force tends to flee from us. Moreover, until The Day of Judgement, The Evils that be will be rampant and free! This is way We alcoholic – drug addicts must stay diligent in seeking God's Will for our lives; for God isn't out to harm or destroy us! This is a reality realness that needs no defense.

54. Bond Eternal

With each passing night and day this alcoholic drug addict sincerely prays to move closer to You Lord God - This action overjoys the Eternal Soul that is me! Everything else in this world is meaningless; for The Evil One is here! And there is no enduring peace anywhere! However God, You Have Blessed me with life, and I shall live it by seeking Your Holy Kingdom. And all people will come to know that all of my ways of living are Your Ways of living; nothing else to myself will I respect! I am an alcoholic – drug addict, and this is my true identity Father God that You Have Blessed me to see. I am forever grateful to You God for this Realization ! I am at Your Service forever – Nothing of this world do I claim – For You Father God Are The True Treasure of my life now and forever.

55. Living Link

We alcoholic – drug addicts must come to a point in recovery where we must consciously ask God to please open up our hearts; we must become humble before God, for we are vulnerable before our known incurable diseases! God's Spirit then can enter us to begin to heal us. "This was my experience". However, it's not a one time event; it must be lived! A positive relationship with God must be sincerely established if there would be any continuous relief from The Evil Diseases of Alcoholism and Drug Addiction! The Forces of Evil are real and deadly; for they have gravitated me for years. By God I've been brought to a position of salvation; however, as long as I live I must work with God; for The Forces of Evil are still rampant and free, and they shall always be until The Day of Judgement!

56. Set Free

I am a spark from The Divine Spirit, placed in a physical shell known as a body. There is a purpose for my existence, and it holds a special meaning that which joins together with all that is good and just! Most of my life I've been ignorant to what my true purpose is. In seeking God I have been given insights and wisdom to why every event happened in my life! God's Power and Knowledge has truly set me free! Before I sought out God and His Kingdom I was bound by The Evil Forces that be! I didn't have a clue to what was happening to me! The truth of Good and Evil has been revealed to me; now I diligently work to help others seek God as I did and still do!

57. The Exposure

No lasting power do I possess. God Has All Power, and He Protects me from The Evil Forces that be, by putting what's in my heart into my head, and this cancels out any evil thoughts that the enemy sends! God is in my heart and He Rests right there; however, I was unconscious of this for a very long time in my life, and The Evil Forces That be had dominion within my mind.

I was powerless to its temptations. Now By The Grace of God, the truth has been revealed to the Eternal Soul that is me! I am now empowered with the defense against the idea of drinking alcohol, or to ingest any other mind altering substances into my body. This Power Is God, and there are no ifs, ands, or buts about the truth that God Has Revealed unto me!

58. Keeping Focus

I will continue to speak about The Evil Forces that be; for they continuously agitate The Human Race! By my observations, it seems that alcoholic – drug addicts are affected more by their temptations more than the rest of humanity. This is why we alcoholic – drug addicts must wholly depend on God for everything. An undying faith in God must be accomplished by us, lest we perish by way of The Evil Forces that be! We must not just be satisfied by being sober and free from any other mind altering drugs; we must strive with all of the energy that God Gives us to further seek His Kingdom. My personal goal is to become an agent of good, with a consistent effort to encourage others to do the same, so that they won't be fooled and enslaved by The Evil Forces that be!

59. Evil Fading

Within the mind of the alcoholic – drug addict, there is a Spiritual War taking place at all times! Only those who possess this malady can relate and agree to the previous statement! We are truly important in the preparation of God's Kingdom to come! There is no other group of people in the whole world who are tempted and manipulated with evil thoughts to hurt ourselves and others than we who possess The Spiritual Sickness of Alcoholism and Drug Addiction.

There is no physical cure for us! However, God Offers a way to salvation and a degree of peace within our minds from The Evil Forces that be! There are many of us who are being blessed by God's Power, and we are in all places on this planet. Depending upon our willingness, faith, and obedience to God's Way of Living, we become powerful agents of good in this life and the life to come!

60. Evil in Motion

Manipulation of our minds, constant disturbance within our hearts, and an eroding of our souls is what happens to alcoholic – drug addicts by way of The Evil Forces that be! This has been happening for centuries! Seeking God and sincerely asking for His Help can and will break The Evil Cycle of damnation. Having an undying faith plus obedience to the way God Wants us to live is a security factor that will keep us protected from The Evil Forces that be! Only God can protect us, fore He Is Above the level of the tormentor! We who possess these diseases which have been given the names of Alcoholism and Drug Addiction are very vulnerable to the persuasions of The Evil Forces that be!

61. Always There

Alcoholism and Drug Addiction – Oh how I find myself not running out of information about these evil relentless diseases that are a part of me ! Each and every waking day I give God thanks for His Directions. I came to learn not to regret the reality of what I am. These diseases are incurable; however, they are treatable, these diseases centers within our minds; there for we must seek out a power greater than our thoughts, lest we are doomed to drink alcohol, or use other mind altering drugs to the death! This is one of the results of untreated Alcoholism and Drug Addiction! The solution to the diseases has key parts that must become a part of the sufferer's everyday life. There must be no reservations in the minds of the sufferers that one day they can stop their practices of total abstinence and they will be all right. This just isn't so; once an alcoholic –drug addict, who can't stop drinking alcohol and using other mind altering drugs, always an alcoholic – drug addict who can't stop drinking alcohol and using other mind altering drugs! This is the stark reality for us!

62. The Same Road

New beginnings; however, I am traveling upon the same road; some doors do close while yet others unfold: "The Most Holy One of Israel Guides me", though my mind hesitates to comply to the orders felt to me from God – The Most High! The good news is that I am sober and free from any other mind altering drug use, and I am better able to respond to my Creator's Will! When I was drunk and high, there was no conscious contact with The Creator of All Things, and my life was stagnant! There was no growth to be had on any levels of my being, only "deterioration." God Allowed my course; however, He didn't Permit my physical death, and for this I am eternally grateful! Now – I am experiencing new beginnings on the same road, and that road leads straight to God Himself!

63. Attack Constant

There is no constant peace of mind for the alcoholic – drug addict in, or out of the recovery process! However, those who constantly seek God for solutions have a better measure of peace of mind, opposed to those who do not seek "The Glory that is God!" We who are alcoholic – drug addicts are easier targets for The Evil Forces that be! It's not our fault that we were fashioned in this way; however, God does Provide Solutions for our many defects. I have found that constantly seeking God for direction, protection, and provisions have proved to be my best defense against my known handicaps! This Evil that is Alcoholism and Drug Addiction seeks to enslave my Eternal Soul! However, I am blessed for I am aware of them and I have God as my defense! But to those who have The Diseases of Alcoholism and Drug Addiction, and have no positive relationship with God, are subject to be tormented over and over again by "The Evil Forces that be!" This is the real truth that I am blessed to tell!

64. The Asking

Those who obey Your Words Lord God, are blessed indeed, and they are a benefit to all who come into contact with them! And those who constantly seek Your Holy Kingdom Lord God become relieved from The Evil Forces that be, and they become as little children who have no fear from those who kill the flesh! Oh, Lord God, if it be Your Will may You please continue to make me an example of Your Greatness - Most Holy One of Israel. So that my fellow alcoholic – drug addict brothers and sisters may see Your Work, and willingly come searching for You Lord God, as a lost child cries and calls out for their parents! May my eyes see and witness multitudes of these examples Lord God, before You lay me to rest.

65. The Beholder

No one can see what another person can see and this is a gift, and a wonderment that God Gives! Now I truly understand the statement, "beauty is in the eye of the beholder." I never realized beauty as I am experiencing it in my own life by way of God's Directions in showing me what's in my heart! There are many qualities of goodness that have been there since my birth; however, I was so distracted by The Evil Forces that be that I never took inventory of me!

Oh, Lord God, thank You for not Allowing me to physically die without showing me these beauties; now I can learn to share them with the people around me, in an effort to make the world a little bit nicer. I am an alcoholic – drug addict and by showing me God my true identity, You Have Enabled me to discover the many intangible beauties about myself! There aren't enough thank you's to thank You with Lord God.

66. The Unfolding

I don't mean to sound bitter and I don't want to come across as being glum; however, the majority of my life so far has not been swamped with many periods of having fun! I am an alcoholic – drug addict in The Recovery Process From God Himself, and I must continue to have a giving heart, or my sobriety will become ever so hard! This is a fact for people like myself; for self-will has brought us to our knees, where we became willing to turn our lives over to the care of God. We couldn't live with our selfish selves one more minute, let alone one more day! There but for the Grace of God do we alcoholic – drug addicts live out our lives one day at a time without the use of alcohol, or any other mind altering drugs!

67. The Transcendence

As I write, I am truly a blessed man; for I am aware of The Evil

Forces that be! God Almighty Has Truly Blessed me with this spiritual insight! The alcoholic – drug addict's mind is where The Evil Forces that be consistently launches their attacks. We alcoholic – drug addicts are vulnerable to their leadings! The Evil Forces that be have been physically killing us through their mental leadings for centuries! However, God Has Designed a way for us to live our lives whereas we overcome these mental attacks and in turn live healthy lives!

Many who knew us prior to sincerely asking God for help, call us miracles, and that we were changed by God Himself. However, we must always seek God's Kingdom; for The Evil Forces that we are still rampant and free, and they will stop at nothing to destroy us!

68. Evil Reality

The Evil Entity that manipulates the alcoholic – drug addict's mind is intangible and deadly, it has one purpose and that purpose is to kill! Its comprehension and identification is subtle; however, it truly exists and it's totally alive! Moreover, God Protects me and Guides me through my heart! My mind is useless operating on self-will alone. I need the perfect directions from God – lest I perish from the constant mental attacks from The Evil Forces that be! We alcoholic – drug addicts have been given a solution to neutralize The Evil Forces that be; however, it must be practiced without fail! This isn't a theory, my resolve comes from my own experiences. I am an alcoholic – drug addict who is being reconstructed by The One and Only Almighty God!

69. Laid Out

What is in my heart and what may come to pass through my mind, is the difference between good and evil! What is the light that rotates in the middle of darkness? What is the darkness without the rotating light? This constitutes life or death for those who possess the entities of Alcoholism and Drug Addiction! The light represents life and darkness represents death! It's a short menu and it's very real! So many die the alcoholic – drug addict death; for they never got into practicing seeking the light that rotates in the middle of darkness! Our Father which art in Heaven, Hollowed be Thou Name...

70. Evil at a Glance

The disease that won't die and it's always a threat to kill – This entity is commonly called Alcoholism! It's evil and intangible, yet oh so real! Relentless are its attacks, this entity is alive and its objective is to kill! Woe to the people who are infected by this evil wretched disease!

This is a spiritual sickness and only a spiritual solution can combat it! The solution must be lived, it can't be ingested or injected physically. Long have I suffered and this is what had to be; however, I am now consciously blessed by God Himself, for God Has Guided me to Alcoholism's Solution!

Now I must pass The Gift from Almighty God forward! Lest I become captive once again by The Evil Forces that be!

*****Thoughts from meditation sessions between volumes 6-7

Peace from within the mind, comes from joy from within the heart. The more my mind centers upon God, the more clearly I can see His Signs. Life is not just limited to the fullest: Life must be lived beyond the imagination! When your life is being lived beyond the imagination that is when your soul is at one with The Orator of Creation! I can't count on my thoughts as being factual every time! Never look to another to understand the inner conflicts or peace you are experiencing. Trust wholly only God!

Essence of Me

Can you burn bright like me? Can you venture into what God Has Given me or do you fear the light in any given day or night? Most of the time I am not even here, for I am destined to sore through the atmosphere! Come parallel with my thoughts, take a step into eternity and feel the joy of the cosmos...

Let me not be remembered by the sweat of my brow, but by the determination of my spirit. May there be peace within your mind, may there be joy within your spirit; for these are the true values of life that may only be felt! Evil can't destroy or diminish these virtues once they are obtained and maintained!

God, me and you

The Mosaic Life

The things that awe me are Eternal indeed, they show themselves to me with unmistakable beauty! A beauty only chosen eyes can see – Oh how blessed I be... By no virtue of my own, yet I've been blessed with the sight of these eternal beauties! A true mosaic of life; its meaning goes beyond my mental comprehension; however, I sense life within them!

I am a writer, my work is for all to see, I am a writer, instructed by God Almighty! My style isn't from any ordinary flux, for my words inspire the hopeless. My words give them hope where there was none. This hope strengthens them to move forward. Only God Can Give The Gift to touch and comfort the hopeless. I am a writer and this is what God Called me to be, in spite of all the evil insanity I have lived through, there but for The Grace of God go I!

Back to reality, if only a little at a time!

Volume - # 7. The Points of Views

1. The Realm That is Me

I believe that there is a spark of energy from God Himself, manifested within all human beings; within me that spark has been growing for years, especially when I started to turn away from worldly things. More and more I sought out The Living God, and one day God's Spirit Whispered to my conscious and said: "Relax in My Spirit."

The honesty of my conscious spoke back to God after a few days stating "God I don't know how to relax in Your Spirit!" I was truthful in my response; at the same time in awe by The Creator of All Life Offering me this great opportunity! Looking at the totality of my life to this point, through God's Spirit, truly uplifts the realm that is me.

2. Selfless Structure

Trust God with all that you hold dear, and have no fear! Hold no defense in your case and God Will Cover you, as you would cover yourself with a blanket to keep warm through the night, Direct no attention to what you think will work or not. Leave this to God, for The Lord God is perfect in all things! You will be up against billions of people who hold none of these principles constantly within their hearts. So you will walk lonely but never alone till death. To obey God, is to trust God, and by trusting God, you begin to conquer yourself.

3. Spiritual Union

Out of the clear blue sky, you came into my life, now everything in my life has changed for the better! Loneliness is a thing of the past, and no longer are my nights long and sad. You are the part in my mind's eye that I have longed to physically see: Oh, God Almighty Has Returned my rib to me! Together new and wonderful places we will travel and see, for you are the missing part that now completes me! God is always good now and to the end of life; oh, thank You God, for Giving me my wife!

4. No Cure at Hand

Diseases are all around mankind; despite the many scientific break throughs. We have accomplished no permanent achievements; fore The Evil Forces that be are rampant and free! Mankind's situation will continue to get worse; for we all are under God's Curse! God's Words are true and He is faithful in all the things that He Has Proclaimed to do. Gentle and Kind God Is; fore if God were evil, none of us would have the opportunity to live. The Evil Forces that be are real and they have life; they are the enemies of God, and this is God's Fight! With mankind there will never be peace until God Himself, Arrest The Evil Forces that be!

5. Mental Manipulation

Oh, what an opportunity The Living God is Allowing me; I get to divulge my experiences concerning The Evil Forces that be! They tempt us human beings through our thoughts all of the time; and many of us fall victim through our actions! For thousands of years The Evil Forces that be have been projecting evil thoughts upon mankind with the intention of destroying as many of us as possible. I myself have come to learn not to trust all the thoughts that come through my mind. Some of them are tainted and evil, and this is the reality God Himself Has Allowed me to consciously see, starting with myself.

Discerning my thoughts has become a constant practice for me; it has allowed me to detect the tainted projected thoughts from The Evil Forces that be. They are a transcend, and they will never cease to frustrate mankind; they are the enemies of God, and mankind have not the power to stop them, only God Himself Can Arrest or destroy them all.

6. God's Door

Alcoholism and Drug Addiction are Evil Entities! Their destruction of human lives was and is devastatingly great! Constantly The Evil Forces that be continue to use their mental projections to misguide their human pray. As I write my face shows concern; for my soul knows the subtle tactics of The Evil Forces that be! Only God Himself Has Graced me this truth; now I pray that alcoholic – drug addicts everywhere will receive this information and fuse it into their hearts!

The Evil Forces that be will never stop their mental projections; so I suggest we seek out God Himself, for our all-around protection. God's Spirit is always here to help us; however, God is a Gentle Spirit, and He Won't Interfere into our affairs, lest we ask Him. Pride and ego are the two factors which keeps us human beings separate from God's All Loving Power. So be wise to know that

The Evil Forces that be will stop at nothing to destroy us. Always remember God's door.

7. My Job

My heart aches and day by day my soul continues to dissipate. I long to leave the body and return home; however, I have a job to do and it's not complete. So I must continue to pray to The Spirit that is God to renew my strength. I don't wish to sound like life isn't good, because it is, I just get so frustrated at times; for The Evil Forces that be are all here! That's the irony of my life; I am to expose these evils and all of their destructive plots. Blessed by God's Power I get new information concerning The Evil Forces that be as I continue my job. My job isn't an easy one; it's not just picking up a pen, and writing down the world's sins. The information I write comes from my own personal experiences, nothing else will count concerning this job The Spirit of God Has Blessed me with.

8. God's Favor

I must stay conscious of God's Will; I must continue to pray for God's Power to help me stay focused. I am sometimes shaky and weak in my mind, the end results from abusing alcohol and street drugs for a very long time. God is my only defense against the mental projections from The Evil forces that be. Oh, thank You for not allowing them to destroy me! I just can't stay still and play it safe, I must continue to pray and seek God's Favor concerning the mental projections from The Evil Forces that be. God Himself Has Delivered me from active Alcoholism and Drug Addiction. Now the rest of my life belongs to the dictates from God! The Evil Forces that be will never stop at trying to destroy me and that's just their job; however, I am now grounded in God, and I am not manipulated by thoughts of fear, I will keep my faith in God, until it's time for me to leave here.

9. Hope Revealed

I have been bound for years, I have been mentally attacked by many fears, with no provocation from me, these are the subtle tactics from The Evil Forces that be. We as mortals have been ignorant of these tactics for far too long. Only the goodness from The One and Only God Can Break us free from this mental and spiritual bondage. So God Himself must be sought out constantly through pray and meditation in order to break the mental projections from The Evil Forces that be. There is no doubt in my soul, about knowing how these mental projections have destroyed billions of people throughout the ages. I write about these evils in an effort to give hope to the readers who can relate, but for years could not formulate the solution, and live it. God is the beginning and the end, and there is nothing that He can't do or un do, this has been my experience.

10. Only God

Weaknesses I do have and strength to support my weaknesses comes from God Himself, and if I am to become a wise man, I must always continue to seek The Lord God Himself. The days we live in are evil, nowhere on this earth is there total safety; fore The Evil Forces that be are all here, and they are destructive in their nature. They will destroy or corrupt anything that is powerless or knowledge less of them. Only God Himself have the power to protect us from The Evil Forces that be. So seek out God's Kingdom, and He Can Provide Strength, and Guidance while we yet live! In reality there are far too many people ignorant of this solution, and they try to combat evil by themselves. The end result is they are not strong enough and wise enough to defeat The Evil Forces that be. That is why God said, "Vengeance is Mine!"

11. A Real Solution

In my heart there lies concern for the many people of this generation, who are still lost to the facts of what is really going on in the world around them! I'm witnessing a great many young kids from the next generation being swept away by The Evil Forces that be, in the form of Alcoholism and Drug Addiction. Oh, how powerless they are when it comes to combatting these evils! Far too many don't grasp the opportunity of the solution! The Evil Forces that be are far more knowledgeable of our human weaknesses than we are; and they use this knowledge to destroy us.

I myself for years have been powerless over their mental projections, and they almost destroyed me. I cried out to The Living God, and I have been Given Power over their mental projections from that night to the present day as I write! Now I possess the solution over the mental projections from The Evil Forces that be, only from The Living God. God's Power is available to all who constantly and sincerely seek His Kingdom.

12. Message to the Soul

The words from a servant of Jesus Christ truly hit my soul this afternoon and I know I will never be the same person ever again! My soul has been invited to relax in The True Living Spirit that is God. There is nothing of this world that has more value than this offering! I know within my soul that the things of this world are temporary and the things of The Spirit of God are eternal. O my friends it took me many years of suffering to be blessed with this spiritual insight. So don't be hard pressed if you yourself aren't there yet in your spiritual journey! If you are reading or hearing this spiritual message, chances may be that The Day of The Lord God, hasn't come yet, and if your heart is troubled or not, may the message of the good news – Eternal Life, inspire your soul! Before You Can see God, you will have to go through Jesus Christ – The Son of Man. So it is written.

13. My Order

God I must constantly seek Your Kingdom; fore The Evil Forces that be are constantly trying to destroy me! Your Kingdom, Lord God, is patience, kindness, compassion, generosity, and love, all of what the devil and his demons are not! For years The Evil Forces that be have robbed me of my time and joy, and almost took my life on a number of occasions! Satan has the power of death and he uses it all the time, I pray never to forget this! The Evil Forces that be are a transcend; however, The Grace of God Has Been Given to mankind with the intension to fulfill the scriptures concerning the promise to Abraham. In actual reality I wholly trust God, and Jesus Christ, and this is the number one order and code, in my life. God, and Jesus Christ were the only ones who cared for me, while the rest of the world through me away like a paper cup, and I pray always to remember this no matter what! Obedience and loyalty to God, and Jesus Christ, is the course I will take, for the rest of my life!

14. The Small Voice

I'm under constant attacks, from The Evil Forces that be, they work so diligently to destroy me! They stress constantly for me to become a material success, while my inner voice speaks softly and tells me to be patient. Oh, how blessed am I, for I'm not drinking alcohol and getting high. Something I did for a very long time and at my end, I almost lost my mind! God Himself Has Relieved me from active Alcoholism and Drug Addiction. However, The Evil Forces that be still remain and they will use their mental projections to confuse, and eventually enslave my Eternal Soul! I must always remember there shall be no lasting peace as long as The Evil Forces that be are permitted to exist in this world. So the little voice is right, for only God Himself Can Make this world a paradise! I must constantly discern my thoughts for some of them are evil, and put into practice for myself the art of patience. It is my experience that only when I am calm, can I hear the small inner voice giving instructions, and I believe that voice to be Jesus Christ Himself.

15. Living Message

I write about what I have experienced; The Evil Forces that be are a negative dark force. They are like vultures; however, the only difference is they eat you while you're still alive! I've been given the power by God to recognize their deadly influences. Writing about these evils are in my power to pursue and do; however, destroying them forever only God Himself Can Do! So we all must endure to the end and commit for ourselves no new sins. The Evil Forces that be are constantly attacking us, even as I write these words. Hate is a very strong word, it is the opposite of love, and love is what God Is, so we must disassociate ourselves with this destructive word! We must take the word hate from the confines of our hearts and souls; for it will soon consume us! We must practice love for our neighbors, this is the command from God Himself. God will either reward or punish us, upon the coming of The Last Day. And The Lord and Master Jesus Christ stands between us and God!

16. Good Things to Come

Good things are not far away, nor is the destruction of The Evil Forces that be. Since being called by Jesus Christ, to write again I've been feeling a sluggish ache in my chest. I truly believe it's the residue from my old sinful nature, still trying to hold territory in my flesh. I am not in bondage anymore from active Alcoholism and Drug Addiction; however, the ism (I selfish me) is still present in me in some ways! I don't know if I'll ever be totally free from the ism (I selfish me) in my character. I know within my heart that this doesn't give me a license to act out! I must continue to be humble under God, and my brothers and sisters within the days and nights left to me. Never must I ever think that it is safe and clear, there shall never be true safety and peace, for The Evil Forces that be are all still here. For now Satan is the ruler of this world; however, his allotted time grows short and the knowledge of The Holy Scriptures are being rapidly sought. So fear not brothers and sisters, and always continue to live righteously, and pray. Take nothing of this world for yourselves and prepare your souls before God's Judgement Day.

17. The Power of God

I have been commanded by the small voice in my soul to study The Holy Bible, and to write what it is in my heart! I am in awe by this spiritual insight I am experiencing! I would have never been called to do this if I were still bound by active Alcoholism and Drug Addiction. There is no doubt in my being; I am being directed by The Most Holy One of Israel and Jesus Christ! This direction takes me away from the desires of this world. In my heart I am experiencing joy; for I'm being guided away from the physical structures set up by The Evil Forces that be. There are many things in this life at present I don't understand and that's okay; for in reality it's The Holy Spirit of God, who direct my way. I consider myself as God's Servant; even though, my flesh is weak, and for years I've been ruled by the sinful nature. This bondage has damaged me in many ways. I believe with all of my heart that there is nothing that God Can't Do, or Un Do! This attitude has allowed God's Power to Flow Through me.

18. My Heart's Chambers

Upon reading most of the book of Revelations, my soul has become weary, I believe the affect is natural; for there will be so much agony, upon God's Fury! Even though, these events haven't happened yet, my heart becomes heavy, for I know in my soul that God Will Carry out what has already been written. My heart is no way heavy for me, but for all those who have died and have been deceived by The Evil Forces that be. However, I will not let myself be gravitated by this; fore there is so much joy in The Almighty God! His Judgments are Perfect. I was also instructed by the small voice in me not for myself to be deceived, saying oh these things are far off, so I can relax, I don't see these things happening while I'm alive! My zeal for The Most Holy One of Israel, and Jesus Christ, must remain wax hot, lest I'll suffer the fate of the unbelievers of God Almighty! This truth I must never forget, I'll hold it, in the chambers of my heart.

19. God – My Master

At this point in my spirituality I consider myself truly blessed. God Has Given me favor while I live in His Sight. He Has Given me the sense to recognize The Evil Forces that be. Especially when they try and tempt me through my thoughts! As I realized the authenticity of God's Gift, I became overwhelmed in my soul. I know within my whole being that The Lord God, and Jesus Christ will never lead me to destruction. The ways of the world are quick and easy; however, in God's Sight they register death and no chance of eternal life! I believe this with all of my heart; fore I've found God's Words to be true. I've seen so much injustice in this world since I've been moved to believe what was written in The Bible has happened and is happening as I yet live. So the ways of this world I will seek not and I will always be uncomfortable; fore the time I live in is evil! However, I was given life and no matter the uncomfortability I must resist the temptations of The Evil Forces that be, until God Himself Says my life here is over.

20. God's Perfect Order

What good is my life here on earth, if I don't obey The One who Allows it? My life isn't my own anyway, I didn't create it. I don't even consciously know when it started and I don't know when it will end. Through this consciousness we human beings call life, I came to believe there is a perfect order to things and somehow from this perfect order there came about a non-acceptance to that order – thus we have The Evil Forces that be! These defiant spirits went against God's Perfect Order of things! They are the cause for the curse that has been placed upon this world called earth.

However, life goes on and unfortunately for mankind physical death also. Through the passage of time The Evil Forces that be have caused oh, so much pain and misery for the human family. Many of us are ignorant to their damaging affects upon our eternal souls. Only God's Perfect Order can save us, lest we perish and suffer the Eternal Fate of The Evil Forces that be. God Is Always Willing to Help Save our Eternal Souls, but we must live to trust and obey God Himself.

21. A message From Jesus Christ

The Spirit of Jesus Christ moves my hand to write these words. Prepare your Eternal Souls my brothers and sisters; fore the war clouds of God's Wrath is near. Seek The Lord and Master Jesus Christ, and God Himself, while They still yet may be found! Don't allow your lives to end without repenting from your sins. The Evil Forces that be awaits to enslave our souls! The time we live in is evil, and so many people are being deceived by The Evil Forces that be, and they are unaware of it. Hear the words of a recovered Alcoholic – Drug Addict, and take heed. The Evil Forces that be are alive, and they are the enemies of God, and Jesus Christ, they will stop at nothing to destroy all of human life, that is why the war clouds are mounting and God's Wrath is coming. Jesus Christ said He Has Not Come to bring peace, but a sword! This is why my hand writes these words. I am a servant of Jesus Christ, and I bring this message from my Master. Prepare Your souls, so that you are not cut off from the gift of Eternal Life, this ends this message.

22. Home at Last

The things that are in my heart is what I call on when I am under attack, the things that are in my heart is knowledge of The Evil Forces that be, so that I may have the power to fight back! Oh, yes I have the responsibility to resist The Evil Forces that be, even to the day of my last breath; and upon following The Lord and Master Jesus Christ, all the events of my life will stand for me as a positive offence against The Evil Forces that be! So what's in the heart of a man, truly determines what he is. He may have the desires of the devil, or he may be one of God's Kids. This is why God Searches the hearts of men!

Jesus Christ and God's Commands are explicit when it comes to my inter actions with the people of this world. All my life I felt different from most of the people here, I never fitted in anywhere down here, and it has been revealed to me why. I am the seed from Abraham, and from finding this out, all the pieces of my former life fit perfectly.

23. Straight to Point

Blessed is the man who can look into a mirror and see his own light! The light that the man sees is a residue from God's Light; for God Has Visited him! God is The Unapproachable Light; there is no darkness in Him! From The filtration of the man's heart who can see his own light, you will find kindness, joy, generosity, compassion, and most of all love! The identity of this man should be called a child of God. God's Children help people all the time, without dictations for payment. The Goodness of God Watches Out over them; for The Evil Forces that be seek to destroy them! Father God Guides His Own, as a mother duck makes clear the pathway, for her ducklings. The summation of this philosophy states, the existences of God's People and then there are the unbelievers of God! Not to forget to mention the people who speak the love of God with their lips, yet in their hearts, they harbor all sorts of evil desires! This is the reality of the many people, who have life on this earth.

24. The Guiding Light

I am not perfect, but every day allowed I ask God to have mercy upon my soul! I have made many mistakes so far while living life; however, I never stop asking God, to help me be better! My Lord and Master Jesus Christ helps me greatly to improve my outlook and attitude concerning all people. The Evil Forces that be influences are all around this world, there is no place where their corruption is not present. Nevertheless, I must let my light shine; for God, Jesus Christ, and The Holy Ghost is my business. To help other souls to surrender to them is the reason why God saved my life. God Himself Chose me to do this service; for my heart was willing, of myself I am nothing. So I walk in The Spirit that is God. Day after day, after day of walking in God's Spirit, He Has Changed my being. I am no longer enslaved, by Alcoholism and Drug Addiction; fore I have surrendered to The Love of God, and His Power smashed the old me! I could have never done this of my own accord. Since my surrender to God, I am now conscious of how The Holy Spirit Guides me around all of the traps set, by The Evil Forces that be.

25. The Intangible Bond

I was instructed by the small little voice in me to study the Bible and then write what's in my heart. Those instructions turned out to be great wisdom; fore my mind seeks to rationalize and sound good! The heart reveals the true substance that's in itself. I believe that small little voice to be God, Jesus Christ, and The Holy Ghost, and it really doesn't matter; for They are All One all the time! They Know all the pain and misery I went through without hardening my heart like oh so many people do. When the hardening of your heart happens; The Evil Forces that be take control of your destiny. With all my pain and misery I sought out The Trinity. From that night, to the present time, God Has Filtered Out my heart and restored me to my rightful mind.

Now all that I am lives in God, and God in me. I am truly blessed to be in conscious contact with The Trinity. There is no shame in me for Them; for They are my best friends! Nothing of this world can ever sever me from Them and when I physically die it will be increased!

26. A Lie in Disguise

God is infinite, don't be fooled by what is taking place in the world around you. While we yet live, we must learn to turn to God, without doubts in our hearts and wholly trust Him. Don't ever lose your zeal, for The Infinite God! Governments, big businesses, and many factions of the world will tempt you to abandon God's Commandments, or keep you from them. All are controlled by The Evil Forces that be! Don't get caught up in their fate! All things belong to God, so don't get blamed, in the judgement of the misuse of God's Property. Seek out the teaching of The Lord and Master Jesus Christ, and if you are honest in your conscious, you will come to know what road to take while you yet still live. All across the world The Evil Forces that be use many tactics to turn people's minds and hearts away from keeping focused on God's Words on how to live their lives in a righteous manner, so that it will go well for them! The story is the same, as it was in the beginning, as it is now. Satan is a liar!

27. Pulling Covers

I am physically hungry right now; however, I can't eat just yet; for the orders from my Master comes first! The truth will always be the truth and a lie will always be a lie, and from the very beginning to the present time, The Evil Forces have always told lies to cover up the truth! I've seen this truth over and over again, and how it has deceived and destroyed oh, so many men! I will press harder and harder with the pen to tell all I know on how these Evil Forces constantly continue their plots, on how they will destroy all men! I will not stand idly by while The Evil Forces that be continue to promote their lies! To have knowledge of them and do nothing would make me just as guilty as they are. My brother and sisters you must bring yourselves to the realization that The Evil Forces that be don't give two cents about humanity! Throughout all of Human History, The Evil Forces that be have stirred up the pot of confusion and mistrust amongst the nations, to get us to destroy ourselves by our own hands! I will always place the truth where the truth belongs and lies where they belong.

28. It Cuts Like a Knife

The words that I am about to write will cause pain for many; however, to some it will be received as a message from a modern day servant that has been long overdue! The Evil Forces that be have manifested themselves in certain people all throughout this world. To discover them all you have to do is look carefully at what they uphold as value, and you will physically see those things cause disease, misery, and death, at a constant rate! People spend their money on these things all the time. They promote these things in their advertisements, as though people are having a good time.

 Woe to the evil spirits who prey on the souls of us human beings. I am just one servant giving this report; however, The Evil Forces that be will rally together to seek to make my life short! The words that I speak cuts like a knife through their territory. The truth opens the spiritual eyes of many. The darkness they love and murder is a common place thing they do on impulse. Jesus Christ is my Lord and Master, God they fear, and God Himself Has Given me The Holy Ghost, and He is my protection, until I leave here.

29. The Enemy Watching

A person came up to me today with a grin and a smile calling me ray, he told me he hasn't seen me in a long while. I looked at the man and couldn't recognize his face, but he knew mine, and the car that I drive. I told him I didn't mean to be rude, but I'm on a timer and I must continue to study my book, he asked me what the book was, and I told him it was the Bible, and he said yea, the real word. He looked at me for about three minutes, while I was trying to find my part where I left off on.

He then got up and said, "We'll see you around ray we'll be waiting for you," while he was walking out the door I glanced up at him from reading my Bible and like a flash, I didn't see him anymore! In my mind I wondered what just happened, and what all of that was all about; and then the little voice in me whispered and said that was just Satan checking you out!

Earlier before I left out from my house, the little voice said be very observant today, by what happens! It's just one more example that I get physically to see, on how The Evil Forces that be are keeping their eyes on me. There but for The Grace of God go I, and I pray to stay giving until the day that I die.

30. A Gift Received While Being of Service

I am not finished in my heart concerning The Evil Forces that be; fore I know The Evil Forces that be wants me to stop my flow of ink concerning the truth about their acts! I haven't even scratched the surface of their darkness. They lost their attempt of gaining complete power of the universe, and now they are running out of time down here! No doubt many people are ignorant of their powers and abilities. This is the strong hold they have over the nations of the earth. Mankind was and still are to the present time easily influenced, by their tactics! The Evil Forces that be are very angry and frustrated at the same time. They are very angry because they lost they spot in the cosmos; They are frustrated, for they still can't find a way to defeat God Himself, with all of His Glory! Just now I had to pause in my writing; for I've never received so many lights in my vision concerning any matter ever before! I just sensed in my soul that The Evil Forces will never repent from their ways! What has been written about these Evils Spirits that be are oh, so true. God Has Just Blessed me to see it for myself.

31. No Heavy Weight

My physical body grows tired, my thoughts start to dissipate, I must hold on in my heart; fore the road of recovery I do take! Only The Trinity Gives me The Power I need to overcome my Evil Wretched Disease! As I entered my early morning meditation, the little voice told me to hold nothing heavy in my heart. Jesus Christ knows out of my heart I do live and my Lord and Master doesn't want me to be in bondage anymore concerning The Evil Forces that be. My life is a Gift from God, and for years I couldn't see it. I was blinded by The Evil Forces that be; and they nearly destroyed me.

I must keep my heart in a humble mode, and listen to the little voice as I was told. As I reflect and look back at the beginning of my life to now, I've always kept things heavy in my heart. I am just now realizing it, I guess I kept my heart so heavy for so long I got used to it. Just the other day my brother in Christ told me to cut myself a break, and now I received the message from my Lord and Master that backs him up, by telling me to hold in my heart no heavy weight.

32. A Practice That Doesn't Have an End

Nothing is impossible when it comes to being placed before God! I have been greatly moved in my soul, within the months of May and June, of the year two thousand and twelve. The Most Holy One of Israel Has Opened Up The Door of my heart! Many truths are now beginning to flow from me. I have locked away many things for years, and now they will be shared! Jesus Christ is my guide who I look to everyday to give me comfort, as I pass through many dark and corrupted pathways. How can I travel in the darkness, without running into an object? The Trinity is my light; I pray to be filled with the everlasting light. The Evils that be now step to the side when they see me coming; fore they recognize The Unapproachable Light that I have access to. I have learned to call on The Unapproachable Light in any given day, or night to give me the knowledge I need to subdue The Evil Forces that be when they attack me! The Evil Forces that be are relentless in their process to destroy, so I have learned to be relentless in my asking for God's Power again, and, again, and again. The Evil Forces that be will never stop in trying to destroy. So I will never stop in seeking God!

33. What's Already There

The blessing of The Lord God are upon me, He Has Spoken to me saying, "don't try and make something that is not!" I was truly moved when He Spoke this to my conscious. When God Speaks to me, it is very simple; however, the simplicity covers many situations that come up in daily living. I am always amazed when The Lord God Speaks to me! It's always a short combination of words, which never leaves my heart and the words always bears witness to be correct when brought up to test any life situation. God Always Speaks to me in a way that I can understand, and He Makes it possible for me to teach. The Evil Forces that be are totally the opposite of what I have just described concerning The Lord God. I learned this by my own hands, by making many mistakes to find out the differences! Up until the present time, God Has Truly Watched Out Over my life and well being, there is no doubt in my heart. So I will take heed and add to my teachings and not make something that is not, but rather use what's already there, to the fullest of its being.

34. Protected Soul

These words are from the heart of a servant. One who was almost destroyed by active Alcoholism and Drug Addiction. The Lord of All Creation Had and Still Has Mercy on my Eternal Soul. He personally interrupted the process of The Evil Forces that be. If I were left unattended to, The Evil Forces that be would have succeeded in my destruction. I would have left this world ignorant of God's Love and Kindness, and The Evil Forces that be would have had authority to enslave my Eternal Soul. I am so grateful to God; however, I have no words to glorify Him with! I can't make something that is not; however, I can make use of what is already here.

What is already here for me is my undying faith in God Almighty, what is already here for me is my loyalty to God's Words concerning all of humanity. As I continue to study the Teachings of my Lord and Master Jesus Christ, my life becomes grounded further in The Trinity. The unbelievers, or deniers of God, will read these words and scoff in their hearts, and roll out from their mouths all sorts of disapproval! You will either love God, or hate him. You can't do both, this is just one of The Teachings from my Lord and Master Jesus Christ that I have found to be the truth. God's Power, Heals my spiritual sickness every day, I simply ask for His Help, and I receive it.

35. Shield From Destruction

Jesus Christ is my Lord and Master, God is my Creator, and The Holy Ghost Shadows over me day and night. Woe unto me if I ever fall from this, in my life; if I ever do I will suffer the fate of The Evil Forces that be! Once again I can't make something that's not; however, I can share with my brothers and sisters my ongoing victory, over active Alcoholism and Drug Addiction. The All Powerful Creator Has Guided me to the solution! There was no price for the solution; however, there are conditions I must always live with.

These conditions cause me to grow. Only God, can make things grow, including me as a living soul. As long as I live, I will be in danger of the mental projections from The Evil Forces that be! It's not something I will ever outgrow. This is when The Teachings from The Lord and Master Jesus Christ serves as a shield of protection from the ongoing traps set by The Evil Forces that be. Temptations are all around to lead the off guard souls into a contract of death. So what has already been sent as a standard for protection must be sought, and once achieved must never, and I mean never abandoned.

36. The Pathway to Life Eternal

There is no sorrow in my heart today; fore The Spirit that is Jesus Christ lives in my heart today. There is no doom and gloom in my soul today; fore The Spirit that is Jesus Christ Guides my Eternal Soul away from the evildoers. Oh, God, tears of joy streams down my face; fore You God, Have Provided an armament of protection for me while I yet still live in this evil place! God, there is nothing that You can't do, and I can see with my own eyes how The Evil Forces that be despise You! The Teachings from my Lord and Master Jesus Christ, Stirs my soul to live and do what is right. Oh, now I can't sit down; fore my soul is heavenly bound. Even though I've got evildoers to my left and evildoers to my right I've learned never to stop asking God, for His Spiritual Insights. God is always on time, and I've grown to increasingly love Him as He Continues to Heal my damaged mind! Now with each passing day that I am being Guided by The Trinity, The Evil Forces of darkness flee more and more from me. However, I must never stop seeking The Unapproachable Light; everything else is anarchy and soon to follow death and damnation.

37. Follow The Goodness of God

Deep is the pit of my unworthiness, it's still not filled up, even to this day as I write. Years have passed since God Has Relieved me from active Alcoholism and Drug Addiction; however, I still catch myself lusting after certain things of the flesh! I believe this will always stand as a shadow in my character. This is why The Trinity for me must always be sought. I've lived irresponsibly for years, and I damaged myself by abusing alcohol and other mind altering substances, for almost twenty years. The consequences of my actions have after affects, and they may accompany me, for the rest of my life. In this respect I must not allow myself any long periods of remorse, or shame . I must continue to in turn and thank God, for His Grace and Mercy, and continue to seek God's Kingdom! If I don't do these things, The Evil Forces that be will use negativity once again to enslave me. I must always practice for myself no form of negativity towards anything, or anybody. My Father in His Heaven is Kind and Merciful to the ungrateful and wicked people of this world, and I as His Servant must learn to be the same way.

38. Movements From The Trinity

I was listening to the celebration of this nation, when suddenly I began rejoicing in my heart and soul over The Lord and Master Jesus Christ; fore The Lord Jesus Christ came not just to free one nation; but to offer Eternal Life to all! I became overwhelmed in my soul, and there was no holing back the tears of joy! All The Host of Heaven was my witness; for there wasn't another soul present when The Trinity hit me! I will never have the old heart of heavy weights ever again. The Trinity Hasn't Touched me like this in a very long time, too long of a time has passed since I felt the way I did tonight. All praise is due to The Trinity forever. I pray this union between myself and The Trinity never to be broken! There can be no greater bond. Most of the time I am not even in this world; however, God Has Given me a job to do, and only God knows when my job is finished. So until then I will continue to spread the good news. In my life I have found God's Words to be true, never once did I find a flaw in them, so God's Words will never come back to Him empty! So if you like life, and want Eternal Life, see to it to seek out for yourself The Lord God's Words, and open your heart to what His Words say, and you will never be the same again – That's if you believe God Is!

39. The Truth About People

The Kingdom of God is within every man woman and child! We are at first a dichotomy of positive and negative forces, whichever side becomes greatest from within us determines our character. This knowledge of what we truly are holds great weight for any individual who is in search of answers concerning him, or herself. Be wise to know that all emotions fall into the slots of positivity, or negativity! To be ignorant of these forces causes individuals to become frustrated and out of control in all aspects of daily living. It has been by my experience from observing people through years; on how the negative is the dominate force in most people's lives. It's more seductive, than its opposite, which is the positive force. The positive force is inviting, whereas the negative force is demanding.

This simply analogy is the total make up of our humanity as we know it. When it comes to the formation of personalities, one force becomes greater, than the other, and individuals are credited by their actions. In simpler terms, they are labeled as being good, or bad in the minds of people. The summation of destiny has a very short menu.

40. End of a Search

No one will believe the things that I can see, and the ability was given to me by God Almighty! I told certain people be for and they shook their heads with compliance, but in their hearts they couldn't bring themselves to understand what was given to me came from God's Hands! So after many years I came to believe that this ability was given to me for a specific reason, and still to this day as I write, it hasn't been revealed to me. It's only in The Mind of God, Whom Holds the answers to the questions I seek. One thing I am assured of is this, nothing bad has happened to me from this ability. On the contrary these objects over the years have truly been a benefit to me; they present themselves at certain times, when something has been known, or conscious to my mind. There have been many days and nights I have contemplated on what I can physically see, and the end results always steers back to God Almighty! So there will be no more searching in my in soul to why I have the ability to see what I can see; I will just continue with the work that God Has Given to me. To help people get connected with The Spirit that is God. God is my business, and all the intangible things that I can see is just a part of it.

41. The Answer to my Seeking

Within each passing day, The Spirit of God Continues to teach me. A day doesn't pass by without God's Spirit Encouraging my Eternal Soul. God's Spirit Lives within me, and He Guides my every step. It took a long time from my life, to surrender to God. God's Spirit Never Forced Itself Upon me. God Is Inviting not Demanding. Living by God's Leadings have truly given me comfort and peace to my soul when I didn't understand something. He Always Sends me into wonderment concerning the whole allowance of my life. By learning to trust God, I have become stable in all of my affairs. Now God, Constantly Sends people to me for council. In each case I intensely listen to them, and in the end I direct them to God, through the power of prayer. The solution to all of their problems rest with The Spirit that is God. The solution will always be God; however, many people will not accept God, as being the answer to their problems. I know this to be true; for I tried to live by self-knowledge for years, and for years I stayed in darkness. Now I seek The Unapproachable Light that is God, and Jesus Christ, now my life has a purpose, and I no longer wonder why I'm here!

42. The Weight of Belief or Denial

The easiest and hardest thing in the world for people to do is believe! Belief carries weight in the outcome of situations. Weight of approval yes, or weight of denial no! When a person believes in something he, or she goes all out to become one with what they believe in. There are no exceptions. Being out rightly talked about, or even laughed at by people doesn't turn their hearts away from what they believe in. Yes the word belief, or denial holds the destiny of every person who had, or has life on this planet. This I affirm from my Lord and Master Jesus Christ! "Whoever believes that My Father in Heaven has sent me will have Eternal Life." He didn't say, whoever has one million dollars saved up in the bank – no, He Simply Said, If You Believe! Oh, how simple is that? Yet the people back there over two thousand years ago still didn't believe, even with all the miracles He Performed which none of them could never do! And as we know they crucified Him! This is why I know that The Evil Forces that be back then were in men, and in the world, and they are present today, and in men! I have truly learned to wholly trust no man, or woman, unless I know within my heart and soul that The Trinity Sent them to me. This is what I believe.

43. Locks Being Unlocked

Through the night my soul became restless, and I couldn't get no sleep, and why I couldn't get proper rest came to my conscious. Upon awakening I was dominated in my mind with this thought. I couldn't no longer walk in the flesh; for now I am being Guided by God away from it! The thought made so much sense to me, I immediately went into prayer and thanked God for always being inside me to help me. In the continuance of my prayer I asked Jesus Christ to give me what I needed to overcome the fact of being a slave to my flesh. In all confidence through my faith, I know I will receive what I've asked for. "No one can come to the Son, unless he is Enabled by The Father!" These words spoken by Jesus Christ has become reality in my life. I abused alcohol and other mind altering drugs for almost twenty years, and at my end, I called out to God, and Jesus Christ for Their Help, and from that night to this day seventeen years have passed, and I have looked to God for His Help and Guidance. Now at this point in my life, God Has Turned me Over to Jesus Christ His Son, so that I may be further taught on how to walk in The Spirit that is God, and to become holy and acceptable to God Himself! As it is written after death, no one can come to God, unless first he is seen by The Son of Man – Jesus Christ! To be with God forever is my soul's highest desire. This is the greatest satisfaction for me!

44. A Child's Truth

I will not talk about The Light too much today; for the ways of darkness, still needs to be talked about! I'll never forget when The Core of Darkness Himself came to visit me as a child. I was so terrified that I rolled out of bed from the top bunk, hit the floor screaming in terror. My mother came immediately into the room to see what happened. I remember, I couldn't even speak; for I was so terrified, and in shock from what I saw! Its form was like a Black Sun, and I mean totally Black, it hovered at the top of my window in my room. After a few seconds it approached me, that's when I screamed and rolled out of bed from it! I'll never forget the terror I felt that night! I was almost seven years old, and I wasn't dreaming, I know what I saw, and I'll never forget it! For years I was in fear of seeing it again. Now I am a fully grown man, and I understand what happened to me. What came to me were The Evil Forces that be, and I darted from them. I didn't know it than, but I do now, I belong to God, Almighty! The darkness is always looking for someone to enter into, to corrupt, and eventually enslave their eternal soul. I am so grateful, to have The Living God Dwell within my body; for it is a temple for Him! Beware of the darkness, which are The Evil Forces that be! Make use of my experience from the little boy lying in bed - run!

45. The Wisdom of The Leaf

One day, I will be as the leaf that falls from a tree; for my soul will leave the body, that was me! I can write this with joy in my heart; for the life that I lead isn't an evil one! Never, in my life did I really want to kill someone, and that's evidence enough for me to know that I am God's Son! With all the killing and hatred in this world I felt very unhappy and sad for the majority of my life. Now I look to and seek God, He Gives me Comfort and Tells my heart that these things must happen first before He Will Bring Order out of chaos! God's Leadings Have Taken me to many peaceful places since I came to Him for answers. The peaceful places I speak of are found in the intangible forces of the universe that are positive in nature! Those same forces; however, have opposites, and those opposite forces are the very reality, which governs this world as we know it today!

So in acquiring this knowledge, it has brought comfort to my heart, and has answered many questions that troubled me, for a very long time. I want no parts of The Evil Forces that be, they are temporary, and soon to be arrested by God, Almighty! So for the rest of my life I will not grovel in my soul, or be sad anymore.

God's Words are just, and He Sits in The Judgement Seat. Take heart brother and sisters, and be glad, always remember that God Himself, Have All The Powers that be, to make, or make not the leaf fall from a tree!

46. The Inside Trek

Once again the whispering of the small voice from within me has manifested itself as reality on the same day that it spoke to me about! What it told me is of no matter to the people who may read this page; however, it has caused me never to doubt its Leadings ever again! Time after time, the little voice has come to be right, and I now label the little voice as being God's Spiritual Insights! Only seekers of The One Living God, will comprehend what I am feeling, or what I feel from day to day. When people begin to seek God, over, and over, and, over again, God, Begins to

Speak to their hearts, then from their feelings, the message turns to gentile whispers within their minds. This is how people get to hear the small little voice giving directions and statements! I possess The Treasure that has no measure; He is available to all, but all will not constantly seek, and this is why God Remains out of most people's reach! I didn't try and make that last statement rhyme, but it's true, just as The Evil Forces that be, lay in wait to corrupt and kill you! This reality I get to see and hear about within each and every God Given Day, it saddens my heart to know so many people end up this way! So forward I will go, without any heavy weights in my heart, Glorifying God along the way, until it's time for me to depart! The endless energy of the color green...

47. Where God Can Rest

In the world where can God Rest His Head? God Doesn't Rest in places built by men. So I'll offer my body not built by men, so God Can Rest His Head; for I am in the world. The offer is a noble one; however, God Will Not Rest, if the conditions aren't holy! After many years of seeking You God, I without a doubt in my heart know that I'm still not holy and acceptable to You yet Lord. However, I know in that same heart God, You Love me Regardless! People come and people go, yet how many people really find salvation? Through many pathways their hearts search restlessly for it. I truly believe the # count on the souls who do find salvation is very low, compared to the many souls who have had life and those who are still living life. When it comes to the fate of humanity, God, You are the only salvation! Man's soul is from God, and God Is Eternal; there for the soul is Eternal also. The Evil Forces that be, stand as a stumbling block, for all of humanity! A man must stay constantly diligent in his prayers to The Lord God, sincerely asking for guidance in everyday situations, so that he may be found blameless, in all of his encounters as he leads the life that God Allows him! After a man routinely does this over, and over, and over again, then maybe, just maybe, God Can Have a Place to Rest His Head!

48. Nothing of Evil

Jesus Christ was oh, so right when He Said, "God Is The Only Good." Nothing can stand as a comparison to Him! He is in the picture frame all by Himself, without any need for change. God is perfect! I will never run out of information concerning God; for He is infinite! I am a thinker, and God's Spirit Always Takes my thoughts from the confines of my physical surroundings. He Avails my soul with oh, so much Wisdom and Understanding concerning the forces that make up His Universe! In conversations with most people I speak not of these things; however, lately in my days people have been coming to me with their relationship problems. I found myself sharing with them basic solutions on how I'm living my life. Before leaving my presents their faces show expressions of wonderment and satisfaction from the information I've shared with them! I know why they express satisfaction from my sharing. I simply translate to them what God Gives to me in meditation. All Glory Belongs to God; He is the rightful owner of it! There is no benefit I can give to anyone of myself, all worthwhile things comes from The Goodness of God! I've learned to rotate the reality, of God's Goodness in my heart over, and over again, and it's as light as a feather; however, it carries visions of solutions as heavy as The Rock of Gibraltar.

49. The Voice From The Heart

O h, Lord Jesus, I feel so tired, but I won't allow my low strength make me disobey what You told me to do ! You Are The Lord and Master Jesus Christ, and I refuse to listen to The Evil One; for he is truly The Father of lies! You Lord Jesus Christ Build me up every day and in every way, and I will continue to listen to You Jesus Christ and obey! Just this morning, The Spirit of God Woke me up real early, and I usually would lay back down and get more sleep; however, God's Spirit Told me to iron up some clothes and go down the road, and listen to The Pastor, of the church speak! The looks I received from the people of the church made me feel like they knew me all my life! One man just loved me with his eyes, after I commented on the fact that he and his wife had been together for a very long time. His wife said fifty-five years; all I could say is God Truly Blessed you, and I said that not to them, but in my own mind! So over the years I've learned to listen to the voice in my heart, instead of the voice in my mind; for there is where Satan tries to deceive us at all times, through our thoughts. The heart of man is where God, or Satan lives, and God Showed this to me today when I looked into the eyes of some of his kids! This is what I've learned today by listening to The Voice of my God when He Said Go, and Listen to what The Pastor has to say.

50. The Story of a Saved Sheep

I can't comprehend the love that I have for The Trinity, just as I can't comprehend the love from The Father , for The Son, just as I couldn't see for a very long time the love The Son have for The Sheep! It's real hard to see these things when you are constantly influenced by The Evil Forces that be. Only the constant seeking of God, has broken The Evil Cycle of confusion and bondage from within me! Day after day, after day for years I had to seek God's Kingdom, in order to be relieved from the bondage The Evil Forces that be had over my soul. Now I live The Kingdom of God without fail; for The Trinity Is Lord over my soul now and forever! The Father, The Son, and The Holy Ghost – Nothing is greater, or more powerful, and has no end to The Glory then They, which is One, thus The Trinity! The perfect order of the universe, soon to be established on the earth. The Evil Forces that be, and all of their house will be gathered together for judgement! I write these words for The Sheep of Jesus Christ, to give them hope and inspiration, so they may increase their faith in The Trinity. Take heed to my example; for I was one of the lost sheep; however, I listened to The Shepard's Voice, Calling me over, and over again! I made it home, and now I am overjoyed and glad!

51. God's Mercy

I know who I listen to during a day; I know who I listened to for thousands of days. I know to whom I was a slave to also, for thousands of days. The latter tries to kill, and enslave me; however, the former Loves me, Protects me, and wants to see me prosper! The former is The Trinity and the latter is The Evil forces that be! I have lived two lives, in one lifetime, and I can't go into eternity with both. One way of being will dominate the other. I am so glad I've learned to despise the latter; The One and Only God, Offered me a way out of slavery, and He Did it when I asked Him and Jesus Christ for Their Help. God Has Been Growing me ever since. The Evil Forces didn't let me go without a fight; they tortured me mentally and emotionally for years. The Lord God Comforted me each and every time, and Gave me a way out of the burning house, which was my mind! I will always be loyal to The Trinity, now and forever! God Has All Power! The Evil Forces are a strong force, but their leadings lead to destruction! I have seen their results over, and over again; starting with my own immediate family. They caused destruction and great sorrow! God Saved my life, in order that I may be a witness of His Power and Grace, not to mention His Glory. God Is The Owner of All Glory Infinitely, not just for a season, as man claims glory.

52. God's Love, and Protection

I do mean to be redundant, and I will continually state over, and over again how The Evil Forces that be are alive! I will continue to cite examples out of my experiences during life, to up hold my findings concerning The Evil Forces that be! First of all they need bodies to work out of! For years they worked out of my body, through my thoughts! If God Didn't Intervene when I asked Him for help I believe I would have been destroyed by The Evil Forces that be, through my thoughts! I can honestly say without no doubt in my heart today, that The One and Only God, Has Changed my whole thought process over time!

As I stated it be for The Evil Forces that be project thoughts! They carry out their destruction through people! They have done this ever since The first man and woman was created! They have the ability to move in and out of people, their goal is to overtake people's hearts, if they can't accomplish this they won't stay long ; however, they will cause as much damage, as possible! That is what happened to me; for years they poisoned my mind, and my actions started to erode my soul; however, they failed at conquering my heart!

All this information was revealed to me through the years, after I asked God, and Jesus Christ for Their Help. The Most Holy Spirit Raised me, and Taught me about The Evil Forces that be!

53. What Most People Don't Know

No one can teach you better than God, He Is The Knower of All Things, there is nothing out of His Reach! I couldn't sleep, and God kept me awake, so that He Could Teach. For days He Told me that someone was going to give me a check, and it was going to be a large sum of money, and I would know that He Is The Lord God! I responded back to God in my thoughts saying; "I already know You are The Lord God; however, Thy Will Be Done." For the past two months everything God, Whispered to my mind has come true, and it isn't going to be no difference in this; for God, never lies!

Right now it's 4:32 am, and I know in my soul I am a very blessed man! I never felt this secure, this joyful, this peaceful, this content, in my whole life, all brought on by that Gentile and Kind Spirit, I call God! He Has Rescued me from The Evil Forces that be, He Has Restored me to sanity, He Has Protected me from foolish me, He Had All Kinds of Patients with me, and He never abandoned me! He took me by my hand, and delivered me to a secure house, where I could finish growing up, and now I am at the stage where I can see God even more clearly than I could in the beginning, when I cried out to Him for help! Oh, what An Awesome God we have!

54. Something Evil Can't Hide

As I write I am weak; however, I will finish this work today; for God, Will Renew my strength! I have learned to depend upon God for everything while I yet still live in this Evil Place! I don't fool myself by what the world projects; for The Evil Forces that be are behind every project! They run this world in every aspect; their hands are in every piece of pie. I don't trust nothing they supply! I see so many people being deceived by what they buy; for the products aren't sturdily built, so people can come back quickly, and buy again! The way most cars are manufactured are evil; they put in sensor lights, to automatically fail after a certain time, and the owner must purchase it, or the vehicle won't pass certain state regulations! So the vehicle is useless until the owner spends the large amount of money to replace the part! The larger they are the more unjust they are! So, whatever the common man needs, they make the prices so high they have trouble paying for the goods. These are some of tactics The Evildoers do! They are materialistic, they hoard money! They don't share with people; for The Love of God, isn't in them! They are controlled by and are children of the devil.

55. When The Spirit of God Moves

When The Spirit of God Moves there is nothing I can do to stay still! I move right with God's Spirit! for His Spirit Is in me and I am in Him! The Light of God's Spirit Shows itself through my own vision! I've heard it said from some people that they saw Lights come from my eyes! These are the Lights from God Himself, He is The Unapproachable Light! I feel so blessed to know that God's Spiritual Glow Flows through me frequently! Lately I've been seeing God's Lights more and more; all brought on by me consciously turning my back on the world around me! Knowing that my salvation isn't down here. The vision of God's Unapproachable Light winks in and out of my physical sight! Now I know why I can't sleep during the early morning light; for The Spirit of God, Moves me to get up and write! There is nothing I can do when The Spirit of God Moves, but to move with Him when He Moves! God Whispered to my mind that greater things I would write in the coming days, and once again The Lord God Almighty was right. It's now 3:57am, and I just completed another beautiful writing from Him!

56. The Transformation

I can't live my life anymore; without giving thanks to God, through Jesus Christ! I, no longer desire the things of this world; I seek The Desires of The Spirit that Is God! There is a feeling of delight in my heart when I feel God's Spirit Moving me! God's Spirit Has Blessed my soul by Placing the desire in my heart to seek out His Son Jesus Christ! For years I use to say to people, I'm no Jesus Christ, I will not turn the other cheek, I will hit you back!

Today I truly don't know if I would hit someone back; however, I do believe I am a lot less selfish than I use to be! One thing I am assured of is this, by seeking The Teachings of the Lord and Master Jesus Christ, I've become truly aware more than I have my whole life about the reality of The Evil Forces that be! It's as though by seeking The Son of Man with all of my heart has caused a chain reaction within my mind, pointing to all the evil practices manifested in the lives of people.

It's a constant awareness concerning many aspects of their

behavior! I am in constant concentration; for The Lord and Master Jesus Christ's Spirit is being poured directly into my soul! I am being transformed by God, through The Lord and Master Jesus Christ!

57. God's Decree

"Stay focused and turn not away!" These were the words whispered to my mind; from The one and Only God, on 7/20/12, during meditation. The Lord God, Left these words on my conscious mind, with the intension to strengthen my will. God, Is oh, so Awesome; fore He Knows my pattern of performance, also He Knows that The Evil Forces that be are right by my side, and in the midst of my presents, to try and tempt me away from my work! By reflecting on my day, I got to see the value of the words The Lord God Whispered to me in meditation on 7/20/12. I rejoice in giving away what God, Gives to me from day to day.

The Wisdom of God, Is Shaping my destiny! My destiny is Eternity, either in The Presence of God , or not! Only Jesus Christ Has that authority; for God Has Already Given it to Him! But right now I am mortal and it overjoys my heart to keep giving away what The Trinity Gives to me.

So, I will keep focused and not turn away! God, Calls me His Son, and as God Being my Heavenly Father, I will not disrespect anyone in my Father's House. Even if they are evil, and disrespectful; for it's not my place to pass judgement on them, that's my Heavenly Father's Obligation, and their outcomes are determined by Him!

58. Guidance, Through a Son, Who is a Servant

Once again The Spirit of God moved me again to pick up the pin and write! I was awakened at 3:52am, on 7/22/12, by a car horn blowing over, and over again, sounding real faint, from a far distance. When my eyes opened the car horn immediately stopped and I looked over at the clock, and it was 3:52am, on the dot! In my heart I knew the car horn blowing was meant for me; one more awakening, by God, Almighty! The Holy Spirit of God's Movements Are Swift, and I've learned to recognize them, oh what a gift! As I stay focused on God's Leadings and turn not away; The Holy Spirit Strengthens me with Spiritual Insights day, by day. I don't try and figure out things anymore; for God's Spirit, Correctly Guides me from my inner core! As I sit here early in this morning pushing this pen, no one in all existence can imagine the joy I feel from within! I never felt this secure and stable in all of my life; and it's not a mystery for God Is Guiding me right. For years I was in bondage by The Evil Forces that be, and I had no means to see my path clearly! Only God's Power Was Able to Set me Free, and now I get to write about the truth so others may seek God Almighty!

59. The Lord God Blessed Me

The Lord God Blessed me and The Lord God Loves me! There were no works from me that made Him Show His Countenance. I will never comprehend The Lord God! As I sit here and write I can feel selfishness and worldly ambitions fall from me; for God's Spirit Is Upon me, and in Him those things have no value! There is no urgency in my heart when The Spirit of God Comes Near to me, and when The Spirit of God Enters into me, I feel like a kid again.

My soul longs to be with Him forever! I'm very sad without God's Spirit Living inside with me! Nothing is worth having if God's Spirit isn't attached to it! Now I understand why I felt so miserable for so many years; for the things I were pursuing had no value, and I belonged to God! Oh, thank You, God; for Allowing me to seek You Lord God. You Are So Patient and Kind; now You Have Enabled me to See Things Clearly. I lived in darkness for years and I was so confused and afraid; I reached the point where as I didn't know what to do anymore. So I called on You, and Jesus Christ for help! Without hesitation, The Lord God Showed Up, and then The Lord God Blessed me and then day, after day, He Increased The Blessings upon me; fore The Lord God Loves me, God, Was Just Patiently waiting for me! Now I don't want to live a second without Him!

60. Life of a Servant

To write is my job and The Lord God Has Called me To serve in this way. I am a doer of The Spirit that is God, not a doer of the spirit of this world! The majority of my time is spent in communion with The Trinity. The things of this world is foolishness to me; Whereas The Things of The Spirit of God is wisdom to me. God, Doesn't Hold Back Anything that is of His Spirit; however, most people seek Him not; they are obsessed by the things of this world! Only when all their resources run dry do they seek out God's Counsel. Most people don't stay in concentration long; for God's Way isn't about instant gratification. They turn away and say, the heck with this God seeking stuff, It's not for me. Why seek God? He never Gives me what I ask for! Here is the statement I hear all the time – there isn't no God! Yea it makes it real easy for them in their minds so they don't have to conform to any moral beliefs! I use to get real frustrated with the mind sets of people like that, not anymore; for my job is to write and help seek out God's Lost Sheep, and guide them to safety which is God Himself! No more time do I spend with closed minded people! My time is limited and my work is ongoing. Only The Power of God Can Change people who are ignorant to His Way, or maybe that's the way they supposed to be.

61. Circle of Protection

The Spirit of Satan came upon my mind this evening, as I was attending a meeting of my fellows, who have, or are still suffering from the bondage of The Evil Forces that be. The Lord God Truly Watches Out Over my soul. I felt the enemy, and asked God to Forgive me. You see God's Spirit Lives inside with me, that's how I was so quick to recognize Satan's Projections to my mind. It was only for a few minutes, but now I see how those minutes were too long of a time. I don't want no parts of The Evil Forces that be, nowhere inside of me! Now I can feel God's Spirit Flowing through me again; anytime I get agitated, it's The Evil Forces that be who are doing their best to upset me. I can feel them and see them in other people all the time. God Calls me Not to let them upset my peace! Hate is a very strong word, and I'm learning how to use this word. I don't use it in my heart when I refer to people; however, I use it with full strength, when it comes to The Evil Forces that be, I hate them, I truly do! The Lord and Master Jesus Christ Teaches on how to defeat evil with good, and I totally agree with The Master; however, the students must have God's Spirit Flowing through them at all times. The students must practice good deeds and constantly seek The Goodness of God! They must become agents of God's Goodness!

62. The Vow

It was Christmas Day, The Year was 1995, I was homeless for eight months. I never want to forget that day; for that day marked the last day I drank any kind of alcohol! I can remember being real sad; for it was Christmas, and it didn't have any meaning for me! I was all alone, in the big old state of California, three thousand miles away from any family members, and that was of no matter; for nobody back there cared, or loved me anyway! I distinctly remember asking God, and Jesus Christ five days earlier to help me; for I couldn't live the way I was living anymore! And on Christmas Day here I was drinking alcohol again, doing the same old behavior! I remembered how I asked God, and Jesus Christ for Their Help five days earlier, and upon the remembrance I became disgusted with myself. I was at an associates house, and immediately I got up and left their house. I remember walking up El Toro Road, and I vowed to myself saying, "I will not drink alcohol ever again, and I will do what God Has Placed before me to do, or I will go on to the bitter end, and drink myself, to the death!" Well the latter didn't happen to me, however, there was a very long period of reconstruction, I had to learn how to live all over again. As I write, I'm a totally different person opposed to what I use to be like on the inside. All as a result from allowing God to go to work on my mind; operating out of the confines of my heart!

63. Folded Away, In God's Spirit

I don't want to die, and be a disappointment to my Maker, I wish not to make God unhappy concerning me in any way! God, and Jesus Christ Have Been So Kind to me, even when I was a fool to myself! So for the rest of my life I will be Their Slave; if They Will Have me. I made this decision from the deep depth of my heart, I want nothing for myself except to Glorify God's Most Holy Name, through His Son Jesus Christ! The road ahead will be lonely; however, I will have joy in my heart. The ruler of this world will try and close in on me, but The Power of God, Will Prevail! The Children of God, will seek me; for from me the truth will flow like a great river, and the children from darkness will hate me; for I will expose their evil deeds! No fingers will I point, but my words will uncover the manifestation of lies. All these things will happen and many more; for it's God's Spirit, that Lives within me. It will be God's Spirit Speaking, not I ! Just as the words the reader is now reading is His, not mine. God's Will, will be done, I am just His Instrument! Jesus Christ's Way of Living will be accomplished through me; for I belong to Them, The Trinity. The rightful owner of everything known and unknown!

64. Food For The Sheep

When A man has no wife, and a woman has no husband what is left in life that is positive? In either case married or single, temptation is always great! The ruler of the world called earth is running out of time to rule! Most people of the world are blind to The Scriptures; however, God Himself is making it possible for everybody to get a chance to repent of their wrong doings, before they leave this earth! It's the end of the world every day for some people; however, I am a Servant of God, and I'll pass this message on. Don't allow yourself to leave this life without seeking your Maker God, He Is Waiting for us to ask for forgiveness! I am not the first Servant that has been Sent to feed The Sheep of Jesus Christ, I am stocked with the food they need to help them survive!

Only God Is The Salvation for our Eternal Souls. So we must prepare ourselves now for The Eternity to come! Either way we will exist for forever; for God Himself is forever, and we are from God! So stop chasing after the things of this world, they are temporary, chase after the things of God's Spirit; fore He is Eternal, Just and Right! Everything you see in this world has an opposite, don't allow yourselves to become the opposite of God! This is the food that I have for Jesus Christ's Sheep!

65. Shades of God's Grace

The early days of freedom from bondage from The Evil Forces that be were oh, so painful; It's like waking up from twenty years of sleeping and realizing you haven't progressed an inch during the last twenty years! The progress you did make was all negative, worthless to yourself and others! The fillings of self-pity and shame consume your mind most of the time, and it feels like it will never end! I can state this oh, so clearly; for that condition of being was me for about six years! The only hope and faith I had was in God Himself! He Comforted my heart from moment to moment with full knowledge of my situation. God's Spirit Encouraged me to keep moving forward day after day; and to always know that He was right there with me, and not to worry about anything! He Whispered to my mind that He Would Provide for all of my needs; however, I was harboring all forms of fear, resentments, and frustrations! This is why I am so grateful to The Spirit that is God to this day as I write the truth about my condition; after being rescued from the bondage of The Evil Forces that be! Only God Himself was able to Transform the damaged soul that I was! God's Healing Power is available to all who constantly seeks Him, and believe He Can Do for them what they could never do for themselves! Always remember God's Ways are not about instant self-gratification!

66. Almost a Waste

From day to day I lived in fear for years; until the point came when I could sense physical death, as one could tell the evening is approaching! Writing about this part of my life always brings me into the state of being humble. In my heart at the present time is the manifestation of loyalty to The Trinity that can't be explained in words! I have loyalty to nothing else like I have loyalty to Them! The Father, The Son, and The Holy Ghost; the soul that is me belongs to Them! My heart burns with fire, when it comes down to the work assigned to me by The Trinity! Nothing of this world matters to me lest it be Their Direction. Jesus Christ Has Given me as well as the other sheep a code to live by, we must honor this code if we call ourselves His Sheep! We are powerless without His Guidance; for God, Has Made Jesus Christ The Head of The Flock! Some of The Sheep are not with The Flock and they are far off in the wilderness, but when The Master Calls, they will come to Him; for they know His Voice. A strangers voice they will not come to, and that was me for years being out in the wilderness. All kinds of voices was calling me, but I didn't go to them, then the strangers came after me, to harm me, but God Gave me Protection, though I knew it not then.

67. Connection to Eternity

As I live one day to the next I can honestly feel The Spirit that is God inside of me! I don't state this to arouse jealousy or confusion, I state this for the common hunger of people who are searching for something in life to actually give them meaning for their lives! That's exactly what I received upon constantly seeking The Lord God, day after day for years without fail. I've learned to depend on God, and trust Him, and now God Trusts me! God Knows I won't flake on a situation, I'm either for something or I'm not! I confide in The Lord God; for I know He Is Faithful, I don't confide in men for they are fallible, and they will break your trust! Part of my job is to be a witness of God's Goodness, so He May Glorify Himself, in the lives of others. The Lord God Doesn't Want anyone who has life to perish! Unfortunately it's already written that everyone won't receive The Gift of Eternal Life! I must not concern myself to much with the future, I must concentrate on the present situation, and at the present time it's not too late to seek out The One and Only God Who Makes All Life Possible! Take the advice from a once lost Sheep. Once you get to know God You'll never want His Presents to leave you.

68. Rhythms in Life

When a rhythm is broken, it off sets so many things; however reinstatement can be achieved again or not, it depends on the circumstances involved! My life is a perfect example, and I'm sure many other people's lives can fit the same outcome if they were examined! Sometimes a rhythm being broken can be a very positive and life changing experience. I know it was for me, when I asked God, and Jesus Christ for Their Help! I was trapped in a Deadly Rhythm, and I myself was powerless to break it! The thoughts of my mind were attuned to an Obsessive Deadly Rhythm!

Only The Creator of All Things Was Able to break it! Today I live by The Guidance of God's Holy Rhythm! Living by the way The Holy Spirit of God Instructs my heart has caused me no ill effects in my soul, with other people, or institutions so far. I sought The Lord God for so long that now I am in rhythm with God. I can actually know when He Is Communicating with me, and I kept that between me and God. He Instructs me to pass on what I have learned, when it's possible. Everything in my life now after seeking God to a rhythm, isn't always a pleasure, or a joy in itself, but by continuing to follow The Lord God's Leadings, has always resulted in the betterment of other people's lives through me. I have learned to give The Glory to God; for I know I am just His Instrument

69. Answers to Common Questions

Oh how confused and ignorant I was for most of my life concerning the fact of who I was, and of other people, who were they, and finally what was life all about? These questions are very commonly asked by most people. However, if people are misled the outcome is corruption! I am sure that's why God Himself Has Implemented His Grace Upon this world, through His Son Jesus Christ. Making it so simple to achieve Eternal Life, by simply believing that God, The Father Has Sent His Son Jesus Christ, into the World to atone for our sins, and to be the model of how to live life! The Lord God, Has Truly Blessed me; for Satan almost destroyed me. The Lord God, Has Been Protecting me for years, and He Still Protects my very life. The difference now in my later years is that I am aware of God's Protection from day to day! The Lord God Calls me to Stay Focused on Him, each and every day, and turn not away! I am not confused anymore, I am not ignorant of myself, or why others are here anymore, and I don't wonder what life is all about anymore. God, Has Given me the answers I sought for years, and the meanings there of! All Life is God's Creation, and whatever direction a soul might take, God Will Be Glorified through His Holiness, and there will be no confusion on The Last Day, Concerning His Glory; however, there will be much sorrow; upon the souls who make up the unbelievers.

70. Solidification to God's Spirit

God I can't go on anymore with any kind of hurt in my heart against anyone! I refuse to complain about the conditions of my life at the present time. I place my soul before You Lord God, with no worries in my heart; for I belong to You, Lord God! This I do of my own self will Lord God that You, Yourself Have Blessed me with! I am in the realization to know that my life isn't my own! I belong to The Unseen Spirit that is God! It's God Who Glorifies Himself Through the body that I possess. I gather up nothing for myself; fore the things of this world are temporary. I am not attracted to temporary things, I am attracted to that which is Eternal! The Lord God Is my friend, and I grew to love and trust Him through His Own Allowance! He Placed a line of communication between my soul and Himself a very long time ago in my youth. As time passed by I've learned to comprehend what God Had Put into place. God's Connection to my soul was never broken, even though all of the bondage of my mental thought processes! The Evil Forces that be failed in their attempt to enslave my Eternal Soul that is me! What saved my life and soul was the remembrance of what The Lord God Told me in my youth never to forget, and always to remember. At the end of my will, I called on it, and God Responded, and I will never be influenced, or manipulated by The Evil Forces that be ever again, so help me God! God Has Restored me to sanity and my rightful mind!

71. Another Spiritual Awakening

In the start of Glorifying God, I will begin with The Head of The Flocks of Sheep and Goats, and He is The Lord and Master Jesus Christ! After seeking God for years The Lord God Whispered in my mind to seek out The Teachings of His Son Jesus Christ, and to follow His way of Living. Jesus Christ Was Perfect in His Life here upon the earth and He is Still that way, and will be that way forever! Jesus Christ Is my Older Brother; for God, Calls me His Son!

My Older Brother Jesus Christ is The Perfect Model for my life, this is why God Whispered in my mind from my heart to seek The Teachings from His Son Jesus Christ! He isn't just The Model for my life, but The Model of Righteousness for the whole world! God Found Favor in Him and Raised Him from the dead, and to be a witness to the whole world that God, Has Power over death by resurrecting Him to life again!

Now The Holy Scriptures are fulfilled through the prophets concerning The Christ! God Has Truly honored my soul by Sending me in search of The Only Man that has been murdered by a mob, and returned to His Own Body that was badly damaged by the crucifixion. The Power of God Run Oh, So Deep, He Has The Grip Of All Power! I consider myself truly blessed to be positively moved by God Himself in this way!

72. Fruits From God's Spirit

I am always being guided positively from The Order of God! When it comes down to giving information about God's Kind and Generous Ways there is no weariness of any kind in my soul. After genuinely seeking God's Kingdom, day after day after day, His Spirit Has Uplifted my soul to a constant awareness of what I am to do from one day to the next! I've learned not to discuss these matters with just anyone; for their hearts and minds are not yet attuned to such things! Nevertheless, The Leadings from God's Spirit Carries through to my heart! This is the outcome from constantly seeking out The Goodness of God. There is no confusion in my emotions for long periods of time, they have become lesser and lesser with each passing day. This has been a long process for me; for I've been miss guided in my mind for a very long time. A good portion of my life was tainted with fears, and resentments from my daily surroundings! I tried to live life like I wasn't afraid of people, places, or things. In my mind I was truly governed by them; however, I played the tough guy roll, which I wasn't! I am truly honored today to be led by The Spirit that is God, and I know who I am today, and I don't have to lie about anything that's going on inside of me!

73. The Road to Salvation

God, there is no worry in You, there is no sadness in You either, this morning I woke up in negativity, and in just a few short minutes of meditation with You God, You Brought me out from that negative mind set! God, You are my treasure that has no measure; oh, how truly blessed I am. I have sought You out Lord God until the road ended up with You Dwelling in my heart;

without an end! God, I wish I could bottle You up, and give you a way to all the people who are in the bondage of self, those trapped by The Evil Forces that be, and those who are just clueless of Your Being! It's my desire; however, it isn't your Will Lord God! God You don't hide Yourself for nothing, it's a reason why Your Conditions are the way they are! You Lord God, Created Everything that has a possibility for existence. God, You've already stated in Your Words long ago, through Your Prophets, in order to obtain The Lord God, one must seek out God's Kingdom! God I can truly see the wisdom in this like I could never see it before! Those who truly love You will constantly seek You over, and over again, without fail; for they truly believe You Are without having to physically see You. Those who don't constantly seek You, won't be Given The Secrets of Your Kingdom. Oh, how Awesome You Truly Are, O Most Holy One of Israel! I am at Your Service Forever!

74. Spirit of Eternal Life

No one of the living from earth can attest to all of the riches and beauties that were at Your Command, yet still You Consented to Your Father that is God, to come to earth, and become poor, to atone for the world's sins, so that we could be Given the opportunity to have Eternal Life, through The Grace of God, just by believing that God, Your Father sent You, His Son Jesus Christ! How can anybody that doesn't have love, comprehend that? No one can have a Greater Love than that. Back in the time of Jesus's Coming, it was foretold that The Christ would be born into the world, and a certain king wanted to kill The Christ. God, Knew of the plot to kill Jesus Christ, so God, Had His Earthly Father Move the family away, until the threat from that king had passed! God,

Has Touched my heart to seek out The Teachings of His Son, some 2012 years after His Resurrection!

The Son of Man is the only road to Eternal Life. I truly believe God Knew I was ready to receive The Spirit, that is Jesus Christ! The Unselfishness of Jesus Christ is not an easy thing to obtain; however, I won't sit around and wonder to myself about myself, and believe in my heart that God Believes in me! No one can seek Jesus Christ, unless he is enabled by God Himself! I know this to be true ; fore Jesus Christ Has said it Himself!

75. The Spirit of God

Wherever I go, wherever I may be moved to go, I know that The Spirit of God is there within me. He Lives in this temple we human beings call a body! He always was inside with me, I was just not constantly taught about the reality of His Presents! Nevertheless God's Spirit Watched Out over my temple and me until I came unto the end of myself! It took thirty-three years and eight days, for me to reach the end of myself. I was pretty badly damaged, at that point of my life. Out of all the things that happened to me and even after all of the disappointments in life, I didn't know it then, but years had passed, and then one day God Showed me that I never hardened my heart to the point whereas I truly wanted to kill someone, or hurt someone really bad! After The Spirit of God Showed me that; I knew in my heart that I was His Son! The knowledge of this empowered me even more to turn away from the ways of this world. As I kept on living God's Spirit Continued to Teach me even more about Himself, and I became amazed from one day to the next, and the process of learning hasn't stopped even up to the day that I am writing this!

I said it before , and I'll say it again, this life isn't my own, it never was. I don't ever want to be misled into that mind set ever again! The Lord God, Created us human being for His Purposes, not for any selfish desires we may be drawn to think!

76. An Evil Tactic Exposed

Oh, Lord God, how the ways of our enemy is oh, so subtle, once again I awoke to a negative mind set ! The enemy spoke to my mind saying, soon you'll run out of things to say about The Lord God, and then what will you do? I just shook my head, not in agreement with the thought, but in the assurance of Satan sticking real close to me; fore I pose a true threat to his hold on the many souls who haven't yet read and studied this material that The Good Lord God Is Giving to me from day to day! No Satan, I won't stop my flow of ink, and The Goodness of God will never run out; if you had feet to be in boots, you would keep on shaking in them!

This soul was once in bondage by you Satan, now I am free and I belong to my Heavenly Father's House, which is The Almighty God, Whom you fear! Satan, your time of rule on this earth is running out! So still more of your mental projections I will expect; for in my heart I know you respect The Many Gifts my Lord God Has Given Unto me. Oh, God, I truly thank You for Giving me The Gift of Discernment, Allowing me to see the enemy for what he truly is. Satan is a liar, he is The Father of lies! This whole excerpt was made possible by Satan trying to deceive me once again through my thoughts! Each time He does it, I will write another!

77. The Calling

Here it's two thousand and twelve years later after that mob crucified You, and Your Kingdom is still forming, You Really Are The King of Kings and The Lord of Lords! There will never be another doubt in my heart concerning Your Kingdom ever again! Your Father Jesus, which is my Father also, Has Whispered to my mind from my heart to seek out Your Teachings Jesus, and with each passing day I grew more humble to Your Spirit Jesus! I truly understand now when the early believers said, we died, and were crucified with Christ, and being that He was resurrected from death to return to His crucified body by God, His Father. We too know that God, Will Raise us too; fore we believe in The Lord and Master Jesus Christ when He said, "He will be The Way to Eternal Life!" Only The Life Giver God, Has Drawn me to seek Jesus Christ! I become overwhelmed in my soul when I contemplate about how much God Loves me. He called my soul to seek out The King of Kings and The Lord of Lords, in an Effort to Show me The Pathway to Eternal Life! God Knows that at this point of my existence I won't just keep this to myself; I will use my tongue and shout about The Good News when I know it will be affective, and God Also Knows I will be silent when I know the telling would be in vain!

78. Joy From God's Spirit

There is no doubt in my soul anymore, about the condition of the position I have grown into! The Spirit of God, Has Been Growing me now for years! All kinds of desires have fallen away from the confines of my heart. Every day I die a little bit more from the ways of this world called earth! I use to think something was deathly wrong with me; for I had no drives for things as I heard others in their desire for things! It truly bothered me for a while. The Spirit of God, Truly Showed me that it was nothing wrong with me, that it was His Spirit who was in my heart, and now His Spirit Lives there, that's the reason why I have no desires for the physical things I'm seeing! I now understand why in many parts of the day and night I am overcome with laughter, and most of the time I am by myself, and I can't stop laughing! You see God's Spirit is of joy, there is no worries in Him, and there is no sadness. God's Spirit is Light and Airy, it's not bound in fears, threats and cursing's. Oh, I am truly blessed, The Lord God's Spirit Chooses to Live inside of me. Oh, how wonderful I feel from day to day, knowing The Lord God Is with me each and every day! There is no better joy than this! Oh, thank You Spirit that Is God!

79. Another Reality Revealed

Why do I feel so sad after feeling so joyful; just one hour earlier? I asked The Spirit of God that Lives within me, and I received my answer. Just as The Lord God 's Spirit Lives within me with all of Its Knowledge, Wisdom, Understanding, and Possession of every intangible emotion there is; so it's in me also! I was just so joyful in listening to my music, that I went to the ends of joy, and when the music stopped, it was as if a brick was dropped inside of me, going from one extreme, in the feeling of joy, to the opposite of joy, which is sadness! Oh, how powerful we human beings really are. The lack of knowledge concerning this, sends an individual into confusion! The Kingdom of God, is an inside journey, and those who never seek it, will always be ignorant of it! This is why God Said, you have to seek The Kingdom, so that a soul my enter into The Kingdom of God! Searching inside myself for years now, has unveiled jewels of wisdom and understanding of God's Kingdom that I could have never ventured into of my own will! Only by constantly seeking God in meditation did I find the solutions to my day to day problems. I had to stop thinking I knew the answers to problems by copying what I saw other people doing. That approach to living life caused a lot of mental, physical, and emotional pain for myself.

80. True Love

Her name was Loleta, I never thought that I would write about her, but I guess God, and my heart did! You can call it what you want, but I know what it was for me, she was the first girl that I truly loved! I was seven, almost eight years old, and now I am almost fifty years old, and I never felt for a person of the opposite sex the way I felt for, and about Loleta, and I don't think I ever will! The joy, the pride, the protection of, I felt all of that about her and for her, and my feelings were never that strong, for any other female ever again! A lot of it had to do with me; for I remember closing up my heart; for I became so sad about the way we were ripped away from each other! We lived on the same block Wainwright Street, I lived on one side of the street and her house was on the opposite side, four houses a part. I'll never forget, we went to Bragraw Avenue School, and her house was on the same side of the school, about fifty-three yards away. We were in school, and the fire alarm went off, and all the classes had to be evacuated, and I remember a teacher saying a house is on fire and the flames are about twenty feet high, and at that moment I said to myself, "I hope it's not my girlfriend's house!" I remember the school letting us go home early, and I found out it was my girl's house, and her and her family moved away, to a different state, and I never saw her, or heard from her, ever again. That experience crushed me, and I stayed crushed for years! I don't think I ever stopped loving Loleta, and I don't think I ever will...

81. The Next Move in God's Process

With the passing of each day now, I can see a little bit clearer the road I was commanded to walk on by my Maker! When God Speaks to me so directly everything has already been prepared for me, the only thing left to do is for me to carry out what God So Gently Instructed me to do. The word command is to harsh of a word to describe The Leadings from God, when He Speaks to me. It's like hearing advice from a concerned friend, who really wants to see me do well in all of my affairs! The road that I can see clearer each day brings joy to my heart that is in no way fleeting! How could it be, when God Himself is Directing my path. The pathway for me leads right to His Son Jesus Christ, my Older Brother!

This is The Most Awesome Gift yet I've Received from my Maker, besides my existence! I already know in my heart that the enthusiasm will grow each and every day now, as Jesus Christ's Spirit Is Poured Into my heart and soul. I'm not trying to contemplate on what my tasks will be, but I do know it won't be from the ways of this world; so I will continue to pray for strength and joy for other people. What I am led to do will be just one more added strength of brightness to the already Unapproachable Light of God's Glory! I never ever want to lose sight of The Things God Has Placed before me, nothing is more important!

82. The Search For Eternal Things

I sought The Lord God constantly for years, to the point whereas a positive relationship has developed, between my soul and God's Eternal Spirit! So many situations has occurred in my life just as God's Spirit Whispered to my mind the outcomes before they happened! I don't believe in coincidences. I've gotten to the point that I don't even leave my house without having a meditation session with The Spirit that is God , and it doesn't stop there, I talk to God all the day long sometimes! I grew to love, and trust God; I believe this relationship was predestined; for when I look at all the situations of my existence it's as though I was guided to seek God, out! The only time when I am at peace, the only time when I am comforted is when I seek out The Spirit that is God. Nothing else in this world captivates my attention, and positively gives me solutions to situations like God does! I'm a thinker, I've been a thinker as long as I can remember and ordinary things don't hold my attention for long periods of time; I have a thirst for knowledge of things, but not things you can see and touch! I guess that's when and why I took up on the search for God's Leadings. It wasn't an overnight process; for I had to deal with the world first, with all of its foolishness, and I was confused and sad for a good portion of my existence! Now I have no interests in worldly things, only to Keep seeking God!

83. The Beginning of The End of Darkness

The world is a beautiful place; however, most of her governments are evil, and there is much corruption here in The United States. The ways of the world are of foolishness, most of the teachings in the schools strive not for the betterment of the world as a whole.

Material Greed is in the hearts of many of its people. Most people of the world aren't consciously sober to this fact! Most people look at making money more important than teaching their children true values and the truth to who really created the world they are a part of, and who sustains their lives from one day to next! No, hoarding money is more important than teaching about the truth of things! Woe unto this world, destruction of all that is seen is steadily approaching! This is the reality that most people want to sweep under the rug and lie to themselves and others by saying, situations here are going to stay stable; no down fall is going to come upon us. Don't try and scare us with those religious things! This is exactly why my God Has Called me to write; fore I will try my best to stay away from public speaking, for the enemy is right there to disrupt, and cause father dissensions amongst the people! So I'll place the truth on paper, and those Guided Souls by God, will be drawn to read its pages, and the enemy will want to burn the pages of the truth, but they will be unable to do so. I will write and tell the truth, and make it available to all those who will thirst for knowledge.

84. Keeping Focused

Oh, Spirit that is God, I at this moment in my existence am full of information that must be digested into my heart and soul as a means for references to Glorify Your Most Holy Name! God, You've Given me so much wisdom in the past few days, it causes me to reflect; for the meanings are so powerful, and by living by what You've Given me has overwhelmed my soul! I've seen the truth in Your Leadings so clearly in every aspect of my daily living, for months now. The enemy has successfully blocked me off from You Lord God for years; however, it's of no avail for Satan; for

Your Spirit Lived with me and through me despite the years of Mental Bondage!

The information I've obtained will serve to Glorify You Lord God in the existence of Billons of souls. There is no exaggeration in my estimation concerning the number of souls who will be helped. The numbers probably will be even greater! I am Eternal, just as my Maker Is! The Work God You've Placed before me is ongoing, and I won't try and force any solutions! All I can do is add to the work that has already been done. I feel so honored in my soul to have been Given this assignment from my Maker! Lord God, my days and nights are oh, so full, and my soul is so happy the purpose of my existence has been revealed to me, and I must keep focused on The Lord God, and turn not away!

85. The Calling From God

I've come to love and trust The Spirit that is God, I always knew in my heart that God, wouldn't ever hurt me; even though, I experienced many hurtful things in my existence, before I truly asked God, and Jesus Christ to help me! My help showed up in the form of guidance from within my heart, I didn't know it at the conscious level then, like I do now! Sixteen almost seventeen years has passed since I first truly asked Them for Their Help. Through the years I've developed a very strong connection to The Spirit that I call God, and He Was and Is The Only Relief I have grown to depend on. Nothing of this world has calmed my soul and healed my damaged my mind other than God's Holy Spirit! Now God's Spirit Has Whispered to my mind to seek out His Son, The Lord and Master Jesus Christ! I am not reluctant to do so, and I haven't been ever since the first day God Whispered to my mind to seek out Jesus Christ's Spirit! Jesus Christ is The Son of Man, and it's a further changing of my character that I must undergo; however, I will take courage! Jesus Christ Is The Epitome of Compassion and Selflessness, we human being have called Him the perfect man; fore He was Blameless Concerning All Things! Now with God Having Great Confidence in me; The Holy Spirit of God Has Sent me in search of His Blameless Son, Jesus Christ! A calling I must never forget!

86. Transcends in Motion

I know I'm not by myself when it comes down to trying to explain happenings that on the surface of things seems impossible! Those incidents are The Workings of God's Spirit! Now unbelievers will laugh and mock at such reports, when people try to explain the things they saw with their own eyes. These people are made to be witnesses of God's Glory! The Holy Spirit Has Been Working in my existence like that for so long now that I'm used to it. There is no big report that I work up in me and say, just wait until I tell so and so what I saw, or just wait until I tell so and so what I saw in a vision, and it happened! These occurrences, when I hear them from people, just makes me smile; for I am able to relate to them and I believe when I hear them try and tell their experience. I said try, because I can just feel the disbelief, from their listeners! That's of no matter though; for I know in the confines of my heart what has happened to them! Sometimes it's not God's Spirit, but the enemy of God, hard at work doing his best to deceive and destroy as usual. I am so happy to report at this time as I write, Satan has no power over me! The Spirit of God Lives inside with me and He Has Made and is Making All The Positive Motion that Makes Up The Apex of my existence. It's God's Glory, not Mines!

87. The Hard Way

Where ever I go, whatever I experience in my emotions, I always come back to rest with The Spirit that I call God! God Has All Power that is known and unknown; I failed time after time when I tried to function in the world without having plugged into The Power that is God! It took many years of my existence; before I learned this simple fact of perfect existence! The Spirit of God Is Totally Awesome; God Knew what it would take to get the attention of His Created Soul, which is me. There where so many times when my existence in this world would have been, or could have been terminated in an instance; however , I truly believe God Himself Protected my existence, as a matter of no doubt I truly know He Did! You see God Protects His Own, and I belonged to God from the very beginning! I wasn't conscious of this for many years of my existence from day to day; however, God, Protected my existence from His Enemies, then He Uncovered my Spiritual Eyes. This Happened when I approached God sincerely from my heart! Thus the process of existing correctly began from that position of my being. I had to truly humble myself before God; I had to learn how to exist in a totally different way. I was totally perplexed for many years. God's Leadings Straightened out my mind and emotions, with each passing day!

88. No Coincidence

I existed in an illusion from the very beginning, corruption and discord were everywhere, I grew up in a place the world called a ghetto! My surroundings were always clothed with tensions and impending drama. This was all I knew for about thirty-two years and three months. Then The Holy Spirit Arranged for me to come to California. My surroundings was totally opposite of what they were in the ghetto; however, the chaos in me was alive and well, but somehow I felt as though I could exist in a place that was totally opposite from what I knew my whole existence! As the days turned into weeks I started to miss my ghetto, but somehow inside of me I knew there wasn't anything left back there for me, but my physical death! The Spirit that is God soon got around to Showing me who I was, and what I had become. The outcome wasn't good, and my journey to rearrange my existence began. Almost seventeen years have passed by, and I've grown in many areas of my existence. Now The Holy Spirit that Is God, Whom I trust with my existence Has Whispered to my mind to seek out His Son Jesus Christ! Through The Years God Has Never Given me instructions to do something unless I was absolutely ready to take on the new directions! My days and nights are truly full with the assignment of love and service The Good Lord God Has Placed before me. Jesus Christ is just one more assignment added to my current assignment!

89. Never Without

A person just asked me a question and he said I see you a lot, what do you do? I responded and said I am God's Servant, and I do what I am Directed to do! The person said right on, Praise Jesus, and then he moved on! Oh, how God's Spirit is always here to help us with any and everything if needs came to be needed! I never really remember seeing that person before; however, he has seen me, and each time he did I had the pen in my hand. You see God Just Used that person to Help me start this writing! My Maker Is everywhere, and He Is at Work all of the time, His Way of Being Has Rubbed off on me, and I feel spectacular! It's positive things I work on all the time now, and The Spirit that is God, Is my Inspiration, He Has Caused me to open up the doors of my heart, and to write about all the realities of my existence.

You see I don't call life my life, it's an existence; for I don't know how I got here, and I don't know when I'm leaving this body, so the reality for me is, I have an existence. The one sure thing of my existence is crystal clear; every time I look to The Spirit I call God, I am Greeted with peace of mind, and signs in my vision that no man, or woman can explain to me what I can see! The endless energy of the color green!

90. Unfinished Business

Once again it's early in the morning and here I sit with my pen, and The Holy Spirit of God. The Holy Spirit of God Awakened me at three thirty-one in the morning to write. When The Spirit of God Moves, I move right with Him! I went to bed three and half hours earlier so tired, I could have sleep the next day away; however, God, said that won't be the case, so here I sit again writing freely with this pen. The Spirit of Jesus Christ Is Upon me, and that's why I couldn't get proper rest; for earlier in the night I almost allowed evil back into my life! A drunken man came up to my car window acting like my buddy and friend, and I told him to leave my presents, but he didn't. I felt my anger level rise from zero to eight, so that's when I started up my car, and left to get that Drunken Spirit from in front of my face! Immediately I felt like I was in the wrong; for I wanted to get out of my car and hit him, but the best I could do was to start my car and move on! Oh, Spirit of Jesus Christ, I Your Younger Brother have so much to learn, and I am willing to seek You out in order that You May

Teach me! It didn't take me long to know that in the man was Satan, Trying desperately to get me to lash out, and commit a sin. Oh, Thank You Spirit of The Trinity, fore now I can see clearly. Satan came upon me boldly to hit me in my weakest spot, but Lord Jesus, You Touched me quickly, to leave that park and lock!

91. The comfort of a Servant

I must be witness to this statement, God, I truly can't do anything that's positive and worthwhile without Your Spirit Leading The Way! Today I honestly inventoried my existence, and the answer was what I just previously stated. There is no doubt in my heart, or Eternal Soul, that will ever stand against what I found in my search! There are multitudes of souls who are truly ignorant to the reality of The presents of God's Holy Spirit. I, Lord God will continue to share within these pages all of the experiences of my existence. In these pages is where the enemy has no power to manipulate the minds of the people! Words carry power and weight, and I, The Servant of God will document the truth, which will liberate the souls it was written for.

I've witnessed and heard about so much needless loss of life that it has caused me to stop watching the news on T. V. This age I am experiencing is evil; I must use every opportunity to help The Lost Sheep of The Lord and Master Jesus Christ! God Himself Has Blessed me by Giving me This Assignment! The Lord God Knows my heart; and it's a joy to me to push this pen, and give away truth and knowledge to God's Children!

92. From no Mortal Hands

When it comes down to being God's Servant, death to this world most happen to anyone who claims the title of being God's Servant! There are no exceptions. The person's heart must become attuned to God's Will, or he, or she will stay focused not concerning The Leadings from God. Obtaining a strong connection with God, and improving on it isn't an overnight process. Individuals must be drawn to God, and sometimes that takes a very long time! There are many distractions in this evil place that cause people to turn away from The Spirit that is God, let alone being drawn to Him! I've said it be for and I'll say it again, I write about no subjects unless I've personally experienced them. I've gotten to the point in my existence whereas I call myself God's Servant! There is no better description for a person like myself. I've grown to love and trust The Spirit that I call God. Unlike anything else that I have yet to encounter, and I know there is nothing greater than God! I see things in my vision that no person can even come close to explain what it is I can consciously see. First of all a person would have to see these things for him, or herself through their own eyes before one could make a comment. That's just one account in my heart that lets me know there is nothing greater than God. When I was in my youth and I almost died God Had Revealed some things to me, and He Told me Always to Remember Them, and I did just that even up to the day that I am writing this!

93. What Man Can't Do

I feel it's an impossible task at times when I consider what I am to write about from my heart concerning The Lost Sheep of The

Lord, and Master Jesus Christ. I guess I'm thinking too much about the people in darkness! So I am going to write about what The Trinity Has Done For me. There was a section of my existence whereas no one truly loved me, or cared about me, and I knew it with my whole heart! This negative estimation of myself from other people was going on for years, not from just one thing I said, or one thing I did, but multiples there of; however, at each and every one of those incidences, I was blinded about my actions. Not until eighteen years had passed from me drinking alcohol, and using other mind altering substances to deal with the inner pain that I was experiencing each and every day. I had no clue that by me picking up that first drink of alcohol at the age of fourteen would set the stage for my existence for the next eighteen years! At the end of that time is when I sincerely reached out to God, and Jesus Christ; for I knew deep down in my soul that myself, or nobody else had power and knowledge to save my existence! I never want to feel the way I felt ever again, and so far I haven't come close to those feelings since I asked from my heart for help! My soul was broken and at the same time also was my heart, and I had nothing else to depend on except The Trinity. Now, and forever I will look to nothing else!

94. No End to the Seeking

Sometimes it's real hard to stay focused on The Spirit of God, especially when so many people around you don't depend on God's Spirit! No matter, I must work harder; for nothing worthwhile comes easy! The enemy of God stays real close to me; fore Satan knows that I have a very strong connection with The Creator of All Things! I constantly have to discern my thoughts; for Satan stops at nothing to try and confuse us human beings! I found out that I must stay in close conscious contact with The Spirit that is God. Satan launches his deadly mental projection attacks nonstop, especially to souls who are not in his power. When I stay close to God through my whole being, I become Protected by God Himself, and the spirit of Satan stands off at a distance; for Satan can't stand The Light of God! Whenever I lax off on my seeking of God, here comes Satan's spirit of temptation, through thoughts projected at my mind! I was almost destroyed by this evil spirit of darkness; however, God's Spirit Saved my existence, and restored me to my rightful mind. This reality of my existence caused me to take a stand, and I chose The Spirit of God, over the spirit of darkness. God's Spirit is The Author of All Goodness, now and forever, so I must never fall for the illusion of worldly success; for if God's Spirit isn't behind it it's worth nothing at all!

95. The Journey to Peace and Knowledge of Self

The closer I come in my mind to You Lord God, the sadder I become, I guess I'm just experiencing the great pain that's in so many of Your Daughters and Sons! God, there's no pain that You don't know about, and there's no sadness You can't fix; however, if Your Sons and Daughters don't seek You, They'll keep on being Spiritual Sick! This is the reality that I've been blessed to see day after day . I use to be baffled by all the insanity I saw, or heard about, now I know why. This world that I exist in is draped in darkness! Ignorance of our humanity is a common factor in the minds of the majority of the people. Before I became a Servant of The Lord God, I stayed drunk and confused concerning the status of the world of which I was a part! Only by constantly seeking The Lord God, was I Given Principles to properly live by, which implemented a physical change in my being. I could have never accomplished the switch from Darkness to Light! My mind was in bondage from all kinds of fears. I was addicted to mind altering substances to the point of being pathetic, I couldn't stop the substance abuse when I wanted to stop, I was constantly depressed and sad. After existing like this for eighteen years I had arrived at the end of myself, and that was the key for me which I so desperately needed! Thus I stared my seeking of The Kingdom of God, which is totally an inside job!

96. Blessings From Faith

I remember walking down Victoria Street so sad I couldn't help to remember parts of my past flashing through my mind, and I couldn't shut the projector off in my mind! It was the month of August in the year nineteen ninety-eight, and I was in the second week of leaving a girlfriend, who couldn't, or wouldn't stop drinking alcohol, and that was included in my decision to leave her, we lived together for one year and a half; however, I didn't want to start back drinking myself! I was miserable, and all alone in California. All I had to keep me going was my faith in The Most Holy One of Israel. God's Spirit was the only drive that kept me from returning to the girlfriend that I had just recently abandoned! I was no angel when it came to abusing mind altering substances, at that time in my existence either. I haven't drank any alcohol since Christmas Day of the year nineteen ninety-five; however, cocaine, marijuana, and cigarettes were still being ingested into my system! Before the end of the month of August in the year nineteen ninety-eight, The Holy Spirit of God, Removed the desires to indulge not in any of the mind altering substances. I remember praying for God to take those desires away from me, and God Did for me just what I asked Him for in my prayers! I never felt the desire to ingest anyone of those substances ever again. There's nothing God's Spirit, can't do!

97. Orders From The Lord, and Master Jesus Christ

The words that I am about to write comes from my Older Brother, The Lord, and Master Jesus Christ! His Spirit told me to be roaring, when it comes to the messages concerning His Sheep! Take heed you Sheep and listen to The Words of Your Shepard Speaking to your hearts! The Wrath of The Lord God Is Near, be not stressed by what you physically see in the world around you! Separate yourselves from the fast track of things that are now taking place on a world wide scale. Steal away and talk to Jesus Christ, and He Will Instruct you on what you must do, no matter where you are on the face of the planet. Place not your trust and hope in no worldly thing, no matter what the circumstances!

Ask The Lord, and Master Jesus Christ, for whatever you may come to need, and believe in your heart that you'll receive it, and it will be Given to you, and upon your receiving it your faith in Jesus Christ will increase! Satan's time for rule is growing shorter, as God's Harvest Comes Closer.

Satan will use all of his tactics to worry you, and scatter you, in an attempt to pick you off, as many as possible, to make you lose faith, and trust not The Lord, and Master Jesus Christ, The Eternal Life Giver! Satan wants to enslave us for Eternity, right along with himself! Exist in Jesus Christ! This ends this message.

98. From The Depth of Satan's Temptation

Long ago, before I called myself God's Servant, a female asked me once, why do you talk about God all of the time? And I had no quick response for her, as a matter of fact, I don't remember answering her at all! At that time in my existence, I wasn't grounded in The Lord God, at all, so the question threw me into wonderment, almost a daze, when she asked it of me! Without even knowing it at the time, God's Spirit, was already in my heart; however, Satan had great influences over my actions, and I was immature by being ruled through thoughts being projected at my mind! Satan was eagerly trying to destroy me; however, I belonged to God, but God's, ownership didn't stop the evil thoughts that were coming into my mind, or from me acting on those thoughts!

I became insane as the days turned into months, and the months turned into years! I became trapped by the mind altering substances I was ingesting into my system, and I couldn't stop no matter what! There was also no turning off the evil thoughts that were coming into my mind, and I started to become depressed with each passing day. This part of my existence is where many people through the age of this evil have lost their existence! Only God Himself, Had The Power to Save them, trust me I know from my now restored mind, "Only From The Power of God Himself!"

99. Ignorance of the Truth

All of God's Creation has a perfect order, and this truth is so evident in everything that I have witnessed, or experienced! The reality of this fact has stopped me in my tracks, especially when I wanted to act out about something. When I was ignorant, or not conscious of this reality I caused a lot of hurt for myself and unfortunately other people. I tried to force my will on people and situations constantly, and the result was always the same, failure and hurt feelings on my part and others. The very upsetting results was that time after time I wasn't learning from the experiences. I was blaming the outcomes on people, places, and things, never was I to be placed under the microscope, and checked for the problem. No, I was always the solution in every case! This behavior went on for over two decades, until one day I got a clue that maybe I am doing something wrong! When The Lord God Guided me to the truth about things, I became devastated, and I stayed that way for a very long time! All that pain, all the misery I existed through, resulted in me truly becoming God's Slave forever. I am not ashamed at saying this! This saying is really the truth – "God, Takes Care of babies and fools", and I wasn't a baby, so I was a fool for a very long time, and now I am loyal to God for forever!

100. No Greater Love

Here in a public place I will begin to write, and the subject is The Lord, and Master Jesus Christ! God Himself, Has Communicated to me to seek out The Christ! For over fourteen years I've been building a positive relationship with The Creator of All Life, and now with His Great Love for me The Creator Has Sent me in search of The Only Perfect Man Whom has ever lived, and who was blameless without sin! In all the years of my existence on this earth, no one, or nothing has shown love to me like this! Jesus Christ Pleased The Lord, God so much that God Himself Turned All Power in heaven and in the earth over to Jesus Christ! The Lord God in His Guidance of my soul Has Caused my heart to become loyal to The Trinity for forever. I must allow nothing to come between myself and The Trinity. I have a new order now, and that is to obey Jesus Christ just as I do God! God Cares for my well-being, and now I have faith that Jesus Christ does also! God's Spirit Has Truly Moved my soul into the best possible position that I could ever be in. No money, no relationship, no property, no illusion of glory, no fame could ever come close to The Honor that God Has Graced me with! The allowance of my soul to seek His Son Jesus Christ – The Son of Man.

101. God's Grace Alive and Well

After building a positive relationship with The Creator of All Life, God's Spirit Has Now Begun to Speak to me through meditation concerning everyday occurrences which happens just the way God Reveals them to me through my conscious thoughts! I marvel in myself day after day over the preciseness of God's Leadings and Statements! God, Holds Back Nothing from those who seek Him, and love Him. I am only here, and I am only able to write about God's Goodness from the simple fact of God's Grace and Mercy, there are no virtues from me! No one is perfect, and I was far from being perfect, I made many mistakes in my existence before I truly sought The Lord God with all of my heart, soul, mind and strength, and for a long while after seeking God constantly, I was still far from the perfect mold! One thing I can say with real conviction, my existence is oh, so much better since I now look to The Lord God for All Guidance!

No worries do I have from day to day, no resentments do I carry in my heart against anyone, and I am content in my soul most of the time. I couldn't claim none of this peace when I was trying to fit into certain sections of this world called earth. All thanks and glory goes to The Most Holy One of Israel My Maker!

102. The End of Self

There was a time in my existence when I was broken and crushed. How can you fix something you can't see? Well that's when I set out to seek something that I couldn't physically see, and I called that something God! My heart was broken one more time, but the finally was my ego and soul were crushed into probably thousands of pieces, this is the best way I can describe my existence at that time! I call that part of my existence, " The End of Self."

There were no more clever ideas that cane into my mind that I would accept! I didn't trust anything anymore that came into my thought process! All I could remember doing from one day to the next was reaching out to The Spirit that I call God with all of my heart, even though all of the negative thoughts and feelings I was experiencing; for I was crushed into thousands of pieces! I stayed in thousands of pieces for a very long time, I believe The Spirit that I call God Is Putting me back together one piece at a time, and it's a very slow process. I came to believe that no one can walk another person's path; however, there are a lot of negative influences that can really determine a person's fate! I have truly existed through the very darkness that exists in this world, Satan almost destroyed me, and he still tries. I exist today in that same Spirit of God I reached out to with all my heart years ago, and I never stopped reaching with All my heart!

103. When a Soul Cries For Help

What is holy? What is right? These are the things I uncover when I write about The Lord, and Master Jesus Christ! The principles I am about to write about aren't popular and they aren't the latest fad; I've been touched by Jesus's Spirit to tell people how I was saved by God's Hand! Jesus Christ, and God are one in the same, and now They Have Chosen me to uplift Their Most Holy Names! I am so honored and I don't look at the work as a chore; fore when I cried to Them for Their Help, They Pulled me back through Satan's Door! Satan's House I was in, and I was filled up with all kinds of sin, but to God, and Jesus Christ it was of no matter; for I was one of Their Lost Sheep that They Had Come to Gather. This They Did, and I am forever grateful, now I must tell my story; for there are other Lost Sheep in Satan's House, who may read these words, and to God, and Jesus Christ they may cry out! In my heart I surly do know that God, and Jesus Christ Would Come and Retrieve them, as They Did me long ago! So I do stress the principles of hope, trust, and faith; and any soul who sincerely cries out to God, and The Lord, and Master Jesus Christ, will Receive Help, no matter the place, or their case. For God, and The Lord, and Master Jesus Christ Searches the hearts of people, not their warped minds!

104. Evil Right Here, Right Now

I am so blessed in my existence, even while existing in the midst of all this evil! God, You Are Always On Point, You Haven't Once ever let me down, or Guided me into a ditch. The evil one never stops his mental attacks, Satan's job is to mutilate and destroy all subjects of God's Creation! Every time Satan tries to send evil thoughts to my mind, I am going to pick up the pen, just as I am doing right at this moment! The people of God, who may read this page will truly understand what is being wrote, and why! My fellow brothers and sister keep your faith in God, Jesus Christ, and The Holy Ghost, and trust nothing, or nobody else wholly, lest you run the risk of being deceived! No matter what the circumstances are, never lose your faith in The Trinity. The Father, The Son, and The Holy Ghost Are your only True Friends that will never deceive you, or cause you harm. They Stand as a Pillar of Strength in the events of all wrong doings being practiced! Don't be fooled by The Evil Forces that be, playing like they really care about your situations, they will smile in your face, at the same time planning your demise. Remember Satan needs a body, or bodies to perform out of, never forget this my brothers and sisters. Satan and his demons are right here, right now amongst us!

105. Self-Destruction

When I write about the years before I truly surrendered to the care of The Lord God, I always feel deep sadness! I always worked real hard at things, but it was always not good enough, and I always felt inadequate! I always wanted to be good at something, and I always came up short! I could have been born in any other place besides The United States, and had an existence much, much harder, so I am not complaining, or whining, but the truth is the truth, and most of the time when I tried to fit into any worthwhile situation, I always failed, and each failure got harder, and harder, to emotionally handle! It got to the point whereas I couldn't handle the emotional pain any longer. I didn't know it then; however, my alcohol consumption started to increase, I was always looking to feel good, doesn't everybody? My existence started to take a direction, I was going down, and I was going down quickly, but I couldn't see it, I just kept hammering away trying to make life work for myself, and feel good at the the same time! Well that never happened, and life was still life, and I became a bigger failure than ever! I was at the end of myself, I had no good ideas left, and that was of no matter; for I didn't trust myself anymore, I was beaten by my own will, yet I was still alive, what was I to do? I was at that time insane, and out of pure desperation, I cried out to Jesus Christ, and God, The Father, by saying "Please help me I can't live like this anymore!" Instantly a degree of sanity returned.

106. Shade of Glory From Jesus Christ

When I think of what Jesus Christ did for the sake of countless souls, it causes me to stop, and appreciate the compassion of God's Son! To know you are going to be murdered in a brutal and savage manner, and still go through with it anyway goes beyond comprehension. I guess that's what you call true love and loyalty to God, His Father! I can honestly say now that whenever I'm about to lose my peace about something, and I hear a small voice say calm down, I know in my heart the small voice is Jesus Christ; for Jesus Knows the evil one is just trying to frustrate my existence. Jesus Christ Has Called me to Relax in His Spirit, and I must, and I will obey The Prince of Peace! Only God, Jesus Christ, and The Holy Ghost Are All that I have learned to wholly trust! I have been so disappointed and hurt by The Evil Forces that be. It was only The Trinity that Has Caused my heart not to harden, and thus become an agent of evil! This is why I've been called by Jesus Christ to Relax in His Spirit! I looked and sought happiness in people, places, and things, and I've never found true happiness and joy in none of those searches; however, just reviewing in my mind what The Prince of Peace told me brought so warm of a feeling in my body I can never forget! When I think of Jesus Christ, I think of joy that has no ending!

107. The Results of Love

Every time I get a feeling inside of myself concerning something outside of myself, and I go and check that something out, and that something turns out to be what I felt, that's The Holy Ghost Giving me Spiritual Insight! The Holy Ghost from God Has Always Been Here; however, I was never seeking God as I do now to receive His Provisions, Protection, and Guidance, and be conscious of it! Now God's Spirit Touches my conscious thoughts on regular intervals! The Spirit of God Is So Faithful, I look forward to connecting with The Force that Holds this whole universe together. The Spirit of God Has Been Watching Out Over me all of my existence, and knowing this in my heart confirms to me I am loved! I must do my best now to make my Creator Glorified by my existence. The Holy Ghost Is So Kind, He is The Guardian of Truth, Knowledge, and Solace. For years, God's Spirit Tried to Guide me, but I was to busy trying to feel good, and satisfy my own selfish self! I was a very foolish young man, and I became more ignorant of The Goodness of God, as the days turned into years! Never did God's Spirit Leave me Open to lose my existence on this earth! With all of my bad choices combined with my selfishness, I beat myself into the ground! God's Spirit Still Never Abandoned me! The Spirit of God Has my loyalty for forever. Nothing, and I mean nothing is more important to me!

108. In God's Hands

Always the same, without change, having no deviation in its purpose, this is the description of the words that come from God Himself! Everything God Has Stated long ago will happen, or has already taken place. The Lord God Is Faithful, and He Will not Mock Himself! I write about these warnings to bring no glorification upon myself, God my Maker Has Charged my heart to write about the truth for this generation. The Creator of All Life Would in no way desire harm to any of His People. Only the enemies of God have desires to harm God's People! In the words that I write, I will preach not; however, I will stack up the truth in piles of plenty, just as lies are told in regularity. It's God's Spirit, that Moves me to push this pen; for the betterment of all people who need their faith strengthened by the example of my existence! I was Protected by God's Spirit, each and every day, for many years. I didn't exist in a very safe place in my early existence, The Spirit of God, Was Able to Maneuver my soul out of the situation I was in! The Enemies of God were earnestly trying to end my existence. I was truly ignorant of The Evil Forces that be, and I state this with all honesty! Only God Himself Has Graced me with the existence that I now experience from day to day. I am Protected, Provided for, and Guided by, The Creator of All Life!

109. Set in Place

For days I've been on edge within myself, concerning The Lord, and Master Jesus Christ! Knowing in my heart I was called by The Trinity to relax in Their Spirit! I didn't know what was expected of me from The Lord, and Master Jesus Christ; however, I was placed in a relaxed state of being recently when a thought came to me that Jesus Christ Was and Is The Healer of the sick and The Light to the world! So at that point I received intuition on what I am to do concerning my day to day interactions with people I may come into contact with. Just the thought of Jesus Christ in my mind provides a healing sensation! Never in my existence have I been so calm and relaxed about things since the pouring of my Master's Spirit into my soul. My sights are clearer now, and my work has solidified before me. Only The Trinity Knows how long my soul has longed for this conformation! Even in the midst of all this evil, I am at home; for I am now grounded in The Spirit of Eternal Existence. This experience is like nothing else I have ever experienced before. These happenings have nothing to do with my will. Only The Loving Spirit of God, Has Arranged, and Allowed all of what is transpiring in my existence to the day of this writing. I am now turned over to The Lord, and Master Jesus Christ.

110. Power at no Cost

I never really knew what freedom was until I feverishly started seeking The Spirit that Is God! I was always at odds with every aspect of life. God's Spirit Released me first of all from the bondage of myself, that was the first release in the journey to freedom. The Spirit that Is God Has Become the most important subject in my existence! Nothing else holds my interest like God's Spirit, first of all I know in my heart that God Saved my existence more times than I actually and consciously know about! In meditation I've Received Insights about people, places, and things that have happened, just the way it was transmitted to me. Those experiences have gravitated me even more to God's Holy Spirit! How can I turn away from such perfection? I've came to realize that connecting to God's Spirit in this way is my destiny. Every event in my existence points to the eventuality of developing a very strong connection to The Creator of All Life! I truly must make this statement through my own experience, anyone who seeks The Spirit that Is God, won't be seeking in vain; however, one must sincerely believe God exists! God Is Always Willing to help people if they are willing to help themselves in the process of seeking His Power!

111. First Contact

Sometimes writing isn't an easy thing for me to do, and this writing is one of those times. I couldn't forget this part of my existence even if I wanted to! I was fourteen years old, and I just made my high school's football team, and that wasn't an easy thing to do! I'll never forget what happened, as long as I exist! I was on the football field at practice, and out of the clearness of my mind, a voice said to me, "you don't really want to do this, go to the coach and quit." I was startled by the voice; however, I did what it said to do. My coach looked at me in amazement, and said - "Son you made the team, alright go inside, mikes in there, and give your equipment to him." When I got inside, and told mike he said man what are you doing? You want to play, I don't want to play, my father's making me play, just go back to the coach and say you didn't know what you were doing, and he'll just make you do a lap! I listened to mike, and in amazement I found myself doing a lap, just what mike said the coach would tell me to do! The voice I heard inside me, Was The Lord, and Master Jesus Christ! Four weeks had passed, and I was going to get my big break, and start in The West Side Game on Saturday; however, that Friday in the J. V. Game against West Side I severely dislocated my left shoulder, and my football career as well was finished; even though, I tried to play for the next two years, I was never the same again, neither was my shoulder. So you see Jesus Christ, was trying to spare me of all the misery I went through, but I didn't know at that time who was talking to me, or who to listen to!

112. Poison Packed Away

There has been so much pain and misery in my existence; that I've come to know without any doubts in my heart now that there is a God, and He is as real as all the disappointments I have faced, but I didn't face them alone; for God, was right there inside of me, He has always been with me. Now I am a mature man , and I am called by God to tell about all of what happened to me, and for me! Sometimes in remembering the past, the pain is as great, as though it's happening in the present time! It's of no matter; for I will obey my Maker, and reveal the truth of my existence. The Creator Knows, my calamities will be blessings for people. For years I was very angry with The Lord God; however, I didn't express my resentments to no one, not even God!

I kept them locked away in my heart, and I tried to move forward in my existence, even though my heart was bogged with a lot of heavy weight! God, Knew of it anyhow, The Spirit of God, was just Patiently Waiting for me to realize I couldn't go on anymore, the way I was travelling! As I look at my existence now, I know God's Grace Was and Is Upon me Greatly; I've seen a lot, and heard about a lot of people who didn't get the blessings, or turned down the opportunity to empty out there hearts!

113. Nothing Compatible

The totality of my being is important; it intertwines with so many things, the numbers become astronomical! At the same time I must not develop a conceited ego and attitude about myself either! I am from The Eternal God, and I must place myself in the right position concerning this truth! So many of us human beings are reckless in our actions; ignorance of what we truly are dominates our souls! Only The Loving Grace from our God can act as an antidote to our confusion and ignorance while we yet live! The Lord, and Master Jesus Christ Has Come into the world to enact just that! So we may receive the chance of the promise of Eternal Life! The totality of The Unselfishness from The Trinity warms me to no end! Just to know I am a descendant of The Majestic Trinity, propels my soul into a gratefulness I can't verbally express! Only The Trinity Knows the compassion of my heart in these matters. There is no comprehension of my views when they are expressed to worldly people; they get lost in the confinements of the world around them! While we are yet in this age of evil, God's Grace Is Still Held Out to all people, and this is The Greatness of The Lord God, and His Kingdom! I His Servant, am overjoyed with gladness; for The Lord God Protected my existence on many occasions while I was in darkness, dancing with The Devil!

114. One and Only

Responsible for every living creature on the planet, Provides food and shelter for them all! Only The Spirit of God, Can Produce such things! No human hands can share in such glory. God's Spirit, Stands Alone, there is nothing like God, and there shall never be anything like God's Spirit, He even states that Himself, in The Holy Scriptures! The Holy Spirit of God Has Made His Will Known to all of the people of earth, so on The Day of Judgement, no one can say, they didn't know, or there was no access to The Words from God! The Lord God, Trusts me today, and I can't describe the feeling in myself, when He transmitted this message of trust to my soul! I asked God about a situation concerning another soul, and His Response to me was, "Do what you feel is right in your heart."

The Lord God, Never Gave me an answer like that ever before. That answer let me know that God Trusted my judgement in the situation! There was a time in my existence whereas I know in my heart now, The Lord God Wouldn't Transmit a response like that; for I was a very sick person, and I needed all the love and compassion I could get in any one session with The All Loving Creator! You see I know first-hand that God's Words are true, and God Himself Is Faithful. God Helped me each, and every time I reached out to Him for help, and God, Gave me whatever was best for me at the time.

115. When the World Ends

There isn't enough money, there isn't enough land, there isn't enough pleasure that can turn me away from obeying The Trinity! I am grounded in The Trinity, nothing can break me away from Their Spirit! All are in me, and I am in all of Them! I am reborn, even though I still exist in the midst of this evil age! I use to be always in a rush to get what I thought I needed for myself. Never was I truly concerned about the next man, or woman. I lived like that for years until I became found out, then people started to close me out of their lives! I became very frustrated, I harbored many resentments against people, places, and things. The Evil Forces that be were in full control of my mind! My saving grace was that I never hardened my heart against people, places, and things! The damage from my conduct over the years had been done, there was no magical cure for my condition, yet The Trinity Showed Mercy to my soul! I became aware of that and I sought God's Help, over, and over again, and I possessed no material things for a long time, about seven years! Despite my slow progress, I never stopped seeking The Lord God, even to the day of this writing, I will never stop seeking The Lord God! God Gave me my existence, and saved my existence, and nothing comes between my soul, and The Eternal Lord God!

116. Only a Few

God, I feel so alone, and I know what this feeling means; fore the true seekers of You, are so few, while the many are consumed by worldly things! This has been the truth as long as I can remember, and the condition of this world hasn't gotten any better! There is a light of truth in this observation which steadies my heart to continue to seek God's Kingdom. So I must endure to the end of my life here on earth and not give in to the come and go fads of this world! The true seekers of God will live by faith, not by sight. Constantly seeking The Living God is the only protection people can get; for The Evil Forces that be are constantly stirring up great distress! A blind man can see it, and he doesn't even need his eyes, all he has to do is listen, and he can hear the discomfort in people's lives! The corruption and death will never end, not until God Himself Powerfully Takes a Stand, and Steps in. It's already written, evil will run its course right up to the day of judgement! God's Words are true, and what

I've stated about what I've seen so far as I've existed in this evil place follows in the righteousness of truth!

117. Negativity Making its Rounds

I feel like something real bad has happened, and I just haven't yet received the news, this is my true feeling as I sit here in my room! My connection to The Creator of All Life is real strong; however, I hope in my heart that I am totally wrong! I've been feeling agitated all the day long, and this felling has carried over into the night, I know in my heart of hearts that something very evil is going on somewhere, and of course it's not right! My feelings never lie to me, so I will intensely seek God, Almighty! The Truth will materialize right before me, so I can see. God, Never Holds Back anything important to me! If it turns out to be some bad news, I just can't roll over and quit, I must seek God's Council and ask for the strength to overcome it.

Good things come, and if you pay attention, those good things leave real quick, I guess God, is just Protecting Them, so evil won't corrupt their Goodness! The agitation I've been feeling is now gone; however, sadness now has taken its place. I get to start feeling this way when I consciously think about the reality of all the evil my brother and sisters everyday must face! So I continue to use the pen, to warn them that Satan is here, and he will use all of his tactics, including fear, to turn people from The Loving Creator of All Life. This Satan will do, until he is arrested, and only God, with all of His Power can do that!

118. A Taste of Forever

Years had gone by since I first meet this person whom had grown to highly despise me. One day this person came up to me and said, "it's your faith, I really want your faith." The faith this person was talking about was not in any person, place, or thing, it was the faith in The Invisible God! For years this person saw me live life without many material things, and yet I kept a smile on my face, and joy emanating from my heart. This person just couldn't understand why that was possible! The only way to receive faith like I have it, is to constantly seek God, no matter what, and upon the seeking, The invisible God Begins to Saturate your soul, and the peace you begin to feel is so unexplainable you begin to thirst for more, and little by little earthly things begin to matter to you not! So material things are of no grave importance to you to possess; for you have tasted a far greater reality! I am free, even though I still animate this physical body, no earthly things have a hold on my soul. The time is coming when I will be with The Infinite God; however, my work here is incomplete! The joy that I have is in the belief and trust in The Giver of all Life; that He Has far better things to Give us than what we are now exposed to! All of what this life is, is merely a test, and oh, so many people fail the test every day! However, The Lord God, Has Great Mercy and Grace, and He Shines it on whomever He Pleases!

119. Mercy From God

My experiences while existing in this evil age is the most valuable things that I have to share with the people of earth! I also know that many people will close their minds to what is being revealed from my experiences in this passage! Only God Himself Can Open their hearts to truth. My job is to tell the truth of my existence; even though, there are a great many things I am ashamed of! I must obey my Maker The Lord God. God Truly Disciplines me as I exist from one day to the next, true freedom of my soul has been the result from learning to believe in and trust The Invisible Maker that I've never physically seen! I never had an earthly father to teach me how to be a man; for my earthly father died when I was fourteen years old. So when it came to father and son things I was a floundering vessel! For the next twenty years of my existence I was out of control, and I became a disappointment to myself and all of my family members. I reached out to The Spirit of God, and He Had Mercy Upon my soul! I was a wrecked human being; however, God Didn't Laugh at me, and Turn me away, I cried bitterly for many days and nights, and The Lord God Gave me solace and Guided my heart what to do one situation at a time, and those experiences is how I know first-hand that God Is Alive and Present with all of His Invisibility!

120. A Message From a Withering Flower

I am like the flower in the fields, one day I will wither away, no more will my fragrance fill the air, no more will my petals provide a pleasant sight! The seeds that I leave behind are my words, words that guide to the true treasure. The One and Only Invisible God, Who Is The Hope of Everlasting Life! His Son The High Priest Jesus Christ Has Pleased The Invisible God by His Behavior, and God Has Turned All Power in heaven and earth over to The Son of Man! I'm stating nothing that hasn't already been written concerning the status of the man who was innocent of any wrong doings, yet was brutally murdered for no good reason, and was raised to life again by God, His Father, who sent Him! I who will one day wither away am leaving this testimony. The hope of the chance for Eternal Life, rests with The Lord, and Master Jesus Christ. Even if you are a person who hasn't been moved to seek The Teachings of The Bible, just know that this is what I was led to by The Invisible Maker God! This information about Jesus Christ is the most valuable part of The Bible I can leave the people that will come after me! The Invisible Maker God Has Allowed me to leave this as a blessing to those who have been touched by Him! God, and His Son Jesus Christ is the opposite, of the flower in the fields that will one day wither away.

121. No Limits

A slot machine in a gambling house has a big payoff called a jackpot, well that's what The Spirit of God Is for me! However, I'll never in this lifetime be able to spend all of my winnings! I'm in the state of constantly being overwhelmed with all of the riches I've been blessed with! There is nothing that can come across my path without me being able to receive the right answer for it! I'm truly overjoyed with the connection I possess with The Giver of All Life! There is one thing I am real sure about, my jackpot was sought after for years, there was real and constant seeking going on, and one day a clear connection was established, and I've been overwhelmed ever since! Now I am seldom ever really upset, I don't worry about the outcomes to things anymore, and I'm almost always calm. Before my seeking I was almost always upset, angry, frustrated, and I lived in fear. I know as a fact of my existence that I by my own virtues haven't accomplished my new existence; fore I didn't have any virtues. I was filled with character defects for years, and my existence wasn't a very positive one. Only by The Powers of God, Was I Transformed from a negative person into a positive one. My personality is constantly changing as I constantly keep tapping into all The Power in the universe, my Treasure that has no measure.

122. To Heed or Grieve

To hear words, or to read words are of one aspect; however, to believe the words you've heard, or read, and do what was comprehended is totally of another aspect all together! What good is The Words of God, if The Words aren't heeded, and actions carried out! To the unabsorbing hearts, God's Words are just words, and they believe not! I must constantly humble myself under The Mighty and Powerful Hand of God! I have been blessed to have tasted the disobedience of recklessness, yet God Graced me by not Allowing my existence to be canceled out because of my ignorance! Oh, how blessed I am, The Lord God, Showed Mercy to me, and didn't Allow Satan to enslave my Eternal Soul! I have nothing to boast about now, and for all time. All Power belongs to The Most Merciful God, and I myself am a witness to this fact! Nothing, or nobody can't ever change my heart concerning The Lord God, and His, and my enemy Satan, and all of his demons and family members. I stress this to the readers of this passage, trust the little knock at the door of your hearts, that Knocker is The Lord, and Savior Jesus Christ, and if you let Him in, your lives will never be the same again. No more will you ever have to worry again, provided you persist in Him, and the leadings He Will Prescribe for your situations. And you must trust and obey Him; even though, Satan will constantly and loudly project thoughts to your mind to do the opposite of The Small Voice in your heart!

123. God Will Wait

When God Speaks to me now, I listen oh, so carefully; His Words Are Just! The Lord God's Instructions Are Straight to the point, there is never any gibber jabber and it's always simple! This is my experience before the years of seeking God. The Lord Jesus Christ, Tried to get my attention for years; however, I was too consumed by chasing the desires of my sinful nature, and trying desperately to fit into a space in this world! Nothing I tried to do came to bear any good fruit, and I became frustrated with my full bag of failures. For fourteen years I had my chance to live successfully as an adult, and I failed at every aspect of being a respectable human being. I didn't know then; however, I know now, The Lord Jesus Christ, was watching out over my life, and He didn't Allow Satan to enslave my Eternal Soul. I stated this be for in other passages, but I must tell what happened again to give the readers hope that God Is Good All The Time, and despite all of your sufferings you may have had in your life, God's Spirit Is Right Here Waiting for you to reach out to Him. The Trinity Loves us beyond our understanding, whereas Satan, just wants to destroy us; fore he himself can't be God. This is the reason for the present condition of the world that is now. So many souls are confused and frightened, and don't know how to live, so I who have been blessed to have overcome this world will leave this message. Put your trust in The Unseen God, and leave it there, then seek God, over and over again from your heart, and one day God Himself, Will Whisper to your mind!

124. God's Spirit – Always Here

The Spirit of The Living God Is Always Upon me now, and I am truly His Servant without any doubts in my heart! The Lord God Has Always been inside of me. I was always sad as a child; for there was always drama in my household, and it terrified me always! God's Love and Protection was always there no matter what. We were poor people, both my parents had to work very hard just to keep a roof over our heads and food to eat. It was the fighting between my mother and father that use to upset me, and I truly believe their behavior damaged me, at that very young age. I always knew I was different from my brother, sisters, and cousins. I was different on the inside; for I knew as a young child something was deeply wrong in the world around me! Now I am almost fifty years old, and the feelings I had as a child were valid, and now I make decisions on the basis of my feelings. Feelings are the intangible gifts from God Himself that I have grown to trust. There are many feelings I get now that I don't take for granted. I don't say to myself like I use to say, oh well it's just a feeling, it will pass; no, each feeling carries a message, and I take the time to decipher the felling received. It has truly brought me closer to The Living Spirit of God which now Lives within me. Every day Now I humble myself under The Living God; for without God's Guidance, I am a reckless and doomed soul!

125. What God Can Do

I have been called by The Living God Plenty of times in my existence. I don't know the number count, and it's of no matter to me; however, I am glad in my heart for God's Grace and Mercy. I've actually seen God's Spirit At Work in people lives on a day to day observation of their lives! Individuals must allow God's Spirit to live the way it desires to live within their physical bodies. Only then are positive changes possible for the individuals.

Changes that will be noticed by all the people who knew them before they reached out to The All Loving Creator. I don't want to mislead anyone; for to live and be Guided by The Living Spirit of God isn't popular in this evil time. Many are called by The Living Spirit of God, but oh so few answer the knock at the door of their hearts by God! I see it often how The Lord God Calls people, but oh so many of them have a deaf ear; for they are attracted to the deathly practices set up by The Evil Forces that be. I must constantly continue to obey The Living Spirit of God, which lives inside my heart. God, Would Never hurt me, or leave me, and I believe this with all of my being, nothing of this world can ever change my heart! I have this conviction in my heart and soul, and by The Powers of Jesus Christ from God, I am dead to the desires of this world, all because I truly believed and trusted The Trinity. God, Has Truly Set me free!

126. The Results From God's Love

My heart will never be settled concerning The Living Spirit of God! I don't even have a son, but if I did, I know I would give my life to protect his! The Lord God, Gave His Only Son, over to murder; for God, Loved the people of this world so much He Sacrificed His Only Son! My heart can never turn away from such Great Love. There is no one, or nothing greater than The Living Spirit of God, this comes from my whole heart, a heart that is attuned to the commands of The Trinity. Now I can see why I came up short every time when I was trying to seek pleasure, why I failed constantly when I tried to be a success financially, why I never got any fame. All because The Spirit of God Truly Loves me, He Knew all of what I sought after was shallow, and soon to be worthless to my being. There aren't enough thank you's, to thank my Precious

Creator! Thank You God, for Showing us that much love and more, oh Most Holy One of Israel! By Your Spirit God Raising Jesus Christ from the dead, we now have a High Priest Who Sacrificed His Blood Once and for All. Jesus Christ Will Hold that position forever! He Truly Is The King of Kings and The Lord of Lords! There is nothing else in this existence for me, but to receive whatever The Trinity Has for me to do, or not to do! I am grounded in Them and They Are Grounded in me, and nothing, I mean nothing, can ever break that! The Trinity Has Saturated my heart and soul, there is no greater joy for me.

127. No Human Power

It matters not my position in this life, it matters not how many material things I may gather up for myself, it matters not the fame I may acquire, all that matters is the decision of The Lord, and Master Jesus Christ! Jesus Christ Holds the fate of my Eternal Soul! He is The Determiner of Eternal Life, or Eternal Damnation! As I keep seeking The Trinity, worldly desires constantly fall from my heart. The more I seek The Trinity, the more my humanity grows. God, Created this universe, and everything I can see, and can't see, so what do I really know? The answer is obviously, very little. I spent so much time trying to be right at everything, and boasting about what little I did know! That type of attitude left me open to all kinds of attacks from people who knew better! That didn't stop me; for I was obsessed with trying to be the best at something, and this went on for years with no success, and through time I had become insane. I backed myself into a corner, and the corner was called defeated! No one to care for, and no one to care for me, I was truly alone, so I thought. It turned out that I was wrong again; for The Spirit of God, Never Left me, He

Was Patiently Waiting for me to reach out to Him, and I did, the decision turned out to be the best decision I've made so far in my existence! As a matter of fact I know it was the best decision I've made in my existence, nothing will ever top that decision. That decision came from a sincere heart, coupled with a broken soul.

128. A Gift From Above

The past is the record keeper of all things, it holds the answers to any questions people often ask about past events; however, many hours of research will have to be spent concerning certain subjects! My past is a very hurtful one to me, and other people; however, The Spirit of God Who Lives in my temple, Pushed to my conscious thoughts to write about this certain incident from my past. It was January the ninth, the year was nineteen eighty-one, I had just turned eighteen years old, the month prior. I'll never forget what happened, it was about 5:45 am, and I had my first car, my brother in law had to go to work, and he didn't have a car at that time, so I decided to be a good brother in law, and drive to his house, and take him to work. Well I got into my car, and something inside of me said look up, and when I looked up there was a hole in the sky! I looked at it for several seconds, and then I looked down, and immediately I looked up again, and it was gone! I was puzzled, and again something inside of me told me to get out of my car, and go around on the side of my house, and I did just that. The sun was coming up, and I looked into the sun, and it was as though the sun was one hundred yards away in the sky, burning oh, so brightly! I think I looked into the sun for about 3-5 minutes. When I looked away I was able to see many different colors, they were awesome. I was moved to tell several people what happened to me, and they looked at me with disbelief, the wonders that I saw from that experience, I can still see today, with many other objects, when they present themselves!

129. The Workings of Satan

What I am about to write about isn't an incident I am proud of, nor should anybody be! The month was January, the year was nineteen eighty-one, I was a new student at New Jersey Institute of Technology, it was the winter break, and I was hanging out with my best friend and my sister, well we wanted to stop home , before continuing our hanging out, so I dropped my friend at his house, which was right down the street from our house. My sister wanted to go and use the bathroom, so I stayed in the car, then my sister came back and said our mother wanted to see me. So I went upstairs and sat on the couch, immediately my mother started hollering and screaming at me about college, and hanging out, and then she said don't look at me like that, and suddenly she rushed me, and started to punch and beat me, I then jumped up, and pushed her away from me, then my sister screamed, and said "don't be hitting mom boy." My sister hit me with a vase, having a baseball swing motion. She missed my temple by less than one half of an inch! I hit the floor on my knees for a couple of seconds, I got up and went to the mirror, I had a knot the size of a small plum, on the side of my head, my mother had ripped my shirt from me, and I left the apartment, and went down stairs, then I came back up the stairs, but they locked the door, I was screaming for them to let me in, and when they did, the city police officers were there, they took me to jail. I almost lost my life in jail, but The Spirit of God Didn't Allow that to happen! All this happened right after I had the hole in the sky experience!

130. Life to no Death

I must never grow weary, or stay stagnated in my heart when it comes to carrying out God's Will for my life! The workings of Satan are constant, and oh, so designed to frustrate and consume The Children of God! All of my sufferings make perfect sense now, and all of the sufferings of God's People makes perfect sense to me now also! So I must constantly continue to humble myself under The Grace of God's Guidance! I along with God's Children are down here amongst all of this evil and corruption by The Will of God, so we must not shrink, and think that The Trinity Doesn't Love us! We who belong to God must become dead to the on-goings of this world; even though we still possess the breath of life. As we still away in meditation with The Lord, and Master Jesus Christ, He Will Instruct us on what we must do from day to day concerning the tasks set in front of us! We as God's Children must come to know in our hearts that Satan will turn up the heat of persecution the more we resist and turn away from his institutions of destruction, and there are many in operation all over this world! Jesus Christ Will Instruct us on what to stay away from and how to turn to Him for what we should do in any situation. We must burn a seal into our hearts that states the words of: "Trust Jesus Christ, He's The Determiner of Eternal Life!"

131. Perfect Union

The Spirit of God Guides me every day, it took many days and nights of seeking God before I really came to know and trust The Spirit of God! Now my purpose in this life has been revealed to me, and it gives solace to my former sad soul! For years I searched so many avenues to find my purpose, and I never found it, and I stayed frustrated for over a decade; that's a long time to stay uncertain to what you need to do. Now since The Spirit of God Has Given me my assignment, my days and nights are oh, so full! Most people can't conceive of God's Power, simply because they don't constantly seek Him. And in their minds God Doesn't Care about them and their lives, some people entertain the idea that there isn't any such thing as a Living Invisible God! Well I myself know without an inkling of doubt that God Is As Real as the air that I breath! The beautiful part about my knowledge concerning The Living God is, I don't have to go and prove it, or argue about it, not even to a single soul. God's Spirit Speaks for itself through my behavior from one day to the next! I am God's Servant, and I do what He Instructs me to do, I am also Jesus Christ's once lost but now found Sheep, and I listen to the voice of my Shepherd, and The Spirit of God that Lives in my temple. The Trinity; Three Equaling One!

132. Perfect Connection

There isn't a dull moment now in my existence; for I am connected to The Trinity, and all of my desires are holy ones, and I am constantly of service to my brother and sisters. I don't force my will in no way upon them. I just share with them what The Holy Spirit of God Reveals to me. Most people I'm finding are being drawn to me, by The Trinity! I am so grateful to be able to carry the message of the good news from The Lord, and Master Jesus Christ. The Trinity Gives me what I need on a day to day basis. They Instruct me on what I need to do, or what I am not to do. I am covered on all sides of my being, I want for nothing, and They place the true value of things within my heart constantly. Nothing, or no one, no matter how hard I searched, could satisfy my soul the way The Trinity does! I am connected to The Treasure that has no measure, and I must continue to humble myself under The Grace and Mercy of God Himself, and continue to do the work He Has Assigned me. The Spirit of God Knows my heart and I don't know what my reward will be. I am Instructed to stay focused , and not to look to the left, or look to the right, but to keep my focus on God Himself! I refuse to test my Lord God, I will obey my Maker and carry out His Instructions for my daily functions!

133. My Truest Convictions

All I have to do is think of the name Jesus Christ in my mind, and I feel sensations in my feet, I can't explain what is happening, but it happens every time! I Truly am Your Sheep Jesus Christ, You have made Yourself known to me in this way! For days now, I keep hearing this phrase echo in my mind. "And greater things you will write." I've just received The Lights from The Holy Place, which confirms in my mind the conviction of the echoing phrase. Just now I came to believe with my whole heart that Jesus Christ Has Known and Protected me my whole life! I recall when I seven, or eight years old, I heard a voice calling my name over and over again, and I wasn't asleep, it happened to me more than a couple of times. The Lord, and Master Jesus Christ's Spirit is in my soul, and my soul is in The Lord, and Master Jesus Christ. Now that I am almost fifty years old, I'm totally sure of it! In my life, The Lord God Himself Spoke to me one time I am assured of, and in His Instructions He Told me not to worry about what color He Was, and to Always Remember The Lights that He Allows me to see! Even through all of my ignorance of myself, and all of the foolishness I chased after, God's Holy Lights were never Taken away from my sights. I know now in the fullness of my heart that I belonged to God before I was even born! The Lord God, and His Son Jesus Christ, and God's Holy Spirit, Will Never Harm the souls that seek Them!

134. In God's Time

I know from the pit of my soul that The Spirit of God Has Freed me from the influences of the evil one! I must constantly seek The Guidance from The Trinity; for the evil one constantly sets traps and snares to corrupt and enslave our Eternal Souls! God's Spirit Has The Power to Defeat the evil one, and it will be done just the way it has already been written about! I must continue with the task The Holy Spirit of God Has Given unto me to do. I always must remember that it's God's Spirit that's in control of everything, and Satan along with all of his demons will be dealt with at the proper time of God's Choosing. I use to become so sad concerning the happenings in my life, and the world as a whole; fore in my young heart I knew the things that I was witnessing in the world was wrong.

I couldn't understand why God Wouldn't Fix it, or Not Allow those bad things to happen anyway. I also knew I wasn't alone in the way I felt concerning the happenings in the world, other people felt the same way I did. Only until I became able to seek The Words from God, and truly believe what was written, did it shed light to why those bad things happened, and are still happening! God Has Truly Shown me that everything in His Creation has a season attached to itself, and that includes Satan, and all of his demons!

135. Exposure of The Evil One

I'm in this world for a specific reason, and that reason isn't to be associated with the operations of Satan! I am an enhancer of the goodness of things, not a destroyer of them. The Spirit of The Living God Protected me through my ignorance of my purpose. Now the fulfillment of my life will prosper through God's Perfect Guidance! All Goodness Comes from The Loving Spirit of God! There are a lot of deceivers in this world of evil, who pretend to be loving and kind, and it's all just a set up to get whatever goodness a person, or persons may possess. I've been hurt and deceived by The Evil Forces that be on many occasions before I became grounded in The Trinity. Most people have the persistence not to keep seeking God's Spirit day after day after day, and as a result they become victims to the snares and the traps set by the evil one and his demons. This is the reality The Spirit of God Has Graced me not only to see, but also experience on numerous occasions. God Has Truly Blessed my soul, and I am fully aware of it. God Is Very Kind and Generous; however, Satan wants you to believe that God Doesn't Care about you, or anybody else. Satan is the director of the physical aspects of this world, that's why Jesus Christ Instructs His Sheep to die to the desires of the physical aspects of the world, including their own bodies. If this is accomplished by The Sheep, They will be able to see Satan and his followers oh, so clearly!

136. Our Innermost Feelings

This message I leave is marked in truth that covers my whole life experience thus far. My innermost feelings never turn out to be false. Before I was reborn I couldn't in anyway live by this conviction. I was like the waves of the sea, moving in whatever direction the wind was blowing. There was no stability in me, or the things I lusted after, yet my heart tried to speak to me often. I spent no time in deciphering my feelings, I was only interested in trying to carry out the next great idea that came to my mind! The only attention I gave concerning my failings were in altering them by way of alcohol and street drugs. The answers to all of my life situations were being transmitted to me through my feelings, but I was ignorant of my blessings! I was blinded by the mental projections from The Evil Forces that be. I was kept in darkness for over two decades. Only by reaching out to The Spirit of God was I able to see clearly, and be Given The Power to get released from my deadly situation! My brothers and sisters it was no magic trick, I had to approach a way of living that I never gave a chance to, and the reality was I had to trust my innermost feelings instead of the thoughts that came into my mind! The instructions from God Are So Simple, but to live without His Guidance from day to day, and without the alcohol and street drugs was virtually impossible for me! In order for me to live a drug free life, and maintain it while being content in my being was only accomplished by learning how to trust my innermost feelings! Only God's Spirit was able to reach my heart and save my life!

137. God's Power, God's Strength

Whenever I think about The Holy Spirit of God, I am always taken to a mindset that isn't concerned, or connected to the outcome of this present world! God's Spirit Always Turns the dial of my heart to humble myself under His Perfect Will. By seeking God's Perfect Will, the thoughts in my mind keep a straight pattern of sanity, which snuffs out the insanity that always tries to on track itself, within the confines of my mind. God's Spirit is able to offset the attempts of the tempter, who never stops at trying to enslave my Eternal Soul. When I study The Words from God, the evil one flees from the makeup of my whole being; for God's Words Holds, oh, so much power. Now when the evil projections come to me from the enemy, I am able to recognize the lies, and I shout out in my voice and say, "Satan get away from me, you have no power here!" When The Trinity Lives in your heart, you can recognize the enemies of God in any form the enemies may take. The Spirit of The Trinity Has Saturated my whole being, God's Holy Lights Are Revealed through me by God's Power.

It's of God's Choosing that His Holy Lights Shines through me. The message I leave now isn't a new message, it's very old; however, it works whenever, or wherever a person may come to find him, or herself. The message is, you must seek God, in order to receive His Power and Strength, and the seeking must come from the sincerity of your heart, nothing else will work! This ends this message.

138. Guided by The Spirit of Christ

Jesus Christ Is The Perfect Example of how to live a just and blameless life; however, so many people have failed to even consider The Lord, and Master Jesus Christ as being the model for their lives. Jesus Christ Was Right When He Said, "the only way people can seek Him, would be if God made them able." There are oh, so many people who don't even truly seek The Lord God, let alone His Son Jesus Christ! This is of no matter that will hinder me not; for I've seen God's Holy Lights, and now I am Guided by God's Holy Lights. Nothing of this world takes up my time, or gets my loyalty! When The Trinity Calls, I am right here waiting for Their Instructions. I am Their Servant, and if it be Their Will I will be Their Servant forever! I've been blessed to have been saved from the enslavement of my Eternal Soul!

Only The Trinity Had The Power to Retrieve me from the enemy's camp. I am reborn in The Spirit of Jesus Christ, and only by God Was That Made Possible! I can see the evil one, oh, so clearly; however, I must continue to obey The Leadings from The Lord, and Master Jesus Christ. I must live the way He Instructs me on how to live! I can't go off on a tangent, and think I know how to handle the enemy on my own power! My Lord Jesus Christ Will Instruct me on how to respond to the enemy; fore He Has Defeated the enemy already. Jesus Christ Knows what I need to do to complete my tasks while I still have the breath of life in me.

139. Don't be Fooled

The time for God's Wrath hasn't come yet, but don't be fooled and say those things God Has Prophesied about through His Prophets are way off, and won't happen in my lifetime, so I'm safe! The end of the world happens every day for some people; however, if your soul isn't grounded in God, or His Son Jesus Christ, your soul will wonder without peace until The Day of Judgement! Only God Knows what will be the fate of those souls! I leave these words behind me in an effort to warn all people who may read my work. God Is Allowing me and Giving me the opportunity to tell the truth by which I have lived through! Satan is real, along with all of his demons, this isn't a fairy tale, that someone made up, to gain a profit. God, and His Son Jesus Christ Are The True Owners of Everything we see, or can't see, Satan was created by God, and also the demons who were once angles before The Great War in Heaven. Satan and 1/3 of God's Angels lost that war, and were tossed here to earth. So don't be fooled, the final destruction of God's Enemies is going to take place. So this is the reason for leaving this message. God Knows that some people can only acquire faith in Him through other people first, so I'll go forward and say, prepare your souls; for we are all from God, and we are all Eternal in essence! Through all of the generations, God Gave us all choices to make. To be free, kind, generous, and loving for forever, or mean dominate, and hurtful, and share not, for a short season, and be damned, and tormented for forever. You see God Is So Kind to us human beings; for He Gives us choices to make on our own- individually. Don't allow the tempter Satan in any way determine your fate.

140. Sections of The Truth

It's tragic on how I get to see with my own eyes in this generation I am a part of, and in the generation upcoming, the growing ignorance concerning The Living God! The young people are losing their lives constantly by the abuse of drugs. Oh, so many people in their forties and fifties are devastated in their minds and emotions from long term drug use, coupled with living in darkness. I am Moved by The Spirit of The Living God to write about the solution to all of these evil things; however, most people will still have a closed heart concerning the truth. Nevertheless I will begin to tell the solution of success from all of the evil that is being practiced in the world today. And in the world until God Himself, Reconstructs this world through His Spirit. Until then we human beings must move to a position, so God, Will Safeguard our Eternal Souls! There are oh, so many people leaving this life having their souls unprotected. The Evil Forces that be waits for the unprotected souls to enslave them! Only The Living Spirit of God Has Given me these Spiritual Insights, so I can warn the people of this generation and those to come. You see, I believe God's Words that are stated in His Holy Bible. God's Spirit Had to Open my Spiritual Eyes in order to be able to see the lies Satan has been using for centuries! I was one of the many people who are addicted to drugs, and one day I received a moment of sanity and I sincerely reached out to The Loving Invisible God. Now after much reconstruction of my whole being, The Spirit of God Is Blessing me to write and leave these Spiritual Truths behind before He lays my soul to rest, or right into Eternal Life. It's all up to God to what my reward will be, and His Son Jesus Christ Holds the key.

141. A Chance to Grow

I'm coming to the end of my forties, and oh, what blessings I've been given. The Invisible and Caring God Has Raised me up from the inside; for I was lacking in maturity! All as a straight result from not seeking God's Directions earlier in my existence. I don't believe in coincidences, I truly believe my chance had come up to get to know and trust The Creator of all life, and I took it, and I held on tightly, and I didn't ever let go. The benefits of my actions are shown through my words of inspiration and the new life that I now lead. The One and True God, and His Son Jesus Christ Is Leading The Way of my life, which Is Their Way of Living. Their Spirit Pushes me to rush for nothing; for They Aren't in a rush to accomplish anything and neither am I. However, when I was running on self-will, I was in a rush to do everything, there was no routine in my life whereas I actually took time to see how I should handle problems that presented themselves. I always pretended like they would just go away. Like I stated earlier, God's Spirit Showed me how to be a responsible human being. I'm writing about these things so that maybe, just maybe someone having similar problems in their existence can one day be Guided by The All Knowing God, and be drawn to read about the solution to my problem, and my problem was I didn't know how to handle my emotions that all human beings get. It really was my main problem for a long period of time in the early part of my life. I had to approach The Living Unseen God like a true and trusted friend. I couldn't connect to God through organized religion; however, God Made it Possible for me to come to Him!

142. What God's Children Must Learn

There is nothing I can write about that has greater meaning than the words from God's Spirit, or that of His Son's Jesus Christ! The Spirit of The Trinity Has Given me the assignment to uplift Their Holy Messages to this generation and the ones to come! The Judgement from The Holy Spirit of God Will Be Just and Swift.

God and Jesus Christ Have Touched my heart in a way that comes from Their Goodness. I've been Charged by Them to give encouragement to the people of my generation and those to come. Seek The Spirit of The Trinity, They Hold the answers to all of the longings of your hearts! This world is a beautiful place, designed and formed by God's Spirit; however, its riches are being exploited by the enemies of God, their season of exploitation hasn't come to a close yet. Grieve not, the evil and unjust acts taking place; fore , God's Spirit Is Just, and He Will Repay The Evil Forces that be, for their astronomical acts of wrong doings. I know in my own heart that it's not easy to hold off from taking matters of justice into your own hands! This is when The Spirit of Jesus Christ must come through the pores of your soul, in order to keep you blameless on The Day of Judgement! We human beings don't have the authority, or power to truly bring justice to the evil one, or his demons. We must learn to trust justice to God's Spirit; for this is His Creation, and God Is The Administrator of all outcomes! There must be no interference on our parts as human beings. Only the true believers in God will keep His Commandments and restrain themselves.

143. Disillusionment of Humanity

I am the first to admit I am ignorant to know all about the beings and creatures in God's Universe. However, I am a human being and I will obey the decrees handed down to us from The Living Spirit of God. That's very noble of me, but I just can't be satisfied with my obedience; for there are so many of my brothers and sisters who are blinded by the enemies of our God! We as human beings are easy targets from God's Enemies. God's Enemies aren't subjected to physical death, like human beings. However, God Didn't Leave us totally defenseless concerning the safeguard of our Eternal Souls! God Has Given us commandments to live by to keep us from further stacking up the sin pile. God Has Even Given us a new code to live by with the sacrifice of His Son Jesus Christ. Who Came Into the world to atone for the sins of the whole world, through His very own Blood! So many people are ignorant to the reality of Jesus Christ's Greatness. The Grace and Mercy from our Creator Has Been Added to this world from His Son's Own Actions, and still many people are ungrateful from God's Non Actions Against us human beings. These are just a few flaws of the human community that I've placed out into the open; however, there are many more! Only by seeking The Trinity does repentance pierce the heart of the seeker. Most people are oh, so concerned with the occurrences happening in the world around them. They consider God almost not at all; for worldly things are more important, and the directions from God Himself becomes almost nonexistent in them!

144. Our Faithful God

The contents of my heart holds great concern for my fellow brothers and sisters, even though I don't know every human being personally; however, I still care about what may happen to them, as a result from their lack of interest of God's Decrees. It's like they almost don't care about how God Is Going to deal with humanity as a whole. This generation that I am apart of act like conditions are going to stay the same forever. It's a real dangerous complacency in the attitudes of people I talk to from day to day. The Forces of Evil, are just lulling the governments of the world to sleep, like situations of the world aren't declining. I am blessed to be able to see the lies that are being told to the common people, on a day to day basis. I will keep seeking The Spirit of The Trinity, always humbling myself to Their Leadings. It hurts my heart to know that the majority of humanity will be destroyed, just as The Spirit of God, Has Already Proclaimed, through His Prophets! Nevertheless, I won't stop writing from my heart. It may be too late for mankind as a whole in its present state; however, God, Is Always Good, and I know from my own experience, God, Will Listen, to the prayers from the sincere heart, so never lose hope, especially when hope can still be found. No matter what your situation may be, no matter how low you may feel, always keep God, as an ace in your pocket. And if you ever pull Him out, He Will Respond to the faith in your heart! I can state this as a fact; for God, Showed up for me, and I'm human just like you!

145. Direction of Protection

I don't know what my fate will be upon leaving this earth; however, I trust The Living God, God's Spirit, and His Son Jesus Christ, now while I yet live! I mustn't concern myself with positions of God's Glory, I must continue to be an excellent servant of The Trinity! God, Has Given me an assignment, and that is where I am putting all of my attention and abilities to the completion of it. Even though the thoughts of the afterlife comes across my mind from time to time. I must keep my focus on The Living Spirit of God! From God I Receive Guidance from one day to the next. When I keep my attention on The Spirit of God, I am in less danger from the temptations of the world, and I am conscious of the lies that are being projected to my mind from the evil one and his demons. The rewards from The Living God Are Great; however, The Evil Forces that be constantly tries to deter me from The Guidance of The Trinity all of the time. The Forces of Evil attacks my weaknesses all of the time; however, The Power of God, Gives me Strength, to cancel out Satan's Mental Projections every time, and the reality of the whole situation is revealed to me by way of soundness from within my mind. Power that I didn't possess before constantly seeking and humbling myself under The Mighty Hand of God! These demonstrations of God's Power, has held me constantly loyal to God, even though the tempter Satan, never stops tempting and trying to get me to abandon The Creator of all life, including his own!

146. The Covering of God

When a soul has the covering of God's Protection, Blessed is that soul; for he, or she is Protected by God Himself! This is how I feel when it comes down to the safety level of my own being. I truly feel as though God Has Protected me all of my life, and I don't believe in coincidences like I stated somewhere in one of my passages. God's Holy Spirit Truly Guards Against Any Harm that has been planned against me! I remember times in the past when I could have truly lost my life; however, God's Spirit Protected me each and every time. Upon pondering on what I just wrote brought me to a position of being overwhelmed in my heart, knowing in my heart without an inkling of doubt that The Creator of all life Cares about me to Protect me all those times, melts my heart! No one alive in all of my forty-nine years have loved me like that except Jesus Christ, and that's it! No one, or nothing will ever love me greater, and I state this in full confidence! I belong to The Living Spirit of God, nothing else, or nobody else will ever get my full attention! Bless it be the souls who are Protected by The Living Spirit of God Himself. Praise The Living God for forever, let nothing get in-between yourselves, and The Living Spirit of God Who Gave and Protects your Eternal Souls! God Will Show you what the true meaning of love is, no one besides His Son Jesus Christ Can Show you a greater love and devotion.

147. Hope Reinforced

The reading of God's Words from His Bible has truly hit my heart in a way like it never has before! The very words from God Himself Has Given me hope like I've never experienced before. I see God in a whole new different shade of light now, His Words

Have Totally Seized my heart! God Called me His Son thirty-one years prior to me reading the readings I read in The Holy Bible concerning The Promise to those who overcome. The hope of receiving The Promise from God burns in my heart now; for God, Already Called me His Son! Being that God Has Called me His Son, now in all rightness I'll call God my Father, and The Lord, and Master Jesus Christ my Older Brother. Now, every aspect of my life makes perfect sense to me; however, the tempter Satan and all of his demons are still on the loose, and nothing, or nobody do I totally trust. I will keep my heart in alert mode, until my Father God, Brings me home. Until then I must continue my assignment.

I must continue to keep my mind attuned to The Will of my Father God, and He Will Show me what I must do from one day to the next! I can feel my Older Brother Jesus Christ's Spirit in my body from day to day now, Jesus Christ Himself Has Manifested His Spirit inside of body, for the simple fact that He Loves me.

This is His Way of Communicating with me, and Our Father Has a Totally Different Mode of Communicating with me altogether, and God Himself Has Established that link to my soul in my youth!

148. The Essence of Things

Oh, how solidified without change is my Father's Creation! Effects of actions are the same every time no matter how many times they are practiced. Evil will always be evil, and good will always be good no matter the time. The manifestation of evil and disease will never leave this world, it will continue to corrupt and decay this world through and through, if there is no power, or order to stop the condition. Throughout history the only known antidote for evil is good! Only the absolute good, can make evil flee. Only by constantly seeking my Father God, do I receive the needed strength to preform my daily functions without being overwhelmed by The Evil Forces that be. Evil in humanity always seeks out positions of power to protect itself, and to dish out cruelty to whomever opposes its position! The death and destruction of this human society hasn't reached maturity yet; however, I can see God's Will oh, so clearly. The Will of my Father God Comforts my soul and makes my heart sing, but the blindness and the ignorance of most people at times irritates me, I personally need to work on that weakness. Father God Exposes the ways of the enemy to me every time I still away and seek His Counsel. Then as I go forward within time, I experience The Teachings God Has Revealed to me within meditation. God's Leadings have been correct so many times, I've gowned to always trust what Father God Reveals to me. Nothing from men do I wholly trust. My Father in heaven Gives me all I need to complete the assignment He Has Placed Before me. He Also Has Deadened within my heart the desires for material gain; my heart use to lust after gaining such things. Now my heart is attuned to Father God's Will.

149. My True Heart

Upon reading The Beatitudes, I found my soul, and it immediately sent me into praising Father God! God's Spirit Always Gratifies my heart and soul by Showing me wonderful things all the time that Gives me hope of being with Him for forever. God Knows I won't keep good news to myself, He Knows that I'll share it with anybody that's willing to hear the good news concerning His Kingdom. My Older Brother Jesus Christ's Spirit Burns in my heart, and within everyday left to me, I will ask Him how to handle situations that will come up in this evil world that I still yet live in. I trust The Trinity with the most precious thing I have, and that's my Eternal Soul! Most people are ignorant to the fact that we come from The Eternal God; there for our souls are Eternal and will exist for forever. Satan has spread his lies by projecting thoughts to peoples mind by saying, "there ain't nothing after death once you die that's it, so get what you can and get it by any means necessary". And this lie has deceived oh, so many people throughout the ages and still to the present time. Father God Said, "you will reap, what you have sown!" The spirit of the evil one is so dastardly, and I hate him, hate is a very strong word and I will stand by it, for I truly do! I am not sorry God, and I am not sorry Jesus Christ, and I am not sorry Spirit of God, this is my true feeling toward the evil one and all of his associates, and I will never change my heart concerning them! Committing an act of evil is one aspect, but being evil is totally different all together!

150. A Brother's Pride

The Teachings of The Lord, and Master Jesus Christ Are Thorough and Holy; He Gave Perfect Instructions on how to become holy and acceptable to Father God! He Left no subject uncovered and when His Work was completed the enemy crucified Him, and God Raised Him on the third day after being murdered to fulfill The Scriptures! He returned from whence He came. His Life Stands as a Guide to the living souls, who desire the Gift of Eternal Life. It's not only what The Lord, and Master Jesus Christ Said, but it also Was His Works that Pleased His Father in heaven! Jesus Christ Never Preformed Unjust Acts, and He Possessed Power at all times to destroy anyone who opposed Him, yet He never harmed anyone! Jesus Christ Truly Was God's Only Begotten Son! No man alive had, or has the power to bring a man back to life after being dead for several days, or a little girl that had been dead for several hours. No, Only The True Son of God Was Entrusted with such Devine Power! Jesus Christ's Own Death Is The Marked Place on how humanity is recording years. My Older Brother Jesus Christ Is The Model for my life. No one in all history gravitates my heart the way Jesus Christ's Spirit Does. Besides The Spirit of The Living God, nothing else gets my total trust and loyalty; Jesus Christ's Life Is The Perfect Example of how to live a holy life. When I just think about The Lord, and Master Jesus Christ, my soul becomes relaxed, and I am vexed about nothing, all activity in my heart is placed on pause; for He Is The High Priest Forevermore, my Older Brother Jesus Christ!

151. The Road I Walk

Sometimes I feel like I'm all alone in this world with nobody to share time with, I'm almost fifty years old, and I have no wife, or kids, and it looks like that's the way my life is going to end up being! I'm not feeling self-pity, I'm just stating how my life actually is at the present time. Father God Is Good All The Time, and my life can change in the blink of an eye; however, my Father God In His Heaven Knows Exactly What He Is Doing, and I totally trust Father God, He Knows what's in my heart! Out of all the things that I am Allowed to see, I know I am not alone, it's just that I've died to the desires of this world, and that's why I feel like I'm all alone at times. This road that leads to The Living God is a very lonely road; for many people don't actually walk it while they have the breath of life! There is no doubt in my heart about The Blessings my Father God Is Blessing me with, I can see very clearly the path that is set before me, and my heart and soul is overjoyed. However, the reality is most people around me aren't walking on the same road I am on! My Older Brother Jesus Christ Was So Right When He Said, "You Can't Serve God and money, at the same time." So I'm going to keep on serving God; for money is of no matter to me, it never was. In the beginning of my life, and for a good while I didn't know who, or what to trust. Now I allow nothing, or nobody, to get in between me, and Father God!

152. Food For The Soul

The Spirit of The Living God Touched me once again as I slept, and when He Awakened me I was filled with awe and gratitude; for God, Showed me in my mind how He's Giving me the opportunity each day and night to do the work to be worthy to be called His Son! This was the "awe" that I felt immediately upon awakening and by pondering the message the attitude of being grateful followed. God Truly Knows How to Feed me spiritually, He Knows what motivates my heart, I can't love anybody greater than I love God! God Himself Is Where my heart is; for years this has been the truth concerning me! I live now to fulfill one of The Beatitudes of The Lord, and Master Jesus Christ, my Older Brother. The work will be difficult, but I already know in my heart I won't be able to stop the amount of joy I will experience from The Spirit of The Living God! All sorts of gifts are available from The Loving Spirit of God. This is why God put as a commandment, "Don't covet your neighbor's house." God, Said this because His Spirit Is Able and Willing to Give Whatever a person's heart can desire without having to be jealous of what his neighbor has! I myself don't know a whole lot of things, but what I am totally sure about is, there is nothing The Living Spirit of God Can't Do. There is nothing too hard for Him! As God Guides me through this evil space in time, I know without a single doubt in my heart that I will endure to the end, and be a success by living my life as a direct result from following the instructions that came from The Words of God and His Son Jesus Christ, on what to do and what not to do!

153. God's Son, That Must be Guided

I stated to The Trinity, and to the readers of my work that I hate Satan and all of his associates, and I said that I would stand by what's in my heart, and I meant what I stated! However, I love The Trinity, and I can't kill a single person, even if they commit evil acts, or they may be just plain evil. I must follow the dictates of The Trinity! My Father God Said, "Vengeance is Mine." And I as His Son must get behind my Father, and humble myself under His Mighty Hand! The temptations are oh, so great to disobey what God, and Jesus Christ Said not to do. I must constantly seek The Trinity for Guidance; for I am weak when it comes to keeping a lid on my emotions and humbling myself. I fall short in other areas also, and I must constantly put myself into check concerning all of God's Decrees. Studying The Teachings from my Older Brother Jesus Christ helps me oh, so much in the core of my heart; His Words Stabilize my emotions. God's Spirit Gives me hope of becoming a better Son and Servant to Him! You see I constantly need The Trinity in order for me to grow and become holy and acceptable to God Himself! I know in my heart I'm a long way off from being holy and acceptable to my Maker! I mustn't hold to much concern about things that will take time and effort to achieve; however, I must stay conscious of constantly seeking The Trinity; for the evil one waits to attack the weaknesses of my being, and that's my experience, not a theory. The evil one and all of his demons are the rulers of this world. I was born in this evil place, but I don't have to be a participant in the evil functions taking place on this planet.

154. The Pattern of God's Directions

You can have riches beyond riches, and gifts beyond gifts, but if you don't have The Spirit of Jesus Christ Burning in your heart, you have nothing at all! You can be rulers of city councils, you can be in charge of whole governments, but if you aren't humble under The One and Only God your accomplishments will come to ruin! The One and Only God Isn't A Mean and Callous Spirit; however, He Is Just and Faithful! Whatever The LORD God Said He Would Do Through His Words, He Will Do! God's Spirit Is Unchanging and this is what His Believers depend on, and they become unchanging in their faith and loyalty to God's Way of Living Life! Everything in God's Creation you can depend on it for whatever qualities they may possess. They are ordered to be the way they are from God Himself! God's Created Qualities will follow their patterns of His Directions; however, to defy God's Orders would bring destruction upon yourselves no matter how long it may take! I see and I've seen evidence to comply with actions of defying God's Ordered Directions! Even with evidence of this fact right in front of people's faces; they still stand in the spirit of defiance! I can truly see The Kingdom of God, Advancing upon this world with a very rapid pace! God's Will, Will Be Done regardless of whatever may be transpiring in the world! At The Proper time nothing will be able to stop the advancing wrath of God's Judgements. The enemies of God constantly keeps a veil over the hearts and minds of billions of people, and this is the reason for my work! The LORD God Has Charged me to place His

Warnings once again out to the people of this generation and the ones to come. God's Orders of things will be accomplished, so take heed and straighten out your lives to fall into compliance with God's Will for your life! This ends this message.

155. What God Has Spoken

Blessed are The Children of God, who are in the earth from generation to generation, to the end of the age! The LORD God Himself Has Charged me to write before I even came out of my mother's womb, and I am oh, so grateful to be His Son! These writings I've been Blessed to write are for The Children of God! I know your sufferings; for I suffer the same things too! The enemies of Father God are everywhere to be found on the surface of the earth; so be diligent in your prayers to our Father God and The Lord, and Master Jesus Christ! The enemies will constantly persecute you, and make you as uncomfortable as possible; however, we must remain blameless and follow the mode of our Older Brother Jesus Christ! Never, and I mean never, fall out from The Love of The Trinity; for the evil one delights in such behavior from God's Children. Our Father Has Great Mercy and Grace, but don't test the validity of our Father God! Always keep in your hearts the certainty that Father God Will Never Leave you, or Forsake you, no matter what; and there is no power the evil one, his demons, or his children can ever cast upon your Eternal Souls. We belong to our Father God Who Created Everything, and Even Allowed the evil one To Become what he has chosen to be! Let not The Forces of Evil cause your fate to become as theirs will be. Their fate will be torment forever! The LORD God Has Said, "You Will Reap, What You Have Sown!" Our Father God Is Faithful and He will Carry out What He Has Already Said.

156. Two Kinds of People

This world called earth is steadily moving into the position foretold by its Maker. I truly am blessed; for I can see the reality of the people who make up the population of the planet. The Lord, and Master Jesus Christ Has Truly Opened Up my eyes concerning the people of this world from one generation to the next. I've always had trouble in my heart when it came to the assessment of people! My Older Brother Jesus Christ Made it crystal clear for me, and now I'll pass it on to my readers! There are two kinds of people in the world; God's Children, and then there are the children of the devil. Reading the words from my Older Brother Jesus Christ Has Solidified the truth in my heart! Now by digesting this newly found truth, it has further caused me to humble myself under The Mighty Hand of God Himself!

My pathway is still the same; however, my sights have been made crystal clear by my Older Brother Jesus Christ! There aren't enough thank yous to thank You with Father God. I truly see now why You told me to seek The Teachings from The Lord, and Master Jesus Christ. Everything changes now within the heart and soul that is me! No more confusion will run through my heart concerning the people who breathes the same air that I breath. There will be no hostility from my being; however, I will separate myself from their presents, and no association will go on and I won't have to lift a finger; for my Father God's Spirit within me will be separation enough; for darkness will always flee from The Light!

157. Instructions For The Believers of God

Being a child of God doesn't guarantee one's self from being blameless when it comes to the actions taken, or not taken in the ordered time of life! A person becomes known by his, or her works. I must constantly seek out The Goodness of God's Spirit; for the evil one constantly sets traps to poison my being with all kinds of tactics, designed to destroy my connection with God! The Children of The Living God must stay diligent in their prayers to The Holy Creator, we must constantly humble ourselves under God's Perfect Guidance! The Lord, and Master Jesus Christ Constantly Stated that we must always check the status of our hearts; fore Jesus Knew what would be the outcome if our hearts became callous. God's Spirit Would Be Closed Off to us, and we would become insensitive to the needs of others. The evil one would continue to whisper lies to us, telling us that God Doesn't Care about us, and He Never Has, so we better forget about all that praying stuff, and get what we can get, before someone else beats us to it! The evil one is very crafty, he can make lies sound so convincing as he projects the thoughts to our minds. The evil one has been lying before man was even created, so he knows when and what to say to our hearts in an effort to deceive us. We can't defeat The Evil Forces that be on our own accord; we aren't wise enough, or powerful enough to conquer him, his demons, or his children, without The Power and Direction from The Trinity. So always know that The Forces of Evil are forever present and will be, until The New Order from God Himself Comes Into Order!

158. The Manifestations of God's Blessings

By the blessings of God's Allowances, I can see my life becoming enriched. His Will for my life becomes clearer to my conscious with each passing day that I humble myself under The Mighty Hand of His Guidance. More and more God Reveals the direction that is so designed for my life. I find myself in almost a constant state of awe! I feel in my sixth sense that there is absolutely no mistake whatsoever in the directions that I'm receiving. I know in my heart without a doubt that God's Spirit Guides my everyday thought process. Now I can tell the difference when the evil one tries to project thoughts into my mind! The blessings from my Father God Grows Now at a steady pace rate; there's nothing greater in this life that I've received except my life! For over fourteen years straight every day and every night without missing a single day, or night have I not sought The LORD my Father God! My claim is genuine and Father God, and all the hosts of heaven are my witnesses, I need no others! The LORD my Father God Knows my heart and He Knows my heart isn't about falsehoods concerning any subject! Now The Spirit of God Is Blessings me Constantly with Spiritual Insights that millions of people wish they had; however, God Blesses Whomever He Pleases to Bless, and I am oh, so grateful for all of His Blessings that Have Been Bestowed upon my soul! As I write, I can feel the enemy tugging at my mind. I can see now how the enemy had me in bondage for all those early years of my life. The Spirit that Is God Has Released me from the binds of Satan's grip! Woe, unto me, if I ever fall from The Grace of Father God's Protection!

159. The Core of The Trinity

Not to the rich, not to the well to do, not to the rulers of governments, but to the sick, to the broken souls, to the ones people cursed, these were the people my Older Brother Jesus Christ Came Into The World to Serve and Give Hope to! I'm moved at this very moment by my Older Brother Jesus Christ, His Spirit Rests in my heart today, along with The Spirit of our Father

God! I desire in my heart to do oh, so many things; however, The Spirit of Father God Tells me Constantly, Turn Not to The Right, or Turn Not to The Left, but to Keep my focus on Himself, and I will do what my Father God Has Instructed me to Do, no matter what! The Teaching of The Lord, and Master Jesus Christ, Always Now Touches my heart and soul, with Awe and Amazement. His Humbleness under His Father and His Willingness to Serve the people who had nothing is the model that I try and live after. I love my Older Brother Jesus Christ, and I never laid my eyes upon Him; however, I know without any doubts in my heart that He Has Saved my life more times than I am conscious of! Right now I am overwhelmed in my soul; for Jesus Christ's Spirit, Is Upon me. The Son of Man is truly The King of Kings and The Lord of Lords, there is no pain that He Hasn't Experienced, and no man alive, or dead has accomplished what He Has Accomplished! Jesus Christ Is Just Like His Father God; They Are Both, in a picture frame by Themselves without any need for change. Only The Trinity Makes my soul Totally Humble on a constant day by day trek. I look to nothing else to copy my life after; I've found Their Spirits, oh, so inviting, never is there anything demanding from Them, I truly love Them!

160. The Gifts From my God

I believe truly in the fulness of my heart, if it weren't for The Grace and Mercy of The Lord God, I would have physically died over twenty years ago, and I am almost fifty years old now. I can't seem to stop saying this in my mind, and I don't ever want to stop saying it. "I truly love You Lord God, You Are my Maker and You Are All I Wholly Trust!" I never ever consciously want to disappoint my God, He's all I have, nothing can ever take the place of my God! I look to God's Spirit for everything; most people can't understand that kind of devotion to something they never saw with their own eyes. I constantly thank The Lord God for All The Blessings I know about and The Ones I don't know about. No one knows what God Gave me, and no one knows what I can truly see, its secrets will always remain between The Lord God, and me! A smile just came across my face; for in my heart Lord God, I know You Protect me as I exist in this evil place. I'm right here Lord God, even though I'm unhappy most of the time, buts that's okay; for the evil one no longer manipulates my mind. God, You Gave me An Assignment, Not to Look to The Right, or Look to The Left, but to Keep my concentration on You Lord God All of The Time! I'm not spending time on trying to foretell the outcome of what You told me to do; for You are my Father God, and I truly trust You! God, You Gave me my Existence, why Would You Ever Want to Destroy me? The evil one is the ruler of this world right now, and I have no more questions in my heart to why I never fitted in anywhere down here. Father God Has Given me my answer!

161. A Song For A Soul to Sing

My body wants to rest; however, my soul presses onward with a steady urgency to reveal what's in my heart. I asked The LORD God this morning to make me like the birds of the air, to give me a song in my heart and be glad about the upcoming light of a brand new day ! To show gratitude to Father God for being oh, so kind to all of us who have the gift of life throughout all of Father God's Creation! How can a soul be ungrateful when he, or she bears witness to a brand new day unfolding right before their God Given Senses? Even the wicked and The Forces of Evil can't deny the awesome beauty of the dawning of brand new days! I will receive a song in my heart; for Father God Always Answers Prayers. I surely am receiving the full blessings from this day; for The LORD God Has Awakened me before the coming of His Light. My body wants desperately to rest, but it will have to wait; for my heart isn't at its emptying out point yet. The tweet, tweet, from God's Little Sparrow awakened me to consciousness one more time; for I drifted away into unconsciousness. My soul won't let me rest until my work is complete, then I can get rest, and go back to sleep! I will praise Father God all this day and all this night; for He Never Stops Giving me Spiritual Insights. I must continue to humble myself like the birds of the world, and know in my heart that Father God Will Always Guide me and keep my Eternal Soul from being sent to hell! Father God Has Given me many good things, and now I'm asking Him to Give me a song to sing!

162. A Way Out of Failure

I call myself God's Servant, and I believe this with all of my heart and soul; however, I don't want to be a wicked servant. I must take what The LORD God Has Given to me, and use it to glorify The LORD God! So I must continue to humble myself under God's Perfect Direction! In the eyes of the world I am a failure; however, in the eyes of Father God, I have an opportunity to shine as brightly as the sun in the sky provided I continue to seek His Perfect Guidance! In all the days of my life, The LORD God Has Protected me; for I was a wayward soul, and I got beaten up a lot of times because of it, but it was of no matter for me; for my way was always the right way! It took over twenty years of misery before I got a clue that I was wrong, dead wrong about a lot of things! It has taken over sixteen years with The Spirit of God Leading the way to help me reconstruct my whole being, and that was very painful every step of the way! Now The Holy Spirit of God, Has Opened Up my eyes to Show me I have nothing positive built up that will produce any good crops! Right now I feel very sad, but The Holy Spirit Told me to Take Heart; for He Has Given me an assignment to do, and if I stay focused on Him and turn not away, and humble myself under His Mighty Hand I'll have some seeds to sow, to bring about good crops! God Is Able and Willing to Straighten anyone out; however, you have to seek God, and learn to trust God regardless of what your present situation maybe, no matter what people may say to you. Constantly seek out The Invisible Creator, and build a positive relationship with The Maker of everything you can see, and everything you can't see. You must come to terms in your own heart that God really exists, and that He Cares About your life, and what might happen to you. This is the first step in seeking The Spirit that is God!

163. Truth, The Freeing Tool

The truth will set you free; also the same truth can hurt really bad if it applies to you, and that same truth can be real funny when it doesn't apply to you, but does to someone else. In either case the truth is the enemy to people who live their lives by pleasing the world! The truth reveals the true nature of things, and the rulers of this world want no parts of that; for they are liars, and they need the truth to stay concealed, so they can continue to deceive the just and honest people of the world. You see the truth will open up the eyes of the masses of people, and they are the ones who are being deceived by the minority who are the rulers, and the rulers are the liars who want the truth to continue to be hidden, so they may stay in power! This is how the evil one has ruled and spilled the blood of billions of just and ignorant people for thousands of years! There is no repentance for him; for he has been a liar before men were created! The Lord, and Master Jesus Christ Has Said this in His Own Words long ago when He Walked the earth! So the truth in any manor will be the tool that can be used to fine out the characters of people in any given situation, and sometimes the deeds of the people are so revealing you don't need the tool of truth at all to see what kind of people you have come into contact with. Now the word truth to The Children of God is oh, so freeing, even though they may have to admit and repent from a lot of wrong doings and self-deception on their parts, and if they are constantly honest with themselves, God's Spirit, Will Place in their hearts to know that the truth will set them free! The world in its present state is a very evil place, and always expect the truth to be hidden when it comes down to issues concerning the masses of people; for the evil one and his family are here to cause corruption and deception, and their specialty physical death!

164. Waves of Confusion and Ignorance

The minds of people are so easily swayed, especially when a decision has to be made from a group of people, and if there is someone within the group who sounds good with the usage of words, that group can be turned to probably do anything that is unjust, and it's worse when it's a mob! When people have no principles of justice to live by; they are easily apt to shed blood when a disagreement arises between themselves and other people. When I truly go over the words Spoken by The LORD God Himself, I become serious of heart; for I believe The LORD God, and I know in my soul that God Will Carry out what He Has Spoken about! Knowing billions of people will be destroyed, doesn't make it easy on my heart to accept! However, I believe in The Spirit of God, and in my heart I know His Decisions Are Just. The people of this generation are very paranoid, and most of them are spiritually sick! Most people have no strong positive spiritual connection with The Spirit of God, or The Lord, and Master Jesus Christ, they are truly lost and confused, and the evil one is so delighted by their confusion coupled with the lack of knowledge to why they are alive in the world. It saddens my heart also to know there are oh, so many false teachings that are taking place. I know these things must happen first, before the new order from God Will Come, and I must not allow myself to become ineffective because of it. I am here to tell the readers that it's never too late to seek God, and ask for forgiveness, I know God Won't Turn Away and Laugh at you. The Loving God Awaits for His Children, or even strangers to seek Him with sincere hearts, and ask for guidance in order to save their sick, or wayward souls. The Trinity Really Awaits the prayers from sincere hearts!

165. The Wreckage of Evil

Every time when I study The Teachings of The Lord, and Master Jesus Christ, I become very sad and observant at the same time. It always upsets me when I reach the part where His Enemies plotted to kill Him, and the physical abuse that was administered to Him! I watched closely how the evil one used the jealousy of the elders, chief priest, and pharisees, to entice the crowd to have the governor Pontius Pilate crucify Jesus Christ, instead of the real criminal Barabbas, even though Jesus Christ was innocent of any wrong doing. The governor even said I will have nothing to do with the blood of this innocent man, he told the crowd it's your responsibility, and the crowd said, "let His Blood be on our hands, and on the hands of our children!" It was pure evil back then that enticed the crowd to crucify the innocent Jesus Christ over the known criminal Barabbas; for it was the governor's custom at the feast to release a prisoner chosen by the crowd. That same pure evil is on the loose still over two thousand years later! I'll never be settled in my heart and soul until Father God Himself Arrest the evil one, and all of his family members! The Spirit of The Trinity Flows through my soul constantly, They Continue to Cleanse me from the contamination of evil that engulfs this world! The Trinity Constantly Protects me from self-deception also; I can't be in any safer hands than Them! I can't express enough on how the enemies of God desires desperately to destroy anything they can that is of God's Creation. The evil one has the power of death and destruction, and nothing, or nobody is safe and secure, as long as Satan is rampant on this earth! Satan has rallied the people long ago to kill God's Son, so in my mind he will use every opportunity to kill anyone, and he has been doing this ever since man was created, and all the way up to the present day that I'm pushing this pen. I said it before and I'll say it again, I hate the evil one, and all of his family members!

166. God The Only Good

Life, any life is a wonderous thing, no one knows what animates a body of something so that it has life. In human beings it's said that the soul is the animator of the body which gives the body movement, or what we call life! Yet no human being alive so far has any proof of a soul being the animator of the body, thus giving it life, nor does anyone alive have any documentation of even knowing what a soul looks like! There are multitudes of things that humanity as a whole are in the dark about. Knowledge of evil is oh, so easy to practice; however, knowledge of good, and the practice of it is totally the opposite! Most people don't take the time and effort to practice the good, and God Himself Is The Only Good! So humanity will stay in darkness, and the evil one and the evil doers will continue to control this world at the present time, and until the end of the age! It will be only the seekers of God, who will obtain the secrets of His Kingdom! This is why The Lord, and Master Jesus Christ Spoke in Parables! You have to seek God, in order for God to Disclose Himself to you! God Himself Is The Holder of all knowledge, and it's only by His Will Does He Disclose any information concerning anything in His Creation! This is why the progress for humanity is so slow; for only a few people constantly seek the knowledge from God Himself, thus evil and darkness reins throughout this world! The only comfort I can give from the realm of the intangibles is the direction to seek out The Only Good, which is God Himself! He Holds the answers to any questions a person may seek. I, as God's Messenger, can only send messages, that is the all of my function.

167. The Spiritual Realm

The Realm of God's Spirit, and everything in the spiritual world consistently stays in my conscious thoughts! Upon constantly seeking The Kingdom of God, my interests in the unseen yet obvious forces in this natural world has increased. The more The LORD God Reveals to my conscious thoughts, the more I realize how little we know as human beings concerning the makeup of everything in existence! Whatever The LORD God Reveals to me, He Knows I will share it with my fellow brothers and sisters. Most people believe things when they can physically experience them with five senses; however their belief system shuts off when it comes to the things they can't experience with the five senses. The area past the five senses is where The Spirit of God Has Drawn my attention to on a daily basis. The knowledge of what I've been exposed to has been overwhelming to me ever since The LORD God Has Captured my attention! By not strengthening the talents The LORD God Had Given me, I stayed a drift in the world. Looking for a place to fit into, and totally clueless to why I was born and what my role was to be while I have the breath of life! I know what the phrase means when people say, "there but; for The Grace of God, go I!" As I said before I almost lost my life to The Evil Forces that be, and that just didn't happen; for The Spirit of God, Intervened, God Demonstrates His Love and Protection to those He Pleases to Show It to! There isn't any doubts in my mind, heart, or soul concerning the presents and existence of The Invisible Spirit known as God! I'm presently experiencing His Presents, as I'm writing this down at 4:08am; fore The Spirit of The Living God Awakened me at 3:38am, so I could finish this passage, and move forward to the next experience that God Would Have me write about!

168. Formula to be Free

Oh, how little is known about The Spiritual Realm, mankind is so shallow in this area of reality; for there is nothing to analyze like in general science, so here is where the wall of prejudice begins in the minds of the scientists, but in the souls of God's Children, the door to the origin of everything is wide open! The Forces of Evil, and the evil one knows this doorway is wide open, and Satan constantly tries to conceal it from the masses of humanity. Through the doorway of The Spiritual Realm is where all truth about everything in existence maybe found. The Land of The

Spirit, where Satan himself is from, is what Satan tries to conceal from the interest of humanity as a whole; for the more one looks into The Spiritual World, the wiser he becomes concerning the world he presently is a part of, and all existence everywhere! The focus comes off worldly things, and attention and concerns are directed to deeper meanings of life itself, and to The True Governor, and Creator of everything. This is the doorway the evil one, and The Forces of Evil, want to remain concealed from the minds of the masses of people on earth! This is why God Said, "Seek The Kingdom of God, and all other things will be added on to you."

God's Kingdom Is Within every person on the planet, and once a person constantly seek these intangible things, knowledge, and truth becomes tangible, within the person's mind, heart, and soul! The Light of God's Spirit Will Expose the darkness the person has been existing in, and evil, fear, and worry loses its grip from upon the person. The person truly becomes free if he, or she persist in seeking the intangible things that make up The Spiritual World! What I've just described is the formula to save our world as we know it today; however, there is no unity, and spiritual success is only granted to those who persistently seek the intangibles of The Kingdom of God!

169. Only From God

No one who has life, can possess any talents, or abilities, unless they were Given by God Himself! Even Satan was Given a time limit by God to roam this earth. God's Spirit Is The Ruler of everything in existence, and the majority of humanity won't hold this truth in the confines of their hearts! Jesus Christ was right, "all unclean things comes from the hearts of men." The Lord, and Master Jesus Christ Never Spoke of anything that was false and self-deceiving, He Said Outrightly that His Power Came from His Father, that was in heaven above. His Ability to Heal the sick, and cause people to see who were blind, and control the elements, were Given to Him, from His Father in heaven! There was never any boasting from Him, concerning His Abilities; Jesus Is Humble, under His Father's Mighty Hand. This is a great lesson for my life, I must become humble, under God's Mighty Hand also, and not boast about my abilities either. God, in all of my life Has Never Taken Away Anything He Has Allowed me to possess, and I praise The LORD God not just for that, but for Being Just to all of His Creation, whether you are evil, or not! God's Will Goes Beyond anything His Created Beings can understand! God Is The One and Only Spirit, to whom there is no comparison, and there shall never be another spirit like Him ever! So I will move forward with the talents my God Has Given me, Assigned Especially for me, and be glad and grateful for His Giving; for no one was able to give me what I possess within this holy temple we human being call a body!

There is no strength I possess that hasn't been Given to me from Father God, nothing is mine originally, all things are from Father God, So Jesus Christ Is Right Again when He Said, "It's better to give than receive." Jesus Knew that nothing was ours anyway, so why not give something of value away to someone; for it will show the love of Father God, that resides in you! Father God, Always Gives something of value to us, without any expectations in return, all Father God Asks of us Is to Treat others as we would treat ourselves!

170. The Realm of Good Is God

There are many things I don't know about in this natural world, and that lack of knowledge comes to be tripled when it comes to the knowledge of spiritual things; however, there is one thing that I am assured of with no doubt in my whole being, and that is God, Is The Only Good! When I hold this conviction in the forefront of my heart, it causes me to humble myself to God's Desire for my life! The selfishness of my heart takes a back seat, and this is progress for me; fore the later was not the former in many aspects of my life for over four and one half decades!

In the light of much foolishness and ignorance, The Creator of all life continued to have Mercy and Grace Upon my confused and wayward soul. Now after fourteen years of seeking The Kingdom of God constantly, I'm able to not only to see God's Grace and Mercy in my own life, I'm also able to see how His Spirit of Love and Concern Covers Over This Whole Universe! So yes The Lord, and Master Jesus Christ Is Right, God, Is The Only Good! There is a whole lot of spiritually sick people in this world, and I know in my heart that God Gives us every opportunity that is possible to assist in the recovery of our damaged souls. I am called by God Himself to offer the way of correct direction to my brothers and sisters as I still have life.

God Himself Has Saved my Eternal Soul from being enslaved by The Evil Forces that be; however, I had to become diligent in following the leadings that The Only Good Placed before me! God Can Only Help when we become willing to trust His Guidance; for God, Gave us self-will; however, we must come to the reality of seeing that we failed over and over again, at our attempt to live our lives successfully! God, The Only Good Is and Will Always Be the correct solution to my existence here in this natural world, and in the spiritual existence to come!

171. When God Calls, I Answer

Here I sit again at 4:19am pushing this pen; for my LORD God Has Awakened me once again to be of service! My Older Brother Jesus Christ Also Was Placed Into Action by The LORD God to be of service to the many! I question The Holy Spirit of God not in anguish by saying, why did You Wake me up this early fore? The Holy Spirit of God Is my Perfect Provider and Guider; there is no long discussion in my heart when The Holy Spirit Reveals Its Directions! Many bits and pieces of my old character still remains in in my heart; and The Holy Spirit of God Has Been Pointing these things out to me on a consistent basis, through my dreams. The Most Holy One of Israel Is So Perfect In All The Things He Does. He Knows How to Awaken me from unconsciousness in such a way that I am not in fear; however, I know in my heart that He Desires something from me. This has been my experience from these early morning wake ups! I'm also finding out that it's a time when I can express my experiences in a clear pathway from my heart! As the days of my life stack one on top of each other now with me constantly seeking The Kingdom of God, I'm receiving a clearer connection from God's Holy Spirit. The clarity is solidifying my new character in such a way that's so obvious to myself and others. I'm starting to experience joy in such a way I truly believe will never leave my heart; it's almost like joy is growing inside of me from one day to the next. I can truly feel The Presents of God's Holy Spirit as I sit here in my room and write! It's now 5:05am, and God's Holy Spirit woke me up at 3:44am, not even two hours have passed and God Has Touched my heart and soul in such a way I shall never forget. Nothing in my life has the power and ability to inspire me like God's Holy Spirit Does, and it's been happening to me frequently now! Blessed am I, to be conscious of Father God's Spirit in this way, only possible by God Himself!

172. God, The Positive Constant

The residue from the selfishness of my desires still has an effect on my being, and I'm so grateful to Have Had The Holy Spirit of God Point this out to me upon an early morning wake up! I can never abandon the spirit of honesty; for the evil one patiently waits to move into my heart with an arsenal of deception. Every night from the tenth hour to the twelfth hour, the evil one, and The Forces of Evil launch their attacks upon my mind with their mental thoughts of projections, I've been monitoring their actions for years now. Only by constantly seeking The Holy Spirit of God have I been able to not fall into the actions from the evil one's temptations! Satan has no power over me; however, he will never stop trying to make me fall away from my Maker! This is why I stress constant seeking of The Trinity; for Satan and The Forces of evil will never cease in trying to destroy The Creation of God, and humanity is included in Satan's plot for destruction! I can feel the disgust from the evil one as I continue to push this pen; for The Spirit of God Is my Perfect Protector, Provider, and Guider, and this angers the evil one oh, so greatly! This is the evil that confronts me on a daily, sometimes moment to moment basis; however, I've learned not to turn away from The Most Holy One of Israel! Now it's eleven fifty-four pm, and I'm starting to feel better in my whole being, this is the reality of what I go through each and every night! It's ok; for I trust my Maker and God Has Never Lied to me. No, not one time in what He Said, or Says from His Mouth, and I hold onto it for dear life; for The Lord

God Is Truthful and Faithful. God Has Done for me what I could have never done for myself! In my life salvation is evident for me, and I am truly blessed by God to actually see this and live by God's Words in the midst of all this evil, in this world!

173. True Obedience

I don't believe in coincidences, I couldn't get any real sleep, so I finally got up, and the clock showed it was three eleven am, I opened my Bible to the page I was to continue my studies, and where I stopped was at the crucifixion of The Lord, and Master Jesus Christ! Until this morning I never knew that they put Him on the cross at three am. Now I know why I am almost at every time awakened somewhere within the third hour of the morning! The Spirit of God Covers All Areas once you make yourself ready to receive the information, and nothing, or nobody can teach you better than God! Nobody in their right mind wants to die, yet The Lord, and Master Jesus Christ Knew that He was not only just going to die, but rather be brutally murdered! Right before they arrested Jesus, He Prayed Deeply three times to ask Father God if the cup of death be taken from Him. So you see He didn't want to be brutally murdered; however, this brutal murder of Jesus Christ was The Will of Father God! By Jesus Christ Following The Will of Father God; God Has Made Jesus Christ The Determinator of who gets Eternal Life, or Eternal Damnation! Jesus Christ Received Glorification from God Himself and the seat at The Right Hand of Father God. All This; for Jesus Christ Turned not Away from what The Creator of All Life Asked of Him. This is the perfect model for the lives of people who have faith and trust in The Spirit of God! The order was a very tall one; for even Jesus Christ Asked Father God if He Would Change His Will; for Jesus Christ, and anyone in their rightful mind wants not to give up the precious gift of life! I thank God Himself for Allowing me to place this message in the proper place, at the proper time!

174. The Holy Spirit of God

Blessed are those to whom The Holy Spirit of God Comes to, or Reveals Itself to! The Holy Spirit of God Is Present in the world, standing ready to help those who seek The Trinity. The Holy Spirit of God's Work Is Never Done when it comes to Being Compassionate and Showing Mercy and Grace to all of humanity! The personalities of people are oh, so various; however, to become holy and acceptable to The One and only God, one must travel a very narrow pathway! People will hate you and your presents, while you sit in a room with non-seekers of The Holy Spirit. Your presents makes them uncomfortable and the seekers of God will know of it! The Holy Spirit of God lives in, or visits your temple, or he doesn't. The Holy Spirit of God Resides with the humble souls. Most people don't ever consider communicating with The Holy Spirit of God, they are too busy trying to grab up all they can out of this world with no thoughts of what God Will Do, or Say about their behavior! A lot of people self-deceive themselves and say to themselves and others, there isn't any such thing as a Holy Spirit of God! I concern myself with them not; for these passages I write are for the believers of and in The Holy Spirit of God. The Holy Spirit of God, Is oh, so Gentile and Kind; He was sent to the world to be The Helper and Guide for those who are in distress from The Evil Forces that be. The Holy Spirit of God Stands as a Position of Strength and Hope to the known believers and worshipers of Father God, and The Son of Man – The Lord, and Master Jesus Christ! The One and Only

God Himself Has Blessed me to uplift this message in this way for this generation and the ones to come. The Holy Spirit of God Guides my every step; for I've humbled myself to ask Him! There is no shame in me whatsoever for depending upon my Holy Spirit of God!

175. The Road to Salvation

God Said He Made man in His Own Image, and I believe this statement with no doubts from within my heart; however, the weaknesses of man is oh, so great, and the sickness of man's soul is even greater! As I further humble myself under The Mighty Hand of God, I can see the once boldness of my ego that was a huge part of my personality. The heights of my ego at times was so great that I use to taunt people. As I look back at my behavior I was insane and out of control for many years! This Spiritual Sickness which I was consciously unaware of has damaged myself and others with mental and emotional affects that time has no power over! The only way to a cure was through God Himself. I had to seek The LORD God, and ask Him to heal me, and then and only then did God Answer my prayer. The asking had to come from the sincerity of my heart; and at the time I was a very sick man. The Good LORD God Has Returned me to the soundness of my mind, I no longer taunt people with my abilities, and I am aware of my recklessness without the continual Guidance from God's Holy Spirit! Holy Is The Spirit of God, All Goodness Comes from God, He Is The Only Good! It's obvious I still have the breath of life; for I'm writing these words, and while I write, I must never forget the weaknesses, the spiritual sickness, and The Forces of Evil that all engulf this world, and all men are affected by them! It's only by The Power of God, can these things be arrested, I myself have been relieved of much evil; however, The Worship of my Father God shall never end from me; fore It's only from God that I've Received Peace of Mind and Calmness in my heart and soul. God Himself Is The Salvation that Eludes most people.

176. The Heart of The Son

The Son of God, Is The Heart of God, all goodness flows from God! His Coming to earth Has Delayed the coming of the new order from God Himself! The Christ Gave His Life, so that all men could have the chance of the promise of Eternal Life. The Lord, and Master Jesus Christ Has Further Gravitated my heart to repentance from my selfish self; I've thought about myself and what's in it for me far too long! Jesus Christ's Life Is An Ongoing Example of how to treat people who breathes the same air as myself. There is no flaw in the actions of His Deeds; He Was of Service to the poor, A Healer of the sick, and A Teacher of how to become holy and acceptable to Father God. Nothing Did He Leave Uncovered while He Walked the earth. He Did His Job to Fulfill The Holy Scriptures, and He Turned Not Away from Father God's Will! His Obedience to Father God's Will Has Inspired me to do the same thing; for God Has Given me a job to do also! After The LORD God Had Risen Jesus Christ from the dead and Glorifying Him by Saying, "Sit Here by My Right Hand, Until I Make Your Enemies Your Foot Stool." I know in my heart that Jesus Christ Does Obey Father God, but The Goodness of His Heart, Makes It Hard for Him to Standby; for the prayers of the many are oh, so great! Even in heaven The Lord, and Master Jesus Christ, Still Obeys The Will of Father God! Even while Sitting on His Throne, The Lord, and Master Jesus Christ, Is Still at Work Doing Good Things, for His Sheep; for He Told Peter after He Had Been Risen from the dead. "Peter continue to feed my Sheep." That was just one of the many directions, The Lord, and Master Jesus Christ Has Given to the people who have taken to themselves the life of obedience, to The Father of All Creation!

177. There's No Better Care

The Spirit of The Living God Has Forgiven me of oh, so many things; I am His Slave Forever! I know surely in my heart that The Spirit of God Has Protected me from destruction more times then I'm consciously aware of. The Holy Spirit of God Lets me know that He Is Present through many signs that I've been Allowed to see through the years! These convictions of The Holy Spirit of God's Presents, has truly sent my mind into amazement from the very first time The Holy Spirit of God Revealed Itself to me and every time after the first! I stay alert now to the times when The Holy Spirit of God Will Reveal Itself to me; God's Spirit Teaches me what I need to do from one day to the next now. The relationship between my soul and God's Holy Spirit has been growing; for I've been putting into practice what The Holy Spirit of God Is Revealing to me. I'm changing at a very steady pace, I feel The Structured Beauty from my Maker, as He Molds my soul from the inside out. The Holy Spirit of God Knows All Things and He Instructs me concerning all things, including directing my thoughts and actions when it comes to interacting with people. This Willingness to first listen, and then take proper actions has taken me years to put into practice; fore I was a wayward soul, and I had to learn the lesson of respecting boundaries the very hard and painful way. There is no doubt in my heart and I know intuitively that The Holy Spirit of God Has Been Protecting me all the days of my life. God's Spirit Is The Sole Reason I am transformed from the way I use to think and act! As I wrote earlier I am His Slave forever, and there is no shame in me for saying it. Nothing in this evil place has treated me better, or cared about my welfare, other than The Holy Spirit of God!

178. What God Gave Me

God Has Given me the beauty of the beginnings of the spiritual realm; learned men and people in positions of worldly fame, all fall way short of what God Has Allowed me to experience! God's Goodness in Itself Sends my mind into wonderment, it brings gladness and joy to my heart, not to forget to mention peace to my soul, all at once in an instant of pondering God! Nothing is more important than obeying The LORD God's Will for my life and the lives of others; blessed am I for having a listening ear, an open mind, and an obedient heart, all attuned to The Will of Father God. The LORD God Is Able to Accomplish Anything within the lives of His Children; nothing is too hard, or too difficult for God to Fix! I can, and will stand by the last statement; for I've personally seen God's Spirit at Work within people, and I've seen God's Spirit at Work outside of people to help people. God Has Made All Life Possible, He Is The Giver of All Life, He Desires the demise of nothing, or no one, God Is The Enhancer of All Life, not the destroyer! In spite of this evil world I was born into, The God of All Life Is Able to Transmit Joy to my heart, and Give me Hope of The New Order from Himself. Every time I seek The Lord God, He Gives me a new tool to add to my tool box for life, or He Instructs me to pick up the old tools and use them when I forget I already have them. God, Always Brings a smile to my face, even if I'm upset; for I've learned to trust God, and I know in my heart that God Himself Is The Cause not for why this world has taken the path that it is on. So I will continue to seek Father God The Only Good, and continue to humble myself, for without God's Perfect Guidance, I will lose my way. The way from Salvation and Eternal Life.

179. Jesus Christ Lives Forever

No ink will flow from the soul of a tired servant. So I will ask my Older Brother Jesus Christ for the strength to carry on with this assignment. Jesus Christ Never Turned Away from telling the truth; even though it may have caused bodily harm to Himself. The word integrity is what comes to my mind every time I ponder The Lord, and Master Jesus Christ! Jesus Christ's Spirit Speaks to my heart every time I get agitated about any situation that causes me to go to an extreme in my emotions. I'm very happy to report on how I rarely go to the extremes in my emotions, since my positive relationship with The Trinity has increased. Multitudes of people through the years from the ascension of Jesus Christ, have turned to Him in their prayers, others have placed their hands on other people to heal them in the name of Jesus Christ, while others have dedicated their lives, to follow Jesus Christ's Pattern of living. It's moderately know as living The Christ Life. Then you have the enemies of Jesus Christ all through the years from His Ascension to the present day, that despise Him! This is why Father God Told Jesus to "Sit here at my right side , until I Make Your enemies Your Foot Stool." Everything has its season, and the drama of this spectacle will surely have its climax! At the present time of this writing there are approximately seven billion people living on this planet. The Lord, and Master Jesus Christ's Name alone is known to at least six billion of them, and the other one billion people are too young to know who He Is yet. No other name in all of history is known to the many souls who lived and died, after Jesus Christ's Death and Resurrection, and those who are alive now have more recognition than The Name of Jesus Christ! The Lord, and Master Jesus Christ, Will Fulfill His Own Prophecy; for good will arrest, or destroy evil, this has been demonstrated throughout all of history. There will be no exceptions upon the process from Father God's Will!

180. The Reality of Many Souls

I am still here, and I'm here only by The Grace and Mercy from God Himself. God's Holy Spirit Is The Binder of This Universe! I don't know about many things; however, I can share about what I've experienced, and still have the opportunity to experience. God's Love and Goodness has no end; His Holy Spirit Will Respond to any soul who cries out for help! God Loved the world so much; He Sent His Holy Spirit to us, to Help and Guide the souls of the world, who truly desires to please Father God, and not continue to sin. The Holy Spirit of God Is Equipped with All Power to Assist the souls who sincerely seeks His Guidance. Unfortunately this world is engulfed with the evil one and all of his demons; most people of the world are contaminated by their presents and are spiritual sick as a result from their evil influences. This exposure is what keeps most people ignorant, or hostile to The Holy Spirit from God. Most people live their lives and leave this world ignorant of their Maker, or deceived by the evil one concerning what the reality is after death. Most people don't put in the effort to seek The Creator of All Things, unless they are in some kind of pain, then they pray the fox hole prayer, "oh God, please get me out of this jam!" Most times The Holy Spirit from God Responds, and Relieves their situation, and soon as the heat is turned down, or off they resume to what they were doing prior to their pain and forget all about God and How He Helped them. That type of attitude towards The Holy Spirit from God is practiced by oh, so many people! The Holy Spirit from God Is Kind and Merciful, and I've come to learn not to be disrespectful to His Great Mercy and Kindness. To really get to know The Spirit from God, one must seek God with all of their mind, heart, soul, and strength! Then and only then Will God Reveal Himself to you.

181. What Everyone Has

God, no one alive, or dead, knows Your Total Will, and God, no one ever will! The LORD God, Has Been Very Good to me, and I won't deceive myself, or listen to the manipulations of the evil one, or the evil doers! One may ask how can you accomplish that, when evil is all around you, and the ways of most everything in the world is run by the evil one? The only way to accomplish such a task is very simple; however, practicing the simple will have to become a way of life, and most people get caught up in the desires for worldly things which cast out the simple very quickly! This is why The Lord, and Master Jesus Christ Said, "What profits a man to gain the whole world, yet lose his very own soul." When it comes to God, I endeavor in no slick schemes to try and out maneuver what God Has Already Said what the outcome will be! In my heart as a child, all I really wanted to do was laugh, play, and have fun; however, as I grew older the fun turned into pain and confusion, and I forgot what it felt like to laugh, play, and have fun! Only by seeking my Father God, and following His Simple Way of Living, have I received again my child like heart, and now I laugh, play, and have fun again. God, Has Done for me Things I could have never accomplished on my own and for that I am oh, so grateful and glad. God, Is my friend that I'll never fully understand, and I really feel that's the way He Wants it to be, and that's perfectly fine by me. There is one thing nothing, or nobody can ever take from me, and that's the love I have for the unseen Father God! That's the beauty of love, and of all the intangible things, nothing, or nobody can separate you from them. This is just one of the true gifts, from Father God, that everyone has, who have life!

182. Not in Vain

Your Coming to earth wasn't in vain, Your Great Love will never fade; Your Disciples Continue to Grow, Your Lost Sheep are constantly being found. Your Banquet Grows nearer as the days and nights add up, while Your Words Continue to Pierce the hearts of many, as they vigorously seek the truth to what was always lied about! The Lord, and Master Jesus Christ's Life, Will Forever Stand, as the perfect example of being holy and acceptable to the One and Only Creator of all life! No way of living can outweigh His Example of compassion and selflessness! Even though Jesus Christ didn't want to be brutally murdered, He Still Obeyed The Will of The One and Only God. Most people from generation to generation have fallen short of what The One and Only God, Has Asked of them! The Lord, and Master Jesus Christ, was oh, so right, when He Said, "all have sinned." The Lord, and Master Jesus Christ, Came into the world to Give us the solution, to our sinful nature; however, the nation He was sent to failed to recognize who He was, and they brutally murdered Him, as it's so recorded! What's done is done and can't be undone; however, the true believers in Jesus Christ, can uphold the truth in every aspect of their lives, and carry the message of good news, concerning

Eternal Life, by following The Teachings of The Lord, and Master Jesus Christ! What was the truth 2012 years ago is the truth 2012 years later! Always know that the evil one, and The Forces of Evil exist, and they will always stand as liars and deceivers, just as they were in the time of The Lord, and Master Jesus Christ, as they are now, in the present time. The evil one will always be rampant, until God Himself` Arrests him, just as God Said He Would!

183. The Protector of God's Children

The Holy Spirit from God Is Everywhere at all times, nothing can happen without His Knowledge of the occurrence, this is just one of His Awesome Features! He Can Contact anyone, or Make Himself Known at any time; however, most people don't actually seek God! God's Holy Spirit Will Respond whenever a soul cries out for help; God's Holy Spirit Lovingly Watches Over all of humanity. I can't write about what I don't know; however, The Holy Spirit from God Makes Himself Known to those who constantly seek His Guidance! The Holy Spirit from God Won't Interfere into the lives of people, God's Spirit Is Oh, So Kind, He Is A Very Gentile Spirit. For years now I've been seeking The Spirit from God, and recently God's Spirit Has Been Communicating with me in ways that has totally relaxed my whole being. The Holy Spirit from God Is Manifesting Its Self through my whole body! Only the true seekers of God will be able to comprehend my experience; I've opened myself to have God Do As He Wills. Only The Spirit from God Knows What my fate will be, I wholly trust The Holy Spirit from God; I know in my heart that God Would Never Harm me. The Spirit from The Living God Comforts souls who have gone through the wringer of torture administered by the evil one, and The Forces of Evil. The Holy Spirit from God Has

Saved my life more times than I am aware of, and God Himself Has Brought this knowledge to the heart of my soul. I am no longer in the dark about the reality of the evil one, and The Evil Forces that be! The Holy Spirit from God Stands As A Protector for The Children of God; however, one must have faith that He Is Here, and Will Assist them in the matters that they have no power over; so believers in The Spirit from The Living God must carry on with the tasks God Has Given Unto them to do, and have no fear of the evil one, and The Evil Forces that be. The Spirit from God Will Protect you, so do your best to shrink not!

184. The Subject That's God

The subject of wonderment, the subject of controversy, the subject of doubts, and the subject that never ends, all this and more has run across the minds of countless of peoples who once had life, or still have life, and that subject is God! It has nowhere been recorded and proven that someone has ever seen God; it has been said that no one shall see God, and live. I truly believe The Holy Spirit of God Himself Is So Pure In His Being that it would kill any person in the flesh instantly, with His Awesome Light! It has been said that God Is The Unapproachable Light! Speaking for myself I don't need to see God Himself, God Has Already Been So Kind, to Allow me to see a great many other things that I know no fellow human being can even come close to describe what The Holy God Himself Has Allowed me to see. So that stops any doubts whatsoever that God Exists in my whole being, and its been that way for over three decades now! God Himself Spoke to me one time in a dream, after I almost lost my life physically, and I never doubted God's Existence from that time on! God, Is The Father of everything and until I realized this fact, I was always in fear; there was never a long period of time in my life that I actually felt safe and secure. I truly believe God Will Make Himself Known to anyone, who sincerely seeks the reality of His Existence. God Is The Point of Origin of everything in existence, and to try and imagine in your mind what is beyond God, can cause a person to lose his, or her mind! No one will know what happened to you, but God Himself. Asking God how to live the life He Has Given to you, and be successful without offending Him, or your neighbors is a task that will take real effort, and discipline. So what good is it to know where God Came from?

185. No Boundaries to Love

No one has been, or will ever be greater than The Lord and Master Jesus Christ! Known to record He Was and Is the only perfect person who has ever walked the face of the earth. Jesus Christ Was Given The Power from God Himself to heal the sick people of the world, and there was a lot of sickness then, as it is now. He Was of Service to the poor and Still Is, He Had Compassion for many, and He Still Does, no other man has come to earth and left that has greater authority! This is why He is called The Lord, and Master Jesus Christ! Not only did He Heal the sick, and Cast Out demons from peoples bodies, and Raised the dead, He Also Taught people how to live wherever He went, and to uphold the Decrees God Has Already Placed before them, from the prophets who have been sent before Jesus Christ! I write these accounts about my Older Brother Jesus Christ in an effort to stimulate the minds, hearts, and souls of many people of the time that is now; for Jesus Christ hasn't returned yet, and it's been over two thousand and eleven years since they hung The Son of God on a tree! The Spirit of God Is So Kind to have Allowed all of this time to have elapsed; for in so doing He Has Given the opportunity to so many souls to live and repent, and place before them the chance for Eternal Life! All praise is do due to The Trinity. There is no greater love for this world, than the love Father God Displays for us. First of all He Created us, and in our denial of following truth and justice, He Still Loved us, mankind became so wicked and vile, God Then Destroyed the earth's inhabitants; however, He Left us a remnant through Noah, and the years passed and the earth repopulated itself, then God Sent us His Son, The Lord, and Master Jesus Christ, and the evil one that's still present in the world rallied sinful men to kill His Son, God, Still Loved us by Sending in Jesus Christ's Place The Holy Spirit, and this is where we stand at the present time!

186. By Faith in Seeking

Always on the watch, always ready to assist, nothing is beyond its reach, this is the gift from God Himself to the world, the gift of The Holy Spirit, to help the children who believe in God! Only a hand full of people on the earth are truly aware of The Holy Spirit's Presents! Most people are ignorant to know that The Holy Spirit from God Was Sent to the children of God, to help them with guidance while living in this evil infested place.

One must truly believe The Holy Spirit from God Is Truly here to help us, most people don't believe that, or even have a clue that The Holy Spirit from God even exist! The Evil Forces that be uses the fact that The Holy Spirit from God remains from the sights of many to say there is no such Spirit, you can't see it, so it's not real! Many have been deceived by listening to such lies; so then people believe they have no Spiritual help! These lies have been told to countless souls. Some people are so deceived to believe that there isn't any God either.

For a very long time I tried to get people to see what I see; however, I've come to learn from The Holy Spirit Speaking to my heart saying, the things I can see came from my very own faith. So now I've come to the point that I don't try and break my back to get people to see the reality of God's Presents; however, I'll go to great lengths to write about it, and those who are blessed to venture into the seeking of God's Spirit, through their faith will be moved, and perhaps this will be honored by The Spirit from God, and God Himself!

I've truly come to learn how God Himself Allows us to make mistakes, so that eventually after all the things we have tried fail us, then we truly move to seek The Spirit from God with a sincere heart, and when this is done, The Spirit from God, Shows us evidence that He is here and has been here before we were even born. If a person reaches this experience in their life, they will be moved to look at many things in this life oh, so differently, it may be the ticket of truth, for that person to be reborn!

187. Where my Heart Is

Intelligence without a body as we human beings know it, this is what a spirit is, totally a reality of what we human being can be someday. The process might take a million years; however, right now human being are in their infant stage! God, Is The Head of everything, and it's only by His Will that anything comes into being or not! God Is where may heart is, and anyone who truly knows me, knows this to be actual and factual. I make no changes in my day to day actions, unless I ask Father God in meditation. Father God Watched Over me my whole life, it's only in the last seventeen years of my life that God Has Blessed me to consciously know this fact on a day to day basis. I know in my heart with no one to actually tell me that I am a very blessed soul; most people don't take advantage of the opportunities that Father God Places Before them so that they may get to consciously experience His Will for their lives, along with His Holy Presents! I don't personally know how God Approaches people; however. I know that God Is Generous and Kind, and He's that way even to the ungrateful and that's something I've seen with my own eyes! In my life when all things went sour, I sought Father God for help, and I received help, and as time moved forward I kept seeking God, and I never stopped the seeking of Father God Himself, and God Kept right on Positively Guiding me through everything that has come into my life, positive, or negative. Now I've passed the point of no return, I look to nothing, or nobody for anything, I trust wholly Father God! I know that I am human and I need human companionship; however, I've learned to make boundaries, for all human beings are fallible, and this isn't so when it comes to Father God. God, Has Never Sought to hurt me in any way; God Is my Perfect Protector, Provider, and Guider, and I love God with all of my heart, soul, mind and strength, all of the time and forever!

188. Bonded to Eternal Life

Oh, how I constantly Thank Father God for sending me in meditation to go and seek His Son The Lord, and Master Jesus Christ! God, Spoke to my heart and mind to do this after sixteen years of me constantly seeking out Himself, God Knew I was ready to receive The Teachings from His Son, Jesus Christ, The Determiner of who will receive Eternal Life, or Eternal Damnation! The Lord, and Master Jesus Christ Has Started to Saturate my body beginning with my feet; now He Has Begun to Work all through me, and I am oh, so amazed and grateful. I am full of zeal to listen to The Lord Jesus, as He Teaches me from minute to minute! He Shows me to continue to humble myself under The Mighty Hand of Father God Himself, something I have no trouble in doing. There are other parts in my heart, The Lord, and Master Jesus Christ Is Having me to take a serious look at, and it's going to take surrender on my part, and a stepping out on faith from me also. I must learn to obey Jesus when it comes to interacting with my brothers and sisters, and especially our enemies! If I am to trust Jesus, as I Trust God, well then I must obey His Decrees also; I can't obey some things He Teaches, I must obey them all! I already know in my heart that matters will turn out for the best; for there is nothing my Father God Can't Do, and if it calls for my heart to further soften itself, well then so be it! I am Father God's Son, and I am The Lord, and Master Jesus Christ's Lost Sheep that has been Guided home, by Father God Himself! As of this writing I am reborn, never to taste Spiritual Bondage again!

189. Destiny Foretold

All that is hidden, all that is unknown, all that is inconceivable, this is the core of The Holy Spirit from God Himself! This has frustrated the evil one before man was even created; and it propels the evil one, and The Evil Forces that be, into an obsession to gain access to all of what God Already Knows! The Wisdom of The Holy Spirit from God, Has no boundaries; God's Holy Spirit is timeless as well, there is no conquer of His Holy Spirit! All things are possible through God's Holy Spirit, all He Has To Do Is Will it, and Whatever His Will Is, Comes into being, or out of existence! I can't report anything about my Maker without His Allowance. God Guides all of my steps; fore I am His Son, and I am bonded in His Holy Spirit Eternally. There is nothing that can occur without The Holy Spirit of God's Knowledge of it, all things are laid bare before God's Holy Spirit, only a fool thinks that God Doesn't See! People who know who God Is, and still defy His Decrees, their punishment will be greater than people who didn't know. The Holy Spirit of God's Creation is Governed by Perfect Order, and to defy that order drums up chaos, and this world that I am currently living life in is in oh, so much chaos, as a direct result from defying The Perfect Order of God's Creation! Thus we have the evil one, and The Evil Forces that be, who help corrupt Man's Existence from the very beginning. God's Holy Spirit, Can't be overcome; His Will for humanity will take its course, no matter how much it's tampered with by The Evil Forces that be, as a matter of fact the evil one, and The Forces of Evil are included in the destiny of mankind's unfolding! The Holy Spirit from God Will Bring Perfect Order to earth, just as He Proclaimed it within The Holy Scriptures.

190. My Father God

I never went hungry, I always had clean clothes to ware, I haven't been mistreated by people constantly, I have hope! All these conditions were supplied to my soul by Father God! I am almost fifty years old, and Father God Still Supplies my every need and more, I don't take anything for granted; for if Father God Didn't Lookout after me I would have been physically dead a long time ago, or wished I were dead. This world at the present time is filled with The Forces of Evil; however, in desperation I sought The Living God, and God Showed up and entered my heart. He Showed me what I had to do, God Gave me hope, God Knew exactly what I needed , and He Still does almost seventeen years later, since I first sincerely sought His Assistance. I've learned to filter out my feelings; for this is how I make better decisions. In filtering out my feelings, I've found precious principles to live my life by. I've also realized that the love from Father God Was and Is Residing in my heart! This let me know that I belonged to Father God before I was even born! This new found knowledge has changed my whole being; my identity has finally been uncovered, I know who I am now, and I know what I must do. I've been living all wrong by competing with my brothers and sisters, instead of being of service to them. I'm Father God's Son, my Father Has Revealed my identity to me; whereas The Evil Forces that be, and the evil one has successfully hid the truth from me for over three and one half decades! Father God through those decades tried to get my attention many times; however, I was a slave to sin, and the most God Could Do Was Protect me from death, until I came to the end of myself! The end of myself was so painful; for the reality of what my life had become devastated me, and there was nobody in my life who truly loved me, only Father God. God Showed His Love by what He Placed before me, and every day after His Direction, I never stopped seeking my Father God!

191. The Appointment

I Always knew something was a part of me, but I could never understand what it was! I always tried to fit into places socially and I would never fit. What was wrong? I asked myself this question for twenty-five years, and I never got an answer that I felt was the correct answer; until my Father God Gave it to me one day after a meditation session. The answer was that I belong to Him, I was not of the world, even though I'm in the world! Immediately I knew the answer was the correct one, all parts of my past life fit perfectly to the answer I received from Father God! Father God Is Perfect in all things, He Knew the proper time to reveal the truth to my heart without me being further deceived by The Evil Forces that be. It took all the experiences of my interactions in life to be able to recognize the truth, when it was revealed to me. Father God Has Given me an assignment, and within my assignment, I was told to seek The Teachings of The Lord, and Master Jesus Christ, and by following Father God's Directions, The Spirit of Jesus Came Upon me, and His Spirit Has Entered into my heart, and Has Begun to Saturate my whole being. I've come to learn my feelings don't lie, only the evil one and The Forces of Evil do the lying through their mind projections, and the evil ones that are their children.

The Devils Kids are amongst God's Children, they tell their lies all the day and night long, causing pain and confusion all throughout the world. Only The Trinity do I wholly trust, as well as it should be in the reality of the world that is now! The Lord, and Master Jesus Christ Is Now the new director of my actions, appointed by Father God Himself.

192. Seek to Find

On the scene, but unseen, in the world, but not from the world, this is The Holy Spirit from God, Sent by God, to Assist The Children of God, until the new order from God, unfolds. The Holy Spirit from God, Stays Hard at Work, Serving The Children of God, and most of God's Kids aren't even aware of The Holy Spirits Presents. I know this as being actual and factual; for The Holy Spirit from God, Has Been Protecting me all of my life, and He Will Continue to be of Service to me; for Father God, Has Sent Him to protect me! He Protects All of God's Kids, I've been Blessed by God Himself to be a witness of His Services. Jesus Christ Was Right, when He Said, "he who belongs to God, hears what God Says, the reason you don't hear is because you don't belong to God." That statement justified the presents of the evil one's kids, they are present all over this world, and they are masters of deception.

The persecution of God's Kids will continue, all the way up to the last day, this has already been foretold. I write these truths for the benefit, of The Children of God, so they may take courage, and seek out The Holy Spirit from God, and He Will Guide them in their day to day lives, and supply them with the things they may need to stand against The Forces of Evil, the evil one and his children. Only God Himself Have The Power and Ability to handle The Forces of Evil, the evil one, and his children, don't try and take them on with your own power; for you will fail, this is war, and it's God's Fight, and we must do The Will of our Father God in this war, the only way to find out what that is for your life is by constantly seeking Father God, and He Will Reveal to you, what you must do!

193. Another Message From The Narrow Road Walker

Men have spent almost all of their lives in search of You, whole nations have gone to war over the sanctity of Your Being and Your Name, and yet most of the worlds people still don't know who

You are, or what Your Purpose Is, and millions of people lost faith in You, and died that way! It's a very narrow road that leads to Father God, and most people don't stay on that narrow road. They lose all interest in the things they can't physically see, and then they wonder off into the seeking of worldly treasures and pleasures. Jesus Christ Was Surely Right, when He Said, " Blessed are those who endure to end." He meant those souls who repented from their wrong doings, and sought out to practice for themselves all of the decrees set forth before man, by Father God Himself. They, in turn, would be rewarded for their obedience; for Father God Is Truthful and Faithful in all the things He Proclaims. The Forces of Evil and the evil one greatly desire to keep The Children of Father God in confusion and fear, they never cease at this function of corruption! Father God, and the orders that He Has Already Laid out for living is the only way to salvation for our souls; for those who aren't God's Kids, can't hear anyway. They will be known by their acts; for they won't have the love of Father God in their hearts, only the concerns for money and positions of power and prestige, this is how God's Kids can recognize the enemies of God, and themselves. Kids of the devil are living right amongst us; don't continue to be deceived by them, unless you don't care about your life after this natural one. I assure you our enemies will also try and deceive us about the afterlife also! These are the things our Father God Has Blessed me to see, and Give warnings about; for I am His Son and Servant, at this particular time in this drama of mankind's existence!

194. Gifts From Father God

I've been awarded the most highest award that I'll ever receive, I was invited to learn from the very best, I'm overwhelmed daily, by the knowledge and wisdom that is being placed before me, oh, how Father God Is Showing His Love for me. I've been Shown by my Older Brother Jesus Christ to continue to humble myself under The Mighty Hand of Father God; this is the wisdom that has been transmitted to me, and I'm oh, so grateful. The things that have been happening in my life are blessings that only The Maker of this world is capable of giving; my whole being is being transformed to a level of consciousness that's only God Given and I am humbled out by the experiences. My feelings now are like I know The Creator of All Life Is Mindful of my actions; so I can't disappoint Father God no matter what. I know that Father God Knows I am human, and that I will make mistakes; however, I feel in my heart that God Wants me to give all of myself when it comes down to the tasks He Places before me. The LORD Father God, Has Been Patient and Kind to me all of my life; the lest I can do is be a sharp tool for God to use, and the most I can do is to keep myself that way always. The only way I can accomplish this is to never turn away from seeking God, no matter what transpires in my days and nights, this principle is the key to growth and prosperity ; for nothing or nobody can teach you better than Father God, this has been my experience in looking to Him, for over fourteen years day and night, without missing a day, or night of seeking Him! So this is the truth that I know about Father God, God, Is Able and Willing to Help me with any situation that may come up in my journey of growing! All I do is what God Said to Do long ago; "ask, and it shall be given to you, seek and you shall find."

195. God's Will For My Life

This message will stand throughout all time, and I tell it for the benefit of the believers in God and in God's Holy Spirit. After many years of seeking God, and asking Him what is His Will for my life? The Lord, answered my question, and the answer immediately placed joy, in my heart; for I somehow knew I was being guided correctly by Father God. The Holy Spirit from God Started Speaking to my mind in meditation sessions, and everything The Most Holy Spirit Whispered to my mind, came to be the truth, and the occurrences humbled me to God Himself. The days and nights went on by, and then I started to have problems with my feet, the circulation wasn't going through like it used to, and one day in meditation The Spirit from the Lord God Said to me, "fear not; for it is I Who Am Manifesting my Spirit in you, through your feet, and when you feel your body shake it is I." Now all I have to do is think about anything pertaining to God, Jesus Christ, or The Holy Spirit from God, and I'll feel Them in my body! Mainly in my feet and legs, or my body will shake, all of this has happened to me, and for me; for the sake of my soul, I truly trust and love The Trinity.

There has been no greater experience that happened in my life besides what God Himself Told me in a dream, when I was a very young man, after I almost lost my life. So you see The Holy Spirit from God, and God Himself, Has Been Protecting my soul all my life, and when I made myself ready, His Holy Spirit, Was Charged to Reveal to me even greater things, by way of God's Holy Will. I know within my heart that The LORD God Has Even Greater Things to Reveal to me at the proper time of God's Holy Will!

196. A Reminder of What Will Happen

I don't believe it, it's a miracle, it's unexplainable, these are the things that are said by people who are ignorant to the presents of The Holy Spirit from God when He performs His Work in the lives of His Children, or believers. God Himself Stays in the fore fronts of my mind ninety percent of the time when I am conscious; He is where I get my strength to handle all of life's situations. It took a long time in my life before I became willing to seek out The Living God, I consider myself blessed by Father God; for He Allowed me the time it took, for me to come to the end of myself. This was the only way I believe in my heart I could have become able to sincerely seek out God's Assistance. God Is Thorough in all He Does, never is something half done when it comes to The Creator of All Life! I've come to learn not to worry; for God Told All of His Children Not to Worry about the present condition of the world; however, He Told us to Carry Out all of His Decrees, and to watch for His Coming; for we don't know the hour He Will Choose to Come!

I truly feel in my heart that Father God, Wishes to hurt no one, or see anyone perish, but the reality is, people will get hurt, and they will perish. I don't say this of my own accord, it's written in The Holy Scriptures that this must happen to rid the world of evil, once and for all, so this writing stands as a warning and a reminder to The Children of God. Take heed and repent if you haven't already, and if you have repented, well then use this message as a reminder that God Is Faithful and True, and He Will Carry Out what He Has Already Proclaimed, now make yourselves ready in His Sights, so that on The Last Day, you will be blameless of any wrong doings! Remember our Father God Is Just and Kind, and He Awaits His People to humble themselves under His Mighty and Powerful Hand! So don't allow yourselves to leave this world, without being blameless concerning God's Decrees.

197. The Full Armor From God

The truth can be hidden only but for so long, confusion amongst God's Children little by little will come to an end. The Evil Forces that be, will start to consolidate their strength throughout the world! Outrightly the children of the devil will publicly denounce my Older Brother, The Lord, and Master Jesus Christ; for Jesus Christ, Is The Way, The Truth, and The Life. The Children of The Lord God, and the believers in God, will understand the words that are written in this passage; however, the evil doers will shun what is written here. Evil always flee from The Only Good that is God all the time, and in the end this will be the undying truth! The Teachings from The Lord, and Master Jesus Christ, Stands as the pathway to Eternal Life; however, the evil one, and all of his family members will use every opportunity to steal God's Goodness away from the masses of people; fore they are already convicted and doomed, by The God of All Created Life. The Forces of Evil, and the evil one want their outcome to be the outcome for most of humanity! Father God, Has The Power of life and death, The Evil Forces that be, and the evil only have the power of death, they can't create life, only The LORD God, Can Create Life! God Created All Life, including Satan's, and all of his family members, and The Lord God Will Have The Last Say About Everything, so don't get caught up on the wrong side of God's Judgement; fore that day will surely come, just as sure as I'm writing these words! Children from God must put on the full armament of protection from God, in order not to be burned by Satan's Fiery Arrows; once this is done , God's Kid's, can withstand anything the evil one, or his family members may attack them with. The Armament is available from The Teachings of The Lord, and Master Jesus Christ!

198. Now I Can See

Oh, how blind the masses of people are concerning The Living God! Most people don't have God's Holy Spirit, Burning in their hearts, and Living with them from day to day! This is the reality of the condition of many people that had life, and are now deceased, and the condition of most of the world at the present time, they don't know The Spirit from The Living God and God's Holy Spirit Burns Brightly not in their hearts, from day to day! This isn't to say that God's Holy Spirit is held away from them, on the contrary God Himself Has Said it many times in the Holy Scriptures, and it has been said by The Lord, and Master Jesus Christ. In order to get to know God, one must seek The Kingdom of God. This is the condition that God Has Set Before His Created Beings; however, oh, so many won't seek The Kingdom of God, and The Holy Spirit from God! I see the powerlessness of my own soul, as I see how many people are walking around in darkness and fear; for I know by my own experience that only The Trinity Is Able to Enlighten their souls. These are just the people I see, in the small area I live; however, I know darkness covers this whole world and some places are in more darkness than others but darkness is still in command! This is the reality of Father God's World at the present time; even though God's Perfect Order isn't being practiced by all of the inhabitants, God, Continues to Grace His People and Show Great Mercy to others! I as His Son will continue to obey The Trinity. Father God Himself Has Done for me what I could have never done by my own direction, I was blind and The LORD God Has Graced me to see, there is no power in all of existence more powerful and Kinder than Father God Himself, this is my experience that grows from day to day in conformation of The Holy Spirit from God!

199. It's So Simple

There is never a stoppage of glory when it comes to the assessment of The LORD God Himself! The evil one constantly provides lies to our minds, telling us that it's time to look to other things, rather continue seeking The LORD God Himself for whatever we may come to need in our daily living! The evil one and his family will never cease in trying to deter us from following Father God. This is the undying truth that I've experienced and seen through the lives of my brothers and sisters for a good portion of my life. Upon the arrest of The Forces of Evil, the evil one, and all of his family members will be a joyous day indeed, The Glory of our Father God on that day will overwhelm every man, woman and child who has ever believed in God Himself! Until then we Children from God must never turn our hearts away from Father God no matter what; nothing in this world, or outside of it should be more important to us than our Father God! We as God's Children must stand as a unified force in God's Holy Spirit, it should matter not wherever we may be in this world, our whole deportment must state – Bonded in The Eternal Living God! Once this happens to anyone of God's Kids, they become living torches of light, and The Forces of Evil will do their utmost to extinguish them! This has been recorded all throughout history, it's nothing new; this is what people fear, so they won't confess their true hearts in public; for they have the fear of losing their lives! This is what Jesus Christ meant when He said, "those who try and save they lives will lose it, and those who lose their lives for My Sake, shall find it." This is the simplicity of our existence; either we stand as Children of The Living God, or we become silenced to the death, by The Evil Forces that be!

200. God's Will, I Will Obey

Jesus Christ Is The Answer to our Eternal Souls; it's of no matter if you believe in Him, or not; He Has already been Glorified by The One and Only True God, with many witnesses watching Jesus Christ Ascending to the heavens within a cloud, after being brutally murdered by sinful men! Jesus Christ Has nothing to gain by our obedience, or not; His Suffering is over, even though His Compassion for our well-being is so great, He never stops like His Father in Giving! The Lord, and Master Jesus Christ Truly Cares about the poor and exploited people, and the numbers are countless. I myself am among the sick and suffering souls; however, I've learned to not stop seeking The Living True God, and God Has Blessed me to seek out His Son Jesus Christ, to further learn how I must live from one day to the next, until it's time to depart from this world! I've come to find there is no such thing as being safe and secure while The Forces of Evil are rampant and free! The Lord, and Master Jesus Christ, my Older Brother is constantly Showing me what I must do from one day to next, on how to be of service to my brothers and sisters, even to the enemies; for there is only One Judge, and He Sits in The Judgement Seat, and that Judge is Father God Himself! There was a time when my heart couldn't and wouldn't even come close to consider the things that The Lord, and Master Jesus Christ, Asks of us!

Only by constantly seeking The One and Only God, Has my heart been changed to consider The Teachings of The Lord, and Master Jesus Christ! Only goodness can come to my life now, as a direct result from obeying The Will from our Father God!

201. Out of True Love

The Holy Spirit from God Lives in my heart, my body, and my soul, as an appointment from God Himself! I don't try and figure out such things anymore; for I trust and don't analyze The Will of Father God! It's only in The Mind of God, why He Sent His Holy Spirit to me in the manner that I received Him! I don't question Father God, or His Holy Spirit, I humble myself to do Their Will! I truly am blessed, I know in my heart that most people don't get to see what I've seen, or most people don't get to experience what I have so far. I've always respected the truth, whether it was in general, or about myself, even if it hurt to know it, I've always respected it. Maybe this is why God, Gave me The Holy Spirit Himself; for He Is The Truth Bearer! Whether that's the reason, or not, The Holy Spirit from God Lives in me, and I am oh, so grateful. There is nothing I can do wrong now, and be innocent of my actions; for I possess The Truth Bearer inside of me, and He Will Testify for me ,or against me, this is the reality of my life now, and it's totally a beautiful thing! In every aspect of my life, Father God Has Always Been right on time and was never late, or early in any situation that I would come to face.

This is why I've come to wholly trust only The LORD God Himself; everybody and everything else has a boundary, as well as it should be! No one, or nothing can have a greater love for you, than The Holy Spirit from God Himself; for He Watches over you, and Protects you from The Evil Forces that be, the evil one, and all of his family members! There is no better protection to safeguard your soul, and Father God Himself Has Done this for me, out of His True Love for me.

202. God's Will Alive and Real

The Lord God Himself Has Truly Blessed me in every conceivable way, and ways that are inconceivable I'm sure! Nothing is impossible in accomplishing when placed before God Himself to achieve success. The greatest accomplishments from man is foolishness, in the sight of God! There is no need to be ashamed of the comparison, that's just the reality of what is; man was created by God, so how can anything man does, be even close to comparison to what God does? The Children of The Living God must learn to place God's Being in the proper place in their hearts, and leave Him there, and watch and observe how God Will Grow your souls through the confines of your hearts. There is nothing any human being can do, or not do, unless they first come from within themselves to advance on any action, or not! It sounds mechanical, but this is the process that happens; I use to try and figure out the outcome of things concerning The Will of God, and I always came up with the wrong answer to what God's Will Came Out to be. I wore myself out trying to match up correctly with The Will of The Living God; God Showed me that He's in a position with no company in sight, and it will always be that way; for He's The Creator of everything known and unknown, and I've come to see the reality of this truth! Everyone and everything falls short from God's Perfect Being; however, there are entities, The Evil Forces that be, and The evil one who desires obsessively to be The One and Only God, and all of them will meet their destruction, at the proper time, and it won't be for wanting to be God Himself, their destruction will come from their disobedience concerning their Maker, and for their mistreatment of God's people, who were deceived by them for thousands of years. There is no escape allotted to anyone, or any force, upon The Mighty Day of The LORD! This is the truth that every denier of

God will face, and their destruction will be oh, so great, I allow nothing to deceive me from this truth, that will one day come to be reality!

203. Leave Nothing Undone

Two thousand and twelve years have been recorded, since the devil's children have rallied themselves together to nail my Older Brother Jesus Christ to a tree, and from that time to the present time of this writing The Forces of Evil, the evil one, and his children have murdered, or persecuted anyone who took a stand for justice, or righteousness after The Lord, and Master Jesus Christ! Believers will Keep on believing and murderers will keep on murdering right up to The Glorious Day of The LORD. I write this for the benefit of The Children of God, and for the true believers in God Himself, never abandon your faith in The Trinity. The season of the deceivers, the murderers, The Forces of Evil, and the evil one will surely come to an end; for The LORD God of Hosts Is Faithful in all by what He Has Proclaimed. The end of the world happens every day for some people, so make certain for yourselves that your life is in correct order, so your soul won't suffer God's Coming Wrath! No matter if you are alive now, or soon to leave this life; everyone no matter what pathway they have taken in life, will reap what they have sown! This is The Order from God Himself, Who Has Created and Allowed all known life, as we human beings have life! God's Son, my Older Brother Jesus Christ Came into the world not as a proud scholar, on the contrary He Came as a Servant to the sick and afflicted people of this world, Jesus Christ also Came to Instruct us on how we need to repent from our sins, and to turn our hearts over to The One and Only Maker – God Himself! From the time of Jesus Christ until now, oh, so many souls have failed to live correctly and become holy and acceptable to God Himself; before their lives here on earth came to an end!

204. Results From God's Holy Spirit

This comes from God's Son, oh, Lord God I've made many mistakes in the life You've Given and Allowed me, I am overjoyed by Your Great Grace and Mercy LORD God; for You've Protected me oh, so many times! God, after my seeking You these last fourteen years constantly, You've begun to whisper to my mind oh LORD God, and I've become overwhelmed in my heart, and my soul has become glad again as if I were a child once more, all because my soul knows who You Are LORD God! Your Spirit LORD God Has Deadened my heart to pursue further the pleasures that are sought after by so many people who are of the world. I pray never to resist Your Spirit LORD God; God, You Raised me from death to life, Your Holy Spirit Has Rejuvenated my soul; for I was dead spiritually. LORD God, I am overjoyed with the assignment You've Given to me, and I've never experienced harmony like this since my youth! I am now bonded in Your Holy Spirit, and nothing of his world has greater importance to me! Life is precious and I love my life; however, I love You God more than my appointed life! There is nothing of this world that can ever take the place of the joy I am experiencing right now, and ever since the first time God, Your Holy Spirit Has Revealed Himself to me. All of what I've stated in this passage has truly happened to me. This isn't some tale to get some dollars; for money is none existent in the place that I shall one day return to, so brothers and sisters, stress yourselves not about anything that may comfort you down here. Always know that our Maker Is The Controller of everything here and after here, so serve one another, don't compete with each other!

205. God's Love and Protection

There is no place in the world I can go now without taking The Trinity with me, They Are Bonded into my soul, I am one with Them forever, God Himself, Graces my soul, for I still sometimes harbor old useless thoughts! Upon recognition of these negative thoughts, I'm learning to repent from them, and immediately ask God for forgiveness. God Knows I am human, and I will from time to time make mistakes; however, I must practice self-discipline, for the evil one always projects his evil and negative thoughts. God Himself Is The Only One Who Can Comfort my soul when I relapse and harbor negative and useless thoughts, and then act on them. Only God Himself Has Been Growing me and Giving me power to overcome my mental weaknesses; these weaknesses have plagued me all of my life! I must always continue to humble myself, under The Mighty Hand of God; and know in my heart that I have these weaknesses, and with God's Power and Direction I can overcome my known weaknesses. The Forces of Evil and the evil one have attacked my weaknesses all of my life; now I am aware of what has been a major problem for me in my life, God Himself Has Been Guiding me from the pit of destruction, the evil one has set for me! God Has Always Given me what I've needed, when I made myself ready to receive His Assistance! The LORD God's Patience Has Always Sent me into wonderment, asking the question to myself, does God, ever get angry? Well I truly don't ever want to find that out! All I know is that God Has Always Delivered whatever I've needed, even when I didn't know I needed assistance, and when I saw what I had, I was sometimes grateful. I am so glad that my attitude toward people, the world, and The LORD God has drastically changed for the positive better, only possible by my efforts of constantly seeking The One and Only God Himself!

206. From God's Hands

Thank You LORD God, Fore Giving The World Your Son, The Lord, and Master Jesus Christ! Even though You Knew The Forces of Evil, the evil one, and his children were going to brutally murder Jesus Christ! The haters that murdered Jesus Christ, are still at large, and their justice hasn't come yet, and they will continue to be jealous of all men, women, and children who continue to seek The Lord, and Master Jesus Christ! The more a person speaks the truth about The Trinity's Decrees, the more The Forces of Evil, the evil one, and his children will rally together to destroy physically the truth bearer! The true believers in Jesus Christ, will follow this principle. "Fear not those who can just take your physical life, but fear The One Who Can Punish you after your physical life has ended." I, who call Jesus Christ my Older Brother, have oh, so much to learn, I use to be a sinner, and a very sick person spiritually. I was called by God Himself to seek out The Lord, and Master Jesus Christ, and within each passing day I was Shown new things on how I must live my life now, so that one day I may become holy and acceptable to The One and Only God! The Lord, and Master Jesus Christ is my teacher; I must learn to obey the directions He Whispers to my heart to do. I will either obey the orders from Jesus Christ, or I won't, there is no middle of the fence; I'm either red hot, or ice cold! Jesus Christ Has Been Appointed by God Himself to be the judge over the living and over the dead; no one can change the decision The LORD God Has

Already Made. There is no one in heaven, or on the earth that has the power to deliver anything from out of The Hands of God! I truly feel genuine love after seeking The LORD God Himself faithfully for over fourteen years, and God Has Called me to seek out The Lord, and Master Jesus Christ, so that I may have a chance to receive Eternal Life!

207. The House of The Holy Spirit

The place from where perfect orders are derived, the place where there are no boundaries, the place that has no chaos, the place where there isn't any stress of any kind. This is The House of The Holy Spirit from God Himself! Within The House of The Holy Spirit from God, all knowledge of all things are stored; God's Great Power Has Created this world we live on, and everything outside of this planet. All existence is directed through, The Holy Spirit from God Himself; there isn't a single occurrence that goes unnoticed by God's Holy Spirit, so every action a person does is instantly known to The Holy Spirit from God! The Forces of Evil for thousands of years has lied to mankind, not revealing the truth about The Creator of All Existence; for These Evil Forces held and still holds a higher position than Mankind's Spirit, thus we have The Evil Forces that be, and the evil one, who still exploits all of humanity. Satan deceived Adam and Eve, and this is the connection to the curse from God Himself! My work is constant today; for I know who my Maker Is, and I listen to His Voice, not the voices from strangers. By seeking The Kingdom of God, I've found who The Holy Spirit from God Is, and He isn't something that is far off, on the contrary, He's Closer to me than my next breath of air. The true believers in God Holy Spirit will be in full harmony to all of what is written in this passage; at the proper time God's Will, Will be Carried Out, and it will be from God's Holy Spirit, that Will Commence all of the changes that Will be Ordered Up By God himself! This All is old information, I'm just giving an update to what will happen; for God Himself Has Charged me to pass on His Message, in this way, at this point in time!

208. The Resolves From The Lord God

Once again I am filled with resolve, there is no ending of God Himself, His Holy Spirit, The Lord, and Master Jesus Christ, or any subjects that are bonded in The Trinity! They are one, The Holy Spirit from God, Has Revealed this to my soul, and the enemies of God are furious; for they are banished from God's Holy Presents! Before God's Kingdom of The New Order Comes, everything here on earth will be in proper position; however, only God Himself Knows when the position will be proper. The Holy Spirit from God, Has Showed me through my feelings how enraged The Forces of Evil are without allowing them to hurt me, and God Holy Spirit Has Enabled this experience several times, now I truly know through my feelings, how The Forces of Evil truly desire to bind my soul, it's like someone restricting my movement in any direction, and when I call on God Himself, I am released! These experiences are resolves to my whole being that The Forces of Evil truly exist, just as The LORD God, truly exist also! I can't make anybody believe; however, I can share my experiences with my fellow travelers. Most of God's Children will take heed to what I share; for they know that what I share is the truth, and the children who aren't God's Kids will mock what I share! It's of know matter; for we are all numbered anyway and marked by God's Holy Spirit. In the event that some non-believers in God, and some children of the devil are turned to the truth, then and only then Will The LORD God Himself Turn to Heal them and Make their paths straight, The Power of The LORD God, runs oh, so deeply! There are always miracles Performed by The LORD God, so I've learned not to close my mind to what I may first experience, when I meet a person. God's Healing Power is Always at work, so I mustn't prejudice my heart towards anyone; for it's only my Father God, Who Sits in The Judgement Seat.

209. The Circle of Love

As God Himself Has Promised Abraham that He would make his offspring in numbers like the dust of the earth, so Is The Lord, and Master Jesus Christ, Is In Authority Over All Souls who have breathed and still breathes the breath of life! I truly believe as it's written about the souls who won't be able to enter, into heaven, and it's said there will be gnashing of teeth. I know in my heart I can't stop that from happening; however, it still troubles my heart, and I know if it troubles my heart, it troubles my Older Brother Jesus Christ's heart as well!

The most I can do with the life that I possess is constantly ask Father God to bless me in ways so I can be of service to my fellows, so that many of them won't suffer the fate, of the gnashing of teeth. I keep thanking Father God for Sending me in search of The Lord, and Master Jesus Christ; for God Knew my heart was ready to receive The Teachings from The Lord, and Master Jesus Christ! There are so many things I don't know, and I don't want to hurt anyone, in anyway, on the contrary I want to help people, so now I truly know why God's Holy Spirit Kept Whispering to my mind in meditation sessions to keep my focus on The LORD God, and not to turn to the left, or turn to the right, but to keep my focus on God Himself! I've been very paranoid for years and I've lived in fear of people for years, I didn't want to get close to people; for they always ended up hurting me in some way, so I learned to keep a good distance, I didn't let anyone get to close to me, because I really didn't want to hurt anyone, or them hurt me anymore.

This was the way I survived; however, now I wholly trust The LORD God, and God Has Turned me over to be further taught by His Son, The Lord, and Master Jesus Christ, and the first thing Jesus Christ pointed out for me to do, was to constantly humble myself under The Mighty Hand of God. I don't know about a lot of things, but God, Jesus Christ, and The Holy Spirit from God, are sure to me, to be a circle of love!

210. No Power From Me

I can't give away the gifts I possess from The Holy Spirit from God, not even to one single soul; however, I can describe to countless souls what The Holy Spirit from God, Has Given to me! I've written about the gifts, I've even told people who I truly respected what God Himself, Has Blessed me with, and it meant nothing to them.

They couldn't see what I see, or feel what I felt, as a result from what I can see! Only The Holy Spirit from God, Can Give to people, what He Has Given unto me; this reality has solidified itself within my heart. There have been so many times in my days and nights I've felt separate from my peers, and I've come to the conclusion that my feelings don't lie; however, I must positively respond to the gifts that God Himself, Has Given unto me, and I've learned that I must allow God, to be God, within myself at all times, and when I do this I get a better understanding of the gifts that God Himself, Has Given unto me! For over thirty-one and one half years The Gifts from Father God, hasn't changed; people, things, and situations have all changed and rearranged themselves, but God's Gifts have never left me.

Whatever God gives me I can depend on; however, what most people have given to me has always blown away with the wind. It took a lot of painful days and nights to realize the difference between the two; I always would get caught up in my emotions concerning God, and the people in the world around me. I've learned to separate God, people, and worldly things, this action has granted me peace in my heart, stability within my mind, and wisdom from God's Holy Spirit! The Holy Spirit from God, Is All Light, and The Forces of Evil are defiant of God's Holy Spirit, they flee from God's Light; for they love the way of defying God's Holy Order of things. This defiance of God's Holy Orders, is why the condition of this world is as it is, at the present time, and The Lord God Himself, Has Vowed, that the end to this world's present condition will come to an end!

211. The Truth About Our World

We are all from God's Perfect Light; however, many of us don't retain God's Holy Light, and we become shadows of our own ambitions ! Some of us have become so blinded by self-deception and conceit that we acknowledge God, The Maker not! Some will say there isn't any God, or I am the god of my existence! There is no humility in these people at all, concerning The Living Creator that's God Himself! This contamination will spread until the coming of The New Order from God Himself; no man, or no earthly power will stop this from occurring. There are intangible forces which influence the hearts of people, they act like a shield, to deflect God's Life Giving Light! The world is cloaked by these forces, and these forces are The Evil Forces that be. Mankind is totally powerless to rid the world of these evil forces; only The Creator of this world can perform such an act. Only by constantly seeking God Himself in meditation was I Graced to see the truth as it truly is, and like it's been so often quoted, "the truth shall set you free." I am free today to be ignorant not, to know what really is the cause of the sickness concerning the world as a whole. I shall never be faint of heart ever again; or become down trodden in my soul, and don't know why.

God Is The Unapproachable Light, and when I sincerely seek His Council, I am Enlightened with knowledge and wisdom that isn't my own, and I can't keep this knowledge to myself, I am Ordered by God Himself, to pass the knowledge onward to the human family. Once freedom is accomplished in the life of a person, and I mean their whole being, being free, that individual stands as a real threat to The Evil Forces that be.

If that person is diligent in his, or her work they can uncover the cloak of evil in the lives of many people; however, Father God, must always be their Guide; for The Evil Forces that be will stop at nothing to destroy the person, and they have an arsenal of ways to accomplish just that!

212. The Reality of God's Protection

I feel The Forces of Evil trying to partition the solidarity of my mind, concerning the assignment The LORD God Has Given unto me! My solution was to pause, and ask The Trinity for strength to refocus my energies on the task The LORD God Has Given unto me. The Forces of Evil, the evil one, and all of his family members always looks for weaknesses in my being, in an effort to exploit them! They have been in motion against my being as long as I can remember, there is no exaggeration in this description concerning These Evil Forces. Every day God Shows me that He Has Protected my life, and continues to do so, I'm just getting to see the facts concerning His Protection! We all have a destiny, mine is starting to uncover right in view of my day to day consciousness, The LORD God, Is Oh, So Amazing! The reality of my life is by The Mighty Grace of God Himself; it's only by God's Protection that I am alive to write these words. There were many days and nights I truly could have lost my life! There is no room in my heart and soul that promotes non-interference from God Himself! His Holy Spirit Was With me each and every day, just as He's Here With me now, as I write these words. The Evil Forces that be are present also, as I write these words; however, I am Protected by The Holy Spirit from God Himself, and all they are allowed to do is watch me, even though they never cease in projecting their Evil Mental Thoughts. Only The Holy Spirit from God Himself, Possesses The Ability to Protect me in the midst of all this evil that has surrounded me all of my life, even while I was in my mother's womb! I am almost fifty years old, and within each passing day now, I want more of God's Holy Presents, and to achieve this I must become more humble in my heart!

213. What I Truly Know

This is the truth that I've found to be oh, so real, and there is no denial in my heart whatsoever, and it has proven itself in my life, over and over again, and that is, "without God's Holy Spirit,

Pumping and Flowing through me, I am nothing, and I'll never feel right in myself ever." Living in this world hurts me most of the time; for I constantly seek The Kingdom of God, and God Reveals the truth about things, and the truth truly troubles my heart. I've been sick for most of my life, and all I have is my faith in God, and many unfulfilled dreams, this is how I know that without God, I am nothing! There is nothing in this world for me; however, God Himself, Gave me life, and no matter how unhappy I am, I will serve my Maker God, He's all I've got! Father God, and all of His Decrees, I've neglected for years; for I was a pleasure seeker, constantly looking to make myself feel pleasure, and I became a slave to it, and it consumed my life for years. One day I received from Father God, a moment of clarity and I literally cried out to God, and Jesus Christ for help, and They Showed Up from the sincerity of Their Spirit, and I began to inwardly change from that night. It's exactly forty-five days from this writing, seventeen years would have elapsed since I got my moment of clarity from God Himself! Each and every day from my moment of clarity, until the day of this writing I've taken steps of true effort from my soul, all to learn that I 'm nothing without The Holy Spirit from God, Guiding my every step! Nothing, or nobody has given me greater knowledge and wisdom than God Himself, and this shall stand as the truth long after I am removed from the body I now possess!

214. Safety and Security From God Himself

Always there, never are my sights empty, even though my vision lessens with my increase in years. Physical sight is one aspect; however, Father God's Presents Reigns All Through my being, I'm never without His Perfect Guidance and Protection, I'm not an orphan! The Evil Forces that be for years used their mental projections to lie to my mind, telling me I had no hope, and that I needed to respond contrary to the hope I was feeling. I stayed constantly confused for many years, I was lost in this world, fear and drama were my every day companions! I didn't know it then, but Father God Was Right With me, as I experienced each perilous situation. All loyalty from my being will rest with Father God for forever, my heart is closed concerning this matter! One day my soul will be totally free, and all thanks will be owed to my Father God, as it is now as I exist in this evil place known as earth! I constantly seek Father God, so my comments will be brutally honest when it comes to the reality concerning The Decrees from Father God Himself. Father God's Decrees Are Sound and Perfectly Designed to bring about order not chaos within the lives of His Created Beings. It has taken many years of decontamination of my being to be able to see and live by Father God's Decrees; now Father God Has Instructed me to study The Teachings of The Lord, and Master Jesus Christ! Only by constantly seeking The One and Only Father God, can souls experience the reality of real joy, whereas no conditions of the world can ever take! The world is concerned with itself, and the rulers are The Evil Forces that be, and they will always place sanctions on the masses of people to keep them in fear, and seeking not The Creator of this world, in an effort to give them solace while living out their lives here on earth, and providing salvation for their souls after they leave the physical body!

215. The Flow of God's Spirit

Here I am LORD, right where You Guided me to be tonight, oh Holy Spirt from God! I will sit at this table and empty out my heart, just as You Commanded me to do; I am God's Son, and it's my duty as His Son, to obey His Orders, all the way up, until He Allows no more breathing of His Air. Here I am LORD, at this table carrying out Your Orders tonight. I can't keep the truth locked away inside of my soul. The Holy Spirit from God, Has Set the stage for my existence; His Knowledge and Wisdom Will Flow from my pen, like the blowing of the wind that has its own end! I am God's Tool that He Will Use, through The Guidance from His Holy Spirit, so give no praise to me; for all credit goes to The LORD God Almighty. I am dispensable carrying a date a of departure of which I am powerless over; however, I am overjoyed with joy in my heart; for The Creator of All Life Has Chosen me to carry out His Will in this way! There is nothing, or nobody in all of my existence that has made me feel the way I do right now, and the continuation of it day after day after day! There is no one like God, Jesus Christ, or The Holy Spirit from God, and there shall never be anything like Them for forever; remember I'm just writing these words, everything here is from God Himself! Take heed of the words that are written here; for they are truthful, and never will they come to be false. Upon reading these words a dagger will pierce your heart, either to heal you, or destroy you, there will be no exceptions upon the gaze of My Holy Words, from my Son, who writes these words from his very own heart; the heart which I Myself Occupy!

216. The Reality of God's Love

I need The Lord, and Master Jesus Christ every day and every night of my life, and there are no ifs, ands, or buts about this statement. I am blessed to see the many flaws in my character at the tender age of almost being fifty! The Lord, and Master Jesus

Christ's Life Stands As A Guide for the actions I need to take, or not take, I'm very critical of myself if I've felt I've made a bad decision, and if I know I made a bad decision I become super critical concerning my behavior. Nothing much ever got accomplished in my life when I couldn't get over the feeling of being guilty. I've made so many wrong decisions in my life, I almost lost hope of every being a decent human being. By seeking out The Teachings of The Lord, and Master Jesus Christ, I can actually feel a difference in my heart within each and every day and night now that The LORD God Himself Allows me. I always become overwhelmed with gratitude on how The Trinity Constantly Demonstrates Grace and Mercy to the whole world; even though this world is contaminated by The Evil Forces that be. The constant demonstration of true love and compassion humbles my soul with a healing force of intuition on how The Trinity Truly Cares about the human family. So my situation is crystal clear, I need The Teaching of The Lord, and Master Jesus Christ to become grounded within my Eternal Soul! I can't seek out any other way of living now; for The Spirit from The Living God Has Revealed His Will for my life and I wholly trust The Trinity, thus my destiny is an open book. The LORD God Has Been Nothing but Good to me my whole life, and there is no exception in God's Guidance to seek out The Teachings of The Lord, and Master Jesus Christ, my Older Brother.

217. The Detour in My Life

A smile registers upon my face with the full knowledge that I am a slave to Father God! I use to be slave to sin, and as it is written the wages of sin is death, and I was surely on the road leading to destruction; however, The Lord God, Placed a detour sign on that road, and I followed that detour sign which led straight to God Himself! The LORD God Had Truly Saved my life in a way that I was consciously able to see after years of seeking His Will for my life! The Guidance from The One and True God must be sought after constantly in an effort not to lose conscious contact; for there are oh, so many temptations in this evil invested place called earth. Even though God Himself Has Increased the levels of Grace and Mercy upon the world, many souls are still lost and confused, concerning the meaning for their lives, and countless others are sick with diseases and disorders, and they die that way in anguish and despair! That was the road I traveled on for a good portion of my life; ignorant to the fact that The Evil Forces that be, the evil one, and the children of the devil, are in full operation all over this world. By constantly seeking The Creator of All Life, God Showed me the truth to why the majority of people living life on earth are lost, confused, sick, and ignorant of His Holy Spirit! The smile that registers on my face is genuine, for I know deep in my heart how God Has Truly Blessed me with the ability to humble myself, and constantly continue to seek out His Holy Presents; without being further deceived by The Evil Forces that be, only made possible by God's Holy Spirit, Entering into my heart! I will never be in the wrong about expressing my experiences concerning The Creator of my life! I am God's Son, and I will promote The Goodness of Father God, every chance Allowed me; there is no other reason for the continuance of my life.

218. Only From God

There are oh, so many things that are in and a part of our human lives that don't always meet the physical eyesight. They stand as a phenomenon, and their existence are demonstrations of God's

Holy Spirit At Work. The reality of these occurrences are as real as the things we can see with the physical eyes! The Holy Spirit From God Is At Work Nonstop in the lives of people, some people are aware of The Holy Spirit At Work, others people find out later on down the scale of their lives, if they are Blessed by God Himself to experience His Holy Spirit At Work. If people of the world could see what I see, they would be in amazement for years, just as I was in amazement by what The Holy Spirit from God Has Allowed me to see, I've spoken about this subject on a few occasions in my passages; however, the gift was given to me and it never leaves my physical sights, nor my mental sights as well. The LORD God Has Given me a special gift, and I can't give it away, not even to a single soul; for The LORD God Himself Made my situation as it is, and no one alive can ever deliver, or change what God Has Set in Motion. So my gift is a phenomenon to me, for I can physically see these objects; however, there is no known way for me to prove to others these objects exists! It's just one of those things that doesn't reveal itself to the physical eyesight of the masses of people; however, in my eyesight these objects are real, but they register not in the ordinary way of determining the existence of something. This is just one of the many beautiful things in existence that hasn't been exposed to the consciousness of many people; I don't know if I'm the only person who can see these objects, and it's only by God's knowledge if there are others. Only God Knows Why He Has Given me this Allowance!

219. God's Revelation to My Soul

What I can actually see is God's Holy Spirit that lives within me, now every aspect of my life for the past thirty-one and one half years makes perfect sense, all actions and responses align perfectly within my heart from the newly revealed knowledge received from God Himself! It's now confirmed in my heart, how my mind is being controlled by God's Holy Spirit, I've been uplifted to a new level of consciousness by this revelation. Peace and calmness settle themselves upon my soul, this new awareness has shut the doorway of my mind that was slightly cracked, now I am truly dead to sin! The Spirit of Jesus Christ Is Truly Within my soul and my soul is within Him. God Himself Has Brought All of this goodness upon me; for I was predestined as being His Son. I must continue the work my Father God Has Assigned me to do, being of service to others is my code, and now it has been fortified by God's Revelation to me on this day of His Creation! I am truly alive with a genuine purpose to breath this air of life; always shadowed by The Trinity, and Eternal Life. God Himself Has Done More Good here than just reveal the truth to me, He Has Further Glorified Himself. Father God Has Increased my faith, He Has Increased my already known diligence concerning my zeal to carry out His Will, and now He Has Also Turned His Holy Spirit Inward on my soul. The results upcoming will be oh, so obvious to all who come into contact with me, or to even here my name. All inspirations from my existence will all go to the already Glory of Father God Himself; for no achievements will be from me alone, and in all reality everything belongs to Father God anyway, I'm just the vessel that God Himself Uses. So I will make this crystal clear, all goodness is from Father God, and all good things will return to Him!

220. Saved by God Himself

I truly know that I was called to write; for my whole being is at peace when I pick up the pen; even though, I know in my heart that God Himself Has the final say concerning all things in the lives of all people! Knowing this in my heart, God Still Places the desire in my heart to write regardless! I am God's tool that He Uses, and my heart and my pen are at His Service! Nothing is mine, I created nothing, and I constantly keep this truth in the front row of the conscious that God Himself Allows me. Souls having not this truth burning within their hearts, have the fear of God not constantly in the front row of their consciousness, this leads to all kinds of trespasses they may commit on their neighbors. Relationships between people, policies, and nations are decaying very rapidly as time moves forward; I can truly see The LORD God's Prophecies through His Prophets coming into view. No, nothing for granted can I take unto myself, the flow of my heart must contain The Spirit of The Trinity; for only by Them do I receive the ingredients I need to be truly useful to my neighbors. My heart must not contain no contamination from The Evil Forces that be; however, from birth the contamination has been increasing, brought on by constant exposure ; just by living life from day to day in this evil infested place has damaged me greatly for years! I became a very sick soul, as I explained in my other passages; only by constantly seeking out God Himself, did God, Restore me to my rightful mind, I was mentally insane for years! God's Kindness and Compassion is what fuels my soul to stay in a position of constant humbleness to whatever God's Will Is for my existence.

The Trinity is where I must keep my focus; lest I become once again trapped by The Evil Forces that be. I am God's Son, and I will stay behind my Father God, and obey His Decrees, all the days of my life.

221. All I Have

All I have in this world that has any true value is my faith in Father God, God Is all I truly have, and He Is The True Treasure that I will leave my brothers and sisters when I leave this body and return to Him! I write these words today in God's Creation, and it just so happens to be the birthdate of my closest girl cousin, whom I love dearly, we grew up together knowing what it truly meant to be kids! We are eleven months and three days a part in time, and she will always have a special part in my heart for forever! Father God Deprives us kids of nothing; for He Provides us with memories that gives us the ability to make time stand still when we reflect on days and nights long gone and spent. We must respect the powers of our memories, for they have the power to generate joy, or pain, oh, how powerful we human beings truly are; however, most people are ignorant, or not always conscious of the powers we possess through the ability to remember! I'm truly grateful that I learned not to shut the door on my past life; even though, there were times when I wanted to, for my memories were filled with many disappointments, brought on by my own actions.

I had to face the fact that my own guidance was no good whatsoever, and I couldn't blame people, places, or things any longer, I had to come to see and realize that I myself was the root cause of all my troubles and failures at living and being successful in this life I was responsible for. So for me my past became a very important possession, for all of my causes and conditions were all set in place nice and neatly in my past life. Only The Love from Father God Brought me to this most needed reality, the truth I could never see on my own guidance; for I was mentally insane for years! Living in fantasy for years in my mind, almost destroyed the beautiful soul that Father God, Has Created. This is why I stated that Father God Is All I truly have, I live by faith, not by sight!

222. The Issue of Life, Only From God

What God Gives no one can duplicate; for the quality is from The Creator Himself, not to forget to mention the uniqueness of what is given. Never is forever and there will never be another soul created exactly like myself, and this is just one of the beautiful examples of Father God's Giving. Everything that has ever been created by God Himself, mankind has done their absolute best to copy, and they always came up short; for Only God Himself Can Create Life, and I won't forget to mention The Evil Forces that be also has come up short in trying to create life! Nothing or nobody can allow the creation of life, let alone create life, other than God Himself! I can imagine in my mind, created beings whosesoever they maybe in this universe has tried to create itself, or life on its own accord, I have no doubt about this in my heart. I truly believe that only God Himself, Possesses the Ability to Create life out of nothingness, this is just another point of reality that mankind can't even come close to getting a solution to! In my mind I feel agitated concerning this subject; for I am human and in my heart I know that we as men fall far short from The Perfection that is God, even the best of us fall short! We will never be equal to our Maker God, nor will The Evil Forces that be ever come close to possessing what God possesses. Mankind doesn't even know what a soul looks like, let alone have the ability to create a soul, this information Only God Himself Has, along with all of His Glory and Majestic Qualities. So The LORD God Himself Will Remain in a picture frame all by Himself for Eternity! So the outcome is the same as it was stated in the beginning of this passage, no one or nothing can duplicate what God Himself Gives. No findings will ever be able to change what Has been written here, and that's a reality that I myself will die with!

223. Talents and Abilities are Gifts not Guarantees

Set to one side to perform many specific tasks, this is the reality of the many souls that are born into the world of God's Creation! Many people fail to find their true purpose to why they were allowed to be born. People are born and then they die; however, before they get here they are given certain talents and abilities from God Himself, The Life Giver. Just because people were given talents and abilities, doesn't mean they will be successful in applying them in their lives; whereas they will become famous in the eyes of the world! This was something I chased after in my mind for years, and I never accomplished anything close to becoming famous in the eyes of the world. I became resentful and confused about my many failures at attempting to be a success in the eyes of my peers and the world. I was always looking on the outside to fulfill the need on the inside, to have a purpose and be needed. I was obsessed with that mind set for years, only to achieve defeat after defeat, until one day I knew in the confinement of myself that I was beaten in all phases of my existence, and I didn't need anyone to tell it to me! My God Given talents and abilities were always with me, securely stored in the very makeup of the soul that is me; however, I couldn't access them and put them into practice to a degree whereas I could make a living by them! I found myself being a middle aged man with nothing in life to share, except my failed attempts at trying to live this life on my own terms. I had to look away from trying to fit into a mold that the world had waiting for me, which was a phantasy that had to be abolished from my heart, let alone from my mind! I had to be reborn, and Only God Himself Could Help me accomplish such a feat, I had no positive guidance, or I wouldn't have ended up the way I did. Only The Loving Kindness from God Himself Has Saved my life for the betterment of my soul, and many others who are, and were placed in my path.

224. From Disillusionment to Reality

I was once free; however, I was miserable in my freedom, now I am a slave to The Lord and Master Jesus Christ, and I have serenity of spirit each and every day. When I was in the world searching for physical pleasure I was always at risk of losing my life, never in my mind did I seriously contemplate it though! Others who were close to me were worried about it far more than I ever was. I believe I was obsessed concerning the pleasurable things the world had to offer. So in actuality I wasn't free at all, I was a slave to anything that made my body feel pleasure! I was bound by The Evil Forces that be, I was caught up in an evil cycle of deterioration that I couldn't break, even when I truly wanted to, I became utterly powerless by being bound for so many years! I was miserable and my life started to take a direction, I was going down, and I was going down very quickly, there was nobody in my corner, no one truly cared if I lived, or died. This is how my life shaped up to be by chasing worldly pleasures, or anything that made me feel pleasure. Physical death was knocking at the door of my soul, and I was blessed to recognize what was knocking, demanding my life! There was nothing left to do, so I sincerely cried out to God, and Jesus Christ for Their Help, and that was the best decision I made in my entire life! Restitution was slow and painful, and there were no significate changes in the exterior condition of my surroundings; however, there were constant rearrangements in my psyche, and this hasn't stopped, even to the day of this writing. This world called earth is cloaked in darkness, and only by constantly seeking The Kingdom of God, can people be brought to the truth about what they need to do concerning their life situations. The tempter is always present, and on duty to poison your life and enslave your Eternal Soul, this is why The Trinity Protects my Eternal Soul on a day to day basis, and being saved from Eternal Damnation has depth and great meaning for me, something I won't ever play around with, or take lightly!

225. God Answers His Sick and Hurt Son

My last lady friend wasn't a believer in God, though we were together for several years, when she left me she said she didn't feel love for me in her heart anymore. I was deeply hurt for over two years, and then one day in meditation, God, Showed me why the break up occurred! My lady friend saw that I loved God, with all of my heart, soul, mind, and strength, and she was never going to topple the love that I have for Father God, in any aspect of my life! We were unevenly yoked, and the break up was just a matter of time and misery on her part; for she never constantly sought out God Himself like her partner did, and still does. When Father God, Revealed this to me, it answered so many other questions in my mind and heart that I never had the answers to. I'm almost fifty years old now, and I might just stay single for the rest of my life; for I won't join with a female unless she has The Spirit from Father God Burning in her soul through and through, lest I won't be attacked to her, my zeal for Father God will never be compromised! I have to be what I was made to be, there is no mistake in God's Order for me. Father God Is my Heavenly Father and I am His Son, and the son does what he sees The Father Doing, where else would I get my knowledge? For years I was misled by the enemies of my Father God; however, my Heavenly Father Protected me from His enemies, and I didn't have a clue in my mind to what they were leading me into. This reality confronts oh, so many of God's People, God Himself Saved my life; for God Loves me, now I must love my Father God by using my life experiences to help save some of my brothers and sisters, by sending them in search of Father God's Holy Kingdom! So there is more than meets the eye, than chasing worldly pleasures; for the love for Father God, and the love for my neighbors, comes before any selfish desires from my heart! I'm also happy to report that since I've been seeking The Kingdom of Father God, selfishness has been decreasing from my being, only possible by listening to Father God in meditation sessions, I truly love Father God!

226. Indispensable Attitude

Believers in The Trinity must constantly stay focused on spiritual matters; for worldly things are constantly on the sneak and creep in an effort to steer the minds of the believers in God, away from God's Plan for their lives! The enemies of Father God are hard at work to destroy The Creation of God in any way they can. The Evil Forces that be consider themselves dispensable; for they have already have been sentenced by God Himself. God's Final Enactment of His Words are all that is left concerning their sentence! So we believers in the Trinity must constantly inventory our motives; our beings must remain one with The Trinity, lest we become useless to The Trinity, and our brother and sisters who are still lost in the darkness. The Trinity is our Guidance and Strength as we live out our lives in this mortal state; faith in all of Their Abilities should remain forever our only needed spiritual food! Dependence upon worldly things must be abandoned, if only a little at a time, and that's how it usually happens with most of God's Kids who begin to see the truth within all things! When the Trinity opened my eyes to the truth about the world through God's Grace, I truly began to seek The LORD God more and more; for there was the feeling of correct guidance and safety every time I would seek out God within my mind. The guidance became so precise within my heart that I wholly trusted what I felt to be God's Leadings, I was being transformed from fear and chaos, to peace and orderly living, something I've never known in my adult life. This experience has changed my life forever and for the positive good. Not only just for my own benefit, but for the souls who will believe my experience and follow my example, and seek out The Trinity for themselves, and one day find out that I was telling the truth throughout all of my words! This mortal life is just a small taste of the promise of Eternal Life that has been written about within The Holy Scriptures!

227. Nothing to Figure Out Any More

I've Reached the point in my life whereas I've made up my heart to try not to figure out The Workings of The God of All Creation! To know that Father God Is my Heavenly Father, and I am one of His Sons, is good enough for me to know, and I don't have to go any further than that. Living by faith, and not by sight is something that took many years to come into my heart to even consider it as a principle to live my life by. For years I spent my days and nights trying to figure out the right pathway to pursue in this God Given Life. I failed over and over again at attempting to live this life successfully. Only by constantly failing at being a success in the world, brought me to my knees, and I was out of self-esteem, then and only then did I turn to The Invisible Force in The Universe called God! I couldn't break away from the fantasies within my mind, I had to run the course of enchantments, placed within my mind by my own ego. I truly believe my ego was responsible for my deep degree of insanity, and when sanity was returned to me by The Grace from God, all my twenties and half of my thirty were used up, and I didn't progress positively in my life concerning worthwhile things, or accomplishments. From that very real position in life to the present time of this writing, I've been engaged in the reconstruction of my entire thought process, Truly Guided by The Invisible Power, people call God! I've been pulled back through the gates of insanity; for I was insane for years. Living in reality was very painful for the first five years of reconstruction, then the pain was relieved just a little bit; for hope had been established within my heart, and I had become overwhelmed with gratitude. My life had oh, so many loose ends; however, through my experiences I came to know that God Was Real, and there were no more doubts within my heart, on how I must whole-heartedly continue to seek The Guidance from The Invisible Power called God! So now I am almost fifty years old, and truly I've learned there is nothing to figure out anymore, and there never really was from day one; however, I was ignorant of this knowledge for years, even the people that were very close to me were powerless to connect me to The Power, that I now live my life by.

228. Slavery or Freedom

All my life I've been a slave without the chains! I was born into slavery; once again without the physical chains. There is no real freedom in this world; however, wherever The Spirit of God Is, there is where freedom can be found! My soul longs to be with Father God, and totally be free; however, I am here right now in the body, and I must do all things to please Father God! I know now why I felt restless for years, and why I was always sad about the state I was in and the hardship of mankind as a whole, it all makes perfect sense to me now. My soul was in slavery without the chains, and the only freedom possible for me while I'm in the body is to keep my mind focused on Father God, at all times. When I'm in God's Holy Spirit, there is no fear, I am like an eagle floating thousands of miles up in earth's atmosphere. I experience true freedom, with no chains, or bracelets around my soul! I can't stop now, I must complete the work my Father God Has Given unto me to complete, the tactics of The Evil Forces that be are oh, so cunning, they truly attracked my being for the last two weeks, with efforts to stagnate my zeal to push my pen, but like always The Spirit that Is from my Father God Has Shown me their evil tactics once again, and now I can flow like the great rivers of the world and not be stagnated with disease like still water! I am alive with a charged up soul, powered by God Himself, planting seeds of freedom; for all humanity are slaves to The Evil Forces that be, and this has been the order, or state of being that is the reality of our world as it has been governed before the birth of The Lord and Master Jesus Christ, up to the present time of this writing! So now I've pointed mankind to the truth about this world, individuals have the choice to remain slaves, or seek Father God, and become free!

229. The Separation

As a believer in God, I am ordered by God to separate myself from unbelievers in God Himself, without having an attitude of holier than thou. I can truly see the difference between believers in God, and non-believers in God, their lives and attitudes are in contrast like night and day! Everything in God's Creation has an opposite, and the example of believers in God, or not opposes no difference. For years now I've lived my life in the search for God's Will for my life truly and honestly, and it's a very lonely road that I walk. Oh, so many people have fallen out of my life; fore they desired not the pathway that I travel on from one day to the next. God's Holy Spirit Guides me and Showers me with knowledge and understanding that comforts my heart along the lonely pathway that I walk. Salvation is at the end of the road; however, I've learned not to despair over the many souls who are suffering all around me, and in the world as a whole. I don't have the power, and the task isn't mine to destroy The Evil Forces that be; Father God Himself only can accomplish that! So I continue to humble myself under Father God's Mighty Hand, and be glad that I am a witness to many things that God Himself, Allows me to see. So you see my heart differs drastically from those who seek not The Holy Kingdom constantly. Nothing in common would I have with a person, or people who seek not and believe not in The Invisible Spirit that is Father God Himself! So it makes perfect sense to separate myself from non-believers in God.

There was a time when I didn't seek God the way I've grown to seek Him, and on recall I can remember my life was bitter, without any salt in it. I was at odds with the world and most people I came into contact with, they were all out to get me, so The Evil Forces that be whispered to my mind and said "get them before they get you"! Father God Himself Has Relieved me from this mania of madness I suffered from for many year.

230. From God Himself

The Lord God Himself Has Showered me with resiliency, over and over again on many occasions of my life experience! If I'm going to boast, it's going to be about the generosity and grace from my Father God. All goodness and joy comes from Him. In my life allowance so far I am a witness to Father God's Grace and Mercy throughout the whole world, God's Spirit Lovingly Watches Over us all, at all times. The Joy of The Trinity, flows through my heart continuously. God's Spirit Overwhelms my soul with the hope of the promise concerning Eternal Life. Pleasures concerning worldly things constantly enters the confines of my mind; however, I've painfully learned to turn my thoughts over to Father God, and it's not always an easy thing to do, it has taken years of practice to get positive results. The I, selfish me that consumed me had run amuck for years! Only God Himself Has Changed my psyche by me constantly seeking God's Spirit and carrying out what God felt to me to do. So it's a two way street, I must constantly seek out Father God, and in turn God Reveals what must be done by me, "faith without works is dead!" Every time I seek out Father God, I'm given new strength; which in turn humbles my Eternal Soul! I've lived two lives; the life of self will, which pushed me to the point of physical death, and now the life of living by spiritual principles, that to which has saved my life and has connected me to The Creator of All Creation, oh, how Graceful God Truly Is! There is no doubt in my soul concerning the reality of God's Holy Spirit Watching out over this world as we know it! The Evil Forces that be are enslaved in the confines of this world, and their sentence from God's Own Words will be carried out in God's Good Old Time. It's only in The Mind of God, when He Will Carry out their sentence. So the saying that God Gives Grace and Mercy to those He Pleases to give it to is the truth. He Surely Gave it to me!

231. Pathway to Salvation

Within each moment of time now, I know the truth of God's Wrath; for I am His Son and I live from one day to the next immersed within God's Spirit! Nothing concerning humanity is kept from my attention; however, in the uncovering of many things I'm finding myself in need of consultation. As I live from one day to the next Father God Guides me, and sometimes He Places people within my midst, in an effort to give me the information I'm in need of. Living by faith, and not by sight isn't an easy way to live for most people. This principle involves a constant contact with The Invisible Spirit called God! For me I call God, Father God; fore He once called me His Son. Nothing comes before Father God, and that's the heart and mind set I've grown to live by. I allow nothing, and I me absolutely nothing come between my being and Father God Himself. There was a time in my life when most of the people I've came to know, through me away like a paper cup. They said nasty things about me, in my face and behind my back, and I thought these people were my friends. O how naïve I use to be, not to forget to mention insane! When I was out of self-esteem and became homeless I then cried out to God, and Jesus Christ, and they didn't laugh at me and treat me like a paper cup. God's Holy Spirit Guided my soul from that night to the day of this writing and I'm no longer the sane naïve person of years ago. The Spirit from The Living God Has Been

Guiding my soul upon my sincere plea for help! I know within my heart how The Spirit from God Was Watching Out over my soul - way before I sincerely asked God, and Jesus Christ for Their Help. From that night to the present time of this writing The Sprit from God Himself Has Been Growing me; God's Holy Spirit Has Been Showing me how to live my life and not to be a problem for my neighbors!

232. Answers From a Sincere Plea

No hope and no God in my life; that was the reality of my being at the age of thirty three. It was my birthday, and I was homeless and nobody wanted to be in my company, I was truly miserable; yet that didn't stop me from pouring whiskey into my system! It was exactly eight days before I fell to my knees and sincerely asked God and Jesus Christ for Their Help. I was truly beaten up by Alcoholism and Drug Addiction and that conviction came from the soul that is me. To admit complete defeat to my own self concerning the usage of alcohol and street drugs took eighteen years of my life to realize. I possess a deadly Incurable disease called Alcoholism, which led to abusing street drugs also. I know without a doubt in my heart that God Himself Drew my soul to the place where I was to discover the true answers to my life's problem. I truly love my Father God and my Older Brother Jesus Christ, my Lord and Savior! I've never seen either of Them face to face, and I don't have to; however, I feel Their Presents now, each day and night allowed to my soul. Now I have hope, and I have God in my life, the feeling is one of responsibility, not only for my wellbeing, but for the wellbeing of my neighbors as well. The LORD God my Father Has Taught me and still teaches me how to live my life from one day to the next, and The Lord and Master

Jesus Christ Instructs me how to treat the non-believers. I am in desperate need of my Savior's Instructions constantly! I've been an undisciplined person for years, and I truly have to work hard at keeping composure when it comes to interacting with my neighbors. Only by seeking God and Jesus Christ constantly, Did They Answer and Begin to Whisper Solutions to my heart and mind. Things that were common sense, but while drinking alcohol and ingesting street drugs, common sense was almost impossible for me to take up, and put into action! Only people who seek God, and Jesus Christ, with their hearts and minds can truly comprehend the joy I experience in my being from one day to the next.

233. Call of Duty

Here it is five twenty am, and once again I'm awakened by The Spirit from God to push this pen and proclaim The Goodness that Is God Himself. These words that I write are formulated for The Kids from The Living God, never give up your faith in The Living God! Always remember this life we are experiencing is taking place in the days of evil, and a Spiritual War is steadily progressing. The Forces of Evil are hard at work to corrupt The Children from The Living God, I am blessed by The Grace from Father God to actually see the corruption and totally be conscious of it from day to day. God Calls me to service in this way, to let my neighbors know that His Wrath is on its way! I am God's Son, a child of light instructed by Father God's Own Spirit to write these words of warnings and encouragements. Look at the world in its present state with all of its technologies; yet millions of people go to bed hungry night after night with no hope in their hearts! How can a world governed by the Love of God allow this to happen? How cans a world governed by the Love of God, seek new ways to destroy their neighbors? How can a world governed by the Love of God, permit same sex marriages? Father God Represents peace and perfect order, not chaos! The proof of my words will be in the seeking of God through your own thoughts, and truth will come to bear on your hearts and souls. The Wrath of God Is Coming to this world, and it's near! I write what's in my heart; for I've been charged to do so by Father God Himself. I can't leave any messages untold; fore I am governed by The Love from Father God Himself, a service that one day I will be rewarded for. The reward Won't be by human hands, but by The Spirit from God Himself, through The Lord and Master Jesus Christ, My Savior!

234. The Seat of God's Judgment

I feel so weak in my body, or my body feels so downtrodden, whatever the reality might be I must continue to move forward. I'm fifty years old now, and my Father God Has Blessed my soul with many Spiritual Insights to correctly live out the remainder of my life! All of what I write is for the benefit of those souls who sincerely desire the pathway that leads to The One and Only God! There is much work people must do to keep themselves holy and acceptable to God Himself; The Evil Forces that be are constantly setting traps to destroy as many souls as they possible can! This was a very sharp reality that I had to learn the very hard way; however, Father God, Has Guided me through the traps set so designed to destroy me. I know deep within my heart on how so many souls are and have been manipulated and enslaved by The evil Forces that be which has spanned for thousands of years! They will never cease at their influence of death and enslavement of human souls; all the way up to the last day. The Grace and Mercy from Father God Runs Very Deep, but take not for granted His Kindness; for God's Spirit Always Searches the hearts of people! The heart is the center of truth, the stage of judgment from God Himself! There will be no mistakes in God's Judgments, so truly take advantage of the time still allowed to you to repent from the wicked ways you may have practiced in the course of your lives! It's never too late to turn from the father of lies, "Satan." God Himself Honors the sincerity from His Created Beings, whether you delight in wickedness, or not! God Will Judge Correctly upon the last day of this evil rein. God Is Merciful and Kind; however, The Evil Forces that be will constantly project thoughts to your mind to steer you away from the truth that is inevitable, everyone who has ever lived will face The seat of God's Judgment!

235. The Truth of my Existence

The Holy LORD, my Father God, Is O, So Awesome! God Reveals the truth about my existence at its proper times! God Reveals what I need to know, when I need to know it. There is no cleverness from myself, or anyone else, it's The Will of The One and Only God! This is what God Himself Has Revealed unto the soul that is me, I've learned to look to my Father God, not to men for what is needed to complete my assignment Father God Has Given unto me. I'm not at all bashing my neighbors concerning the good things they may possess, and I'm convinced that my Father God Has Allowed them those good things, so God Is Able to Provide them for me also, if it be His Will. There is no desire in my heart for an abundance of material things, my heart's desire is to help my neighbors connect to The Unapproachable Light, that is

God Himself! I am not a preacher, or a teacher who has been ordained, but the love from Father God flows through my veins. Nothing or no one can teach me better than my Older Brother Jesus Christ, or The Holy Spirit from God Himself. I seek constantly to keep myself Godly, evil is all around me, at all times always seeking to cause confusion in my life! This is the reality of this world called earth, and Father God Has Called me to separate myself from the evil doers, and proclaim His Glory and Goodness wherever I am guided to be. I know why I am here on this planet, at this time of God's Awesome Creation, nothing, or no one can steer me from the truth of my existence. The Holy Spirit from God Himself Guides my every step, I live to carryout Father God's Holy Will Only; there is no other reason for my existence here on this planet! It took many years of living in darkness to find out the reality of my existence, now Father God's Eternal Light Guides my soul to salvation, and in the process many other souls will be saved. Only from God Himself Is Goodness Demonstrated through the faith and work of one soul multiplying power to bring to many other souls as well.

236. The Presence of God's Will

The Grace from our Holy Father God Has Been Laid on thickly upon the whole world; fore God, so Loved the world that He Sacrificed His Only Begotten Son! Before that time to the present time of this writing the world never cared about the will of God! God's Holy Spirit truly Showed me the truth about the condition of this world called earth. The situation is going to get worse; however, I am called by Father God to continue the work He Has Given unto me to do. I must never shipwreck my faith in The Trinity, no matter what may transpire within my allotted days and nights! To trust and obey The Will of Father God Is the most important responsibility I will ever have in my existence. Nothing, or nobody comes before The Will of my Father God, starting with my own selfish self! I've grown into the attitude I possess within my heart concerning my Maker, and I desire in my heart to be more like Father God, with each breath allowed me. I must become a living breathing example of love and service, and do my best as The Lord and Master Jesus Christ Guides my heart and soul. The enemies of Father God are all throughout this world, yet Father God with His Great Mercy Desires not to destroy them, but rather give them the opportunity to repent, and Father God Would Heal them. This is the reason for the lives of all people born into the world. Satan, and one third of God's Angels which are now called demons are so entrenched in their disobedience, they consider not repentance. Nevertheless Father God Calls His Children to be kind and be wicked not, and practice compassion to all souls encountered! The Will of God Is of Peace and Perfect order, not chaos and confusion. So all who answer the call from Father God will turn their hearts and souls to the rhythm of God's Movements!

237. My Part in Life's Drama

I can't make anyone believe the reality that is so plain to me concerning the existence of The One and Only Living God! God's Presence is in my plain sight, even when I close my eyes, God Is Present. I don't expect the masses of people to believe me; however, this message is for those few who do! God's Goodness is an open book; even though many people don't read the pages. Then there are some who do read the pages but don't retain the information, and they remain in darkness! This condition of not successfully connecting with God The Creator has been going on for thousands of years. I don't know the outcome of the things that have been, or what the outcome will be for the things to come, all I have is my experience and knowledge to know that I am God's Son. I can't speak for anyone else; however, I know without a shadow of doubt in my heart what The Holy Spirit from God Has Spoken unto me. I hold God's Words Near and Dear to my soul, God Is Faithful in Everything He Proclaims, and I need no other being's testimony to give me faith, I have my own! The reality of true believers and doers of God's Holy Decrees are oh, so few, and I must constantly keep myself humble and alert to my Father God's Will for my existence. I was sent to earth to help many lost souls connect their souls to The All Powerful God of All Life! Through all of my sufferings, God Has Shown me where I came from and what I was sent here to do! Until I came to realize that God Himself Is The Beginning and The End of Everything, I was just like a dead leaf, toasted along by the blowing of the wind, with no structure, or base. My position in this life has been made crystal clear by Almighty God Himself! Now I must continue to do what God Has Brought me in the world to do. I consciously know that I was sent by The Unapproachable Light, to be a light to many souls suffering in the darkness of this world!

238. The Consciousness I Must Keep

I must always hold true to what God Has Told me to do! When I feel uncomfortable within myself, it's a sure sign I'm slacking in my work concerning The Good LORD God, and what He Has Placed before me. It's so easy to get caught up in worry and not stay focused on what God Has Instructed me to constantly work on! My Father God, Is Oh, so Merciful to me; for God Always

Allows Atonement for my weaknesses. However, I must continue to put my best efforts forward, and not take The LORD God for granted! I will not put my Father God to the test, despite my many short comings in this life so far. I must continue to live each day with humility, asking Father God for the power to carry out His Will in each day allowed to me. I've been given my life for the sole purpose of helping others and to Glorify Father God in the same instance! Subtle, are The Evil Forces that be, and I must train myself never to forget their efforts to corrupt whomever they can. Father God Has Charged me with the responsibility to bring knowledge and truth to this generation, acting like an echo from The Lord and Master Jesus Christ, my Lord and Savior. I must become like a shotgun blast that repeats itself, hitting as many souls as I can concerning knowledge and truth about The Unapproachable Light that is God Himself! No one can deliver out of Father God's Hands, or stop what Father God Has Set in motion. I've truly grown to live my life by this principle, and nothing has ever proven it false!

239. No Glory for Me

I can't be something I'm not; The Lord and Master Jesus Christ Spoke to my soul when I was very young; however, I didn't realize it was Him until many years later. Most things I had to learn the very very hard way; for I was confused in and about life at a very young age! Now that I live my life by Spiritual Principles, my emotional set hasn't been of rage in a very long time. The LORD God Always Comforts my soul no matter what's going on in my life! It took a lot of trial and error before I learned to humble myself under The Mighty Hand of Father God! There must never be any complacency for me; its effects are very damaging to me;

for Satan always tries to frustrate me through my thoughts! Most times I feel like I've been set aside; for my Father God Has Truly Shown me that the ways of the world are death for me, coupled with punishment after death. This revelation is something I don't play with, or think its relevance is false! I've come to realize when The LORD God Speaks to my heart, the message is the truth and it's for the benefit of my soul. I've also came to believe that I can't be selfish with the leadings from God's Holy Spirit. God Has Charged me to pass on the knowledge and truth that He Has Revealed to my heart! There is no exaltation ever for me, I've learned never to exalt myself, that has brought only defeat for me in most situations of my past experiences. All glory belongs to Father God, nothing belongs to me, everything is an allowance from Father God Himself. Woe unto me if I ever fall away from the truth of things! Blessed am I to know where all power emanates from.

240. The Leadings from Father God

Human life on this earth isn't for a very long stay, and without warning, or even with it our human lives can be easily taken away. Very fragile and precious human life is, and once it's gone its gone! God The Heavenly Father Constantly Touches my heart, keeping me focused to write about all the experiences I've encountered while being in the physical body. For one day I will be gone too; however, my experiences can be of value to those who are still here and those yet to come. Everyone's life has a meaning attached to itself, and I must constantly keep focused on my own meaning; my meaning falls into the content of "mine your own business". My mind is negative and my heart is positive; when both are combined on any subject they produce a positive solution, these solutions are directed to construct good things; fore my heart is positive; however, if my heart were negative, my solutions would be directed to support evil things. The heart of a human being is the orator of all emotions, and I'm so glad that I haven't allowed my heart to have become hardened concerning all the evils I've faced so far! I can speak to this end concerning my present psyche, "I wholly trust The Invisible Spirit known as God, and I've come to learn how to humble myself daily, under God's Mighty Hand". At the present time of this writing I am fifty years old; however, it has taken me up to the age of thirty four to actually surrender my will and life over to the care of The Invisible Spirit Called God! I've also came to learn that God Himself won't force His Way of Living on no one; even though, God Desires to see no one perish, or come to a horrible end of life. Nevertheless, we all die, but it doesn't have to be in fear, shame, anguish, guilt, or sin. The Holy Spirit that Is God Has Given me Hope of The Promise of Eternal Life! There isn't a greater reward than that, so I continue to keep my heart attuned to the leadings from Father God Himself.

241. Actions on The Road to Judgment.

Deception is so easy; however, staying focused on The One Living God, is oh, so hard! This world is crippled by the influences from The Evil Forces that be. I'm not talking about the physical world, I'm referring to the hearts of men and women throughout the whole world! Oh, so many people are being deceived in so many ways and there aren't conscious of it. Their very souls are in slavery, and they are in denial about the reality of their lives. They are influenced by The Evil Forces that be! Everything in this world order is based on competition and if you don't have enough skills, you are turned away, and sometimes treated very harshly. Many don't even get a chance to compete, and they are treated worse than animals in a zoo! All brought on by greed and the fear not of The One Living God! The exploitation of the masses of people has been going on for thousands of years, and this is the tactic Satan and his followers have been using throughout the ages. Death threats and actual murder have been and still are the tools they use to keep the grip of fear constant amongst the masses of people! This tyranny will continue and get even worse, all the way up until Judgment Day. The children from God, must prepare themselves and fear not; fore Almighty God Will Fall Short Not in Protecting us! Those who trust in The All Mighty God have nothing to fear! There is nothing The Almighty God Can't Do! Children from The Living God hearts must burn bright and fear not The Evil Forces that be! Children from God are not from this world; even though, they are in the world. God, Knows His Own, as well as Satan knows his own. Those who read these words will know without a shadow of doubt, to whom they belong. As sure as God Himself Has Allowed this whole drama of life to unfold, there will be no stoppage of Judgment Day!

242. The Holy Charge From The Lord God

I am charged by God Himself, I am an agent guided by God's Goodness; Father God Is my Master! The business of minding my own business is a full time job, and yet oh, so many things are left undone! Living life on life's terms was something that was very foreign to me; for almost forty years. I had a real hard time accepting things as they really were, I always thought I could change things, or make them better. I've learned lessons the very hard way, I couldn't positively change situations on my behalf no matter what, or who I tried to manipulate. Even if I did get my way, it never lasted for any long length of time. I would end up right back at the start line, and sometimes I would be further back from the original start line and then I would become superbly frustrated. Within forty years of living life, disappointments where not long between each other, yet I didn't allow my heart to become hardened; even though my heart was broken several times! The Spirit from The Living God Kept Right On Healing me and Encouraging me to keep moving right alone, despite my many failures. If it weren't for The Spirit from The Living God, I wouldn't be writing what I'm writing at this very moment. There were oh, so many times all I could do was just hurt on the inside; however, God Himself, was always there, and He Never Allowed Satan to damage me beyond repair! So I say to the masses of people who are in so much pain and distress, never shipwreck your faith In God Himself, or His Only Begotten Son Jesus Christ, They Are Always Here, and They Will Never Abandon you, no matter how hard Satan and his family members temp you to hurt yourselves and others. Seek out The Holy Spirit that Is God, over and over again, and one day God Will Charge You, as He Has Charged me, and you shall never be powerless over this world ever again! Woe to the people who turn back after being Charged by The One and Only Living God Himself. "Test not The LORD God Himself!"

243. The Light of my Heart

What I feel in my heart at this exact moment I expect no one to comprehend; for the feeling I feel is transmitted to me from The Holy Spirit Himself! No one can open what God Seals, and no one can close what God Leaves Open! I write these words to strengthen the confidence in The Children from God; for for many trails are to befall on the living souls of the earth, as it was foretold through Jesus Christ's Apostle John. Prepare your souls; for each man and woman ever born will have to give an account for the lives they have led! The Holy Spirit Himself Has Touched my heart to write these words. I am God's Son, and I am a tool that Father God Uses to touch those who He Has Pre Determined to read these words! The things I can see and the things that I feel are all intangible; however, they are oh, so real, they are the allowances from God Himself. I've truly come to realize how blessed I truly am. Father God Has Also Charged me with the responsibility to pass on the knowledge that He Has Entrusted me with. I am not to keep my light under a bed! I must put my light on a stand, so others may see clearly as they pass along in the darkness. This is the order from my Heavenly Father God! The work my Father God Has Placed Before me has no equal, this is what I was born to do! I would have never found my purpose on my own accord. I had to humble myself, and seek The Kingdom of God, then and only then did Father God Bring my destiny into the light of my heart! Father God Has Truly Demonstrated to me more than once, on how He Can Make A Way, when there was no way possible in sight! Father God Can Truly Make a way, when there is no way. I've never been truly sure about something in all the days of my life as this.

244. The Key to be Forever Free

I must constantly practice for myself self-discipline, no one can safeguard my soul, I must constantly humble myself when it comes to seeking after perishable things; for that would be a shameful end concerning the soul that is me. Idolatry would be in full effect within my heart! For years and still to the very time of this writing I have to safeguard my soul from those evil tempting thoughts. Once again the solution is living by Spiritual Principles, I have found that I can't live my life with peace in my mind and joy in my heart without staying connected to The Spirit of God Himself! God Has Given me my being, and to be in disharmony with Him only causes me pain and anguish, not to forget to mention a great many other negative and destructive emotions. For almost forty years of my life, The Evil Forces that be have stolen many days and nights of my life away from me, by making me ineffective in many areas of my God Given Life! When I became aware of what had been happening to me through The Grace from God, I became very resentful towards The Evil Forces that be; however, God Has Shown me not to poison myself further with hate and to always remember that "Vengeance is His." Peace in my mind and joy in my heart have been growing everyday within my being since I've been doing my best to obey Father God Himself. The LORD God Constantly Blesses me with many worthwhile things in my character and at times I become overwhelmed with gratitude to know in my heart that God Is my Heavenly Father, and I am His Son! I write about the truth of my life, to give hope to my fellow brothers and sisters whom have been tempted also by The Evil Forces that be, and are looking for a way out from enslavement concerning their Eternal Souls. To enslave our Eternal Souls is the will of Satan, and he will stop at nothing to accomplish this objective. Only The Power from The One Living God Can Vanquish the hold that Satan and his family members may have on your Eternal Souls!

245. The Road Less Traveled

I will grow weary not, I will continue to reveal the truth about the intangible forces of this universe! This is what I've been called to do, and I won't allow The Evil Forces that be make me sit down, and do not what The Lord, and Master Jesus Christ Has Instructed me to do! I can steadily feel The Evil Forces that be, and their influences from within people with regularity. For years I didn't know why I felt uncomfortable around people, especially in a crowd; however, The Spirit that Is God Has Given me my answer. The Forces of Evil influence the minds and hearts of people with subtle precision and they are very crafty with their tactics! I've learned to discern my feelings and I came to know within my heart how The Spiritual Realm and justice is closing in on this world as we human being know it to be. The Lord, and Master Jesus Christ Is Alive and Well, and He Patiently Is Obeying His Father's Command, "Sit by my side, until I Make Your enemies Your Foot stool". Only The Almighty God Knows when that will come to be; there for I must live my life by being humble, under The Mighty Hand of God! I believe my Older Brother Jesus Christ, for I've seen The Evil Forces that be, and I know that I am God's Son also! So over and over again I will continue to write, and tell about the reality of The Evil Forces that be, I will stop at nothing to continue to give accounts of their presents. The Evil Forces that be are all liars, they will smile in your face while planning your demise, you can only trust them to kill you. They are master deceivers, but those who are in Jesus Christ, can recognize with regularity, who they are, without any doubts of a false identity. Jesus Christ Constantly Lets His Sheep Know who, and where the wolves are. Oh, so many others get slaughtered by The Evil Forces that be. Even those who know who Satan and his family member are sometimes get their blood spilled by Jesus Christ's Enemies, and this has been going on for centuries. Worry not for justice and God's Judgment Day will become a reality. Father God Is Faithful in Everything He Proclaims.

246. Integrity, by Constantly Seeking The Kingdom of God

I must keep on pursuing what I believe in my heart to be the right things to pursue, if I am incorrect about anything, The Spirit from God Himself Will Let me Know it! I don't know what my status is in The Eyes and Mind of God Himself; however, the most important thing in my life to do, is to continue to constantly humble myself, under The Mighty Hand of The One and Only Living God! The Son of Man, Jesus Christ, The Holy Spirit from God, and God Himself, are all that I wholly trust, no other beings will I ever wholly trust. This is the foundation stone of my soul, and since I've made this my directive, nothing has shattered me emotionally to the point of a melt down! This straight and narrow pathway has been one of the best decisions I've made in my existence so far. I make this statement with the full conviction from my soul. The usage of this principle has been the most secure and stable element in my life since I've come to live by it! I've found that anything that is positively connected to The Trinity is totally trustworthy. No falsity at no point is ever intermixed with its character. So in my heart I can never fall away concerning what has been written about The Lord, and Master Jesus Christ. His Life, Death, and Resurrection were all true accounts that I can never push away, and say they had, and they have no meaning. Those accounts are the examples of God's Awesome Power of Life! I've said it be for and I'll say it again, Satan, and all who are connected to him are liars, and they will be punished for their acts, just as The Faithful Lord God Has Stated in His Bible. So forward my soul shall march upholding the truth that has been told, and constantly uncovering the lies that have been believed for centuries, until the day of my departure! This is the meaning for my life, and I constantly had to seek The Kingdom of God to finally see the truth, and believe what was revealed before my heart. There is no falsity in The Holy Spirit that Is God!

247. God Himself Is The World's Only Cure

God Is The Only Good that constantly remains good, and God in my heart shall always be the only good! God Himself Is The Epitome of goodness, I was drawn to seek out The Spirit that is God, the world had beaten me to the point of destruction. I never want to forget about The Evil Forces that be, their influences are responsible for the current condition of this world called earth. For over four decades I could never really understand the world that I have existence in. The world itself is truly awesome, with its perfect order of being, everything is in harmony with each other, except for the beings called human beings. Harmony is severed when it comes down to the masses of humanity, and it's still this way as I'm pushing this pen. The nations of this world have been in total chaos for thousands of years, for they never could keep The Perfect Orders from God Himself. I am a witness to the corruption that plagues this world, I am Charged by my Heavenly Father God Himself to write about the accounts that I've witnessed in my existence! There are so many places I can begin at; however, I will start at the one that I was born into, and that constitutes the attempt of genocide of a people who wouldn't give up their rights to exist within a nation that was very hostile to them! I can remember when I was A very young boy always being frightened; for the adults and older people of my community were mostly always agitated, and I didn't know exactly why. As I grew older I saw there were different kinds of people, and they were different in appearance and soon after I learned the meaning of the word colored and somehow colored was taught to be bad and white was to be good! This confused me for a long time, for I belonged to the colored group, and I truly didn't want to hate, or hurt anybody, so I stepped back, and watched the hurt being administered from one side to the other, and I don't have to tell the outcome; fore it told on itself. Racism is just one more of the many tactics used by The Evil Forces that be, and years have gone by from me being that young boy, and racism is still being practiced, on a world wide scale!

248. Message. From an X Wayward Soul

I can't change what The Lord God Has Already Stated what the finale outcome will be; however, God Himself Has Given me the ability to write, and I will use all of my talents to help my neighbors see the righteousness of Father God's Decrees! My job is to pile the truth up into piles of plenty; there for my neighbors to examine what has been written. Only God Himself Has The Power to Change the hearts and minds of the wayward souls of this world. I myself am nothing without The God of All Creation Leading my path; for I use to be one of the wayward souls of this world! I was gullible to the many thoughts that came to my mind. The Evil Forces that be kept me in darkness for years, by way of their mental projections. The Spirit from The Lord God Has Delivered me from an obtuse angle of discernment, to a very acute angle of discernment from within the confines of my mind. This process has changed my life for the positive good! God's Power Has Enlightened me, and His Light Has Begun to shine itself upon every dark corner of existence. I myself have become humble as a result of the knowledge that has been revealed to my soul! It took an undying willingness from my soul to constantly seek out The Kingdom of God. Then, and only then did God Himself Bless me with a very acute angle of discernment concerning all thoughts that came and come into the confines of my mind. So the track that I now travel on is the track of truth and uprightness, there is no better way for me to live out the remainder of my days and nights on this planet called earth. The forth coming has already been revealed by God's Prophets. Justice, will truly come to life, and everything that has been written concerning judgment of the dead will also truly come to be reality! So I am truly a reminder to my neighbors of this generation with all the compassion from my heart, please take heed; for Father God, Won't Mock Himself! This ends this Message.

249. No Stones Unturned

The Lord God's Will, will be done, so everything in operation that's not in accordance with, or from Father God's Will, will be uprooted! This has been stated by The Lord and Master Jesus Christ- Mathew fifteen verse fourteen. This statement alone has answered so many questions in my mind, and I see the evidence all over the face of this planet! Nothing will prosper unless God Himself Has Placed His Stamp of Approval on it, all things belong to The Loving Spirit that Is God Himself. I've lived in darkness for many years of my life, The Lord God Has Opened Up my Spiritual Eyes, now I can easily see the deep corruption of this world. This corruption can only be remedied by The Power from God's Holy Spirit. God's Prophets along with The Lord, and Master Jesus Christ have already foretold the outcome that will soon come to be a reality for this world. There is no doubt in my heart concerning the actions I must continue to uphold and live out the remainder of My life by. I am truly guided by The Trinity, my message of God's Love is crystal clear, there is no salvation in me.

I however, am the tool that God Himself Uses to Give an Account of His Great Mercy from the very example of my own life. Everything that I've ever written about is the truth, this is the calling for my life. Everyone who has the gift of life was placed here for a specific purpose. The Lord God of All Created Life Is Perfect, without ever making a mistake. So I pose this question to the readers. Search your hearts and ask yourselves this question. For what purpose did God, Place me on this planet? If you really believe there is a God, this question if it already hasn't been pondered, will leave you in deep feelings for a very long time, especially if you are a sincere person. In order for people to truly find the answer, they would sincerely have to seek out God, and ask! In my own experience it has truly taken me many years to really find the answer to the question of why am I here? The Evil Forces that be have been running interference through my thoughts for years, and they still do; however, The Maker of my life Has Truly Given me the truth about myself, and the world around me, and before the end of this world, God Himself Will Leave No Stones Unturned!

250. Evil and its Multiplying Affects

As I continue to see all of the injustices taking place in this world, I myself mustn't become bitter; fore eventually my heart would turn to stone! I must keep faith in Father God, and trust in my heart that God Himself Will Make Right all that has been wrongfully done. I can never place myself in God's Place, or I too will be in the wrong! Father God's Decrees Were Given to mankind thousands of years ago, and those same Decrees must still be obeyed now, thousands of years later. There is no reward, or benefit in disobeying The Decrees from God Himself, if disobedience is the outcome from the actions people take, only Father God Himself Will Know what their fates shall be! God Almighty Searches the hearts and minds of all men. My soul constantly seeks the truth about the origin and make up of things, I know in my heart that my Father God Has Fashioned me in this way. I can't be secure and prosperous in something I'm not! So when I study The Teachings of The Lord, and Master Jesus Christ, there are never any conflicts in my being as a whole. This is how I know that Jesus Christ Has Spoken and Still Speaks the truth; fore the truth needs no defense, and He Never Defended Himself With The Power He Possessed. The evil within the devil's children brutally murdered Him! God Himself Has Blessed my soul to see the truth as it really was and still is to this day, right up to the very moment of my writing this sentence. The children of the devil will always use lies and deception to keep the truth of God's Wrath hidden from the hearts and minds of the masses of people! I've borne witness to the truth of their tactics, by observing humanity so far from Father God's Blessings. Being ignorant within the midst of evil doers, I myself was almost destroyed by The Evil Forces that be on numerous occasions; however, The Mighty Hand of The LORD God Protected me and Provided a pathway for me to exit out from. There are oh, so many places on this earth designed to kill The Children from God.

251. The Persistent Seekers

The way to salvation has already been shown to the inhabitants of this world called earth; however, through the years this saying has been the truth concerning humanity, "many are called, but oh, so few are chosen, or many are called, but oh, so few respond to God's Calling." I can't become stagnated with the truth concerning The Trinity; the light of true knowledge saturates my whole being! God Himself Has Called me to uplift the truth once again, by way of the pen. The Teachings from The Lord, and Master Jesus Christ Is The Pathway to The Living God. By following Jesus Christ's Example, souls will connect up with The Maker and Sustainer of their Lives as they are living them! The inspiration I'm writing about isn't new, its timeless; for Father God Is Timeless. I can't make anyone do anything, but what I can do is share my life experiences. I do this for my fellow neighbors who live this life with me, and for the souls who will be left after The Mighty Lord God Decides to lay me to rest! I wholly trust The Trinity, They in no way would ever hurt me, this is how I live my life, I've grown to know They Are Alive. I don't ask anyone to believe what I believe; however, what I write about are true occurrences that happen in my existence! If my neighbors take the leap of blind faith and constantly seek The Kingdom of God, as I did and still do, they will never view the world and all existence the same ever again. I've truly experienced how Father God Awaits the sincere seekers of His Existence. One must be prepared for The Evil Forces that be; they will constantly use their mind projections to steal your zeal away from your attempts to seek out The Creator of All Life. You must be persistent, that is why I used the word constantly; for if you keep seeking God, the devil will flee from your conscious thoughts!

The persistent souls will gain a true connection to God Himself, and like I said my neighbors will never view all existence the same ever again; for God Himself Will Bless them with an acute angle of confirmation from within the confines of their hearts and minds!

252. No Greater Importance

No one, not even The Son of Man Jesus Christ Knows the day and the hour when The Holy Spirit That Is God, Will Come and Judge this world! God's Wisdom Is Unapproachable, His Ways Are Always Generous and Kind. I don't know exactly when; however, I've reached a point in my seeking of God Himself whereas I wouldn't want to go on living anymore, if I couldn't seek God anymore. The Power That Is God Is my life, God's Holy Spirit Has Been and Still Is Oh, So Kind to the soul that is me. All God Has Ever Felt to me Is to be kind to all of my neighbors, no matter what, even if they are evil! The Holy Spirit That Is God, Always Overwhelms my heart, even in my dysfunctions I tried to do my best to please God! Most times I would come up short in my behaviors; however, God Would Always Listen to me in my prayers, and God Never Turned me away and hurt me with the feelings of being no good and to never come before Him ever again! No, there was always a feeling of deep concern ; especially when I knew I did something wrong, I could feel it all around me; even though, I didn't know what it was at those certain times as I do now. It was Father God's Loving Presents, and I never got away with bad actions; for God would make my wrongs exposed to certain people, who He Knew would chastise me and guide me back on the right path. So you see there is no substitute for The Loving Presents of God Himself, this is what I've found by constantly seeking the Kingdom of God. The Spirit of The Living God, Patiently Waits for His Created Beings to seek out the reality that is He. Never is there any pressure involved from God's Holy Spirit concerning His Created Beings. There is nothing we created beings can to do to hurt God; however, there are numerous things we can do to hurt ourselves and others! God Himself Has Restored me to my rightful mind, so I am able to see the truth concerning many situations in life. The Life of The Lord, and Master Jesus Christ Is The Best Example I have to study from, in order to become holy and acceptable to Father God Himself. I truly desire to please my Maker, Father God's Will Is All That Truly Matters in my life, nothing else has greater importance to me; even though, there are other important things in life.

253. The First Steps of Being Reborn

I can't change what I am; however, I've learned to seek out The Kingdom of God, to live my life to the extreme of the abilities Father God Has Given unto me. There was a price to pay in order to receive the correct pathway that I know travel on. I first had to abandon myself from depending on people, places and things, and that took almost four decades to learn how to do! There was a wall of selfishness that I constructed for three decades, along with willful pride. From the inside of my being all of this had to be destroyed, and new self-worth had to be built; this process was slow and very painful, there was no way I could have accomplished this on my own power and direction. I needed and wanted a brand new way of thinking and living; however, I didn't know at that time how to accomplish it, all I knew was that I couldn't live the way I was living anymore. So I pulled out the ace that I had in my pocket, and that ace consisted of God Himself on one side of the card and Jesus Christ, God's Son, on the other side of the card, at that time I was thirty three years old. I openly invited The Spirit of The Trinity, into my existence on that very night, in the month of December, in the year nineteen ninety five. From that night forward it became my responsibility to continue seeking The Invisible Force in The Universe people have come to call God! No peace in my mind, or heart were long standing for many days and nights, I was easily agitated by people, places and things; for my wall of selfishness and willful pride was still very much intact. Only by constantly seeking God Himself Was I Instructed on how to consciously start to breakdown the wall of selfishness and willful pride. It became the hardest thing I ever had to do in my life up to that point; nothing of my self-deflation came easily! My failures wouldn't let me rest, the thoughts of them would constantly come into my mind, they truly overwhelmed me on many occasions, making me ineffective for hours and sometimes days at a time. My progress was very slow, and my tormentor The Evil Forces that be would loudly speak through my thoughts, telling me it's not worth it, and not to continue any further. Fortunate for me, even though I didn't know it at those times, on how The Spirit of The Living God Was Already Manifest within my heart, and I had begun not to listen to my thoughts and commit actions from them that were adverse from God's Will for my life, I was reborn!

254. When Reality Strikes

Oh God, I truly became overwhelmed from studying The Teachings from The Lord, and Master Jesus Christ, especially when I finished reading Mark chapter seven, verse number twenty. Almost all of those evils I have done, and some of them I have practiced. I know that I am not perfect oh God; however, You call us to be, fore You are Perfect, oh LORD God. This revelation has truly shook me up and brought what I must do to the fore fronts of my heart. I truly see now God why You Told me to keep my focus upon You at all times. I know within my heart at this very moment that I am still alive only by Your Grace and Great Mercy, oh Precious Father God! The Evil Forces that be are very powerful and subtle at the same time; in no way will I ever be safe by being disconnected from Your Holy Spirit LORD God. There is no doubt in my soul, I truly know The Evil Forces that be want sincerely to enslave my Eternal Soul, and they have tried on many occasions to have that accomplished by my own hands, or someone else's! I was brought to awareness within The Recovery Process from The Grace from God to discern my thoughts, now God's Holy Spirit Has Grown me to discern my heart as well. I write these things from my being; for this is what God Himself Has Called me to do! Our deeds follow us after we physically leave the body, this is why all of God's Prophets Were Sent to warn the masses of people, so their fates wouldn't match that of Satan and his fellow evil doers. I am just one soul, and I will continue to tell the truth as Father God Transmits to my heart what I am to write about. The Holy Spirit from God Flows through my heart as I write the words with this instrument called a pen. The Lord, and Master Jesus Christ, Is The Key to Eternal Life, no one can see The Father, unless they first come through The Son! Take advantage of the time The Maker God Is Allowing us, don't let Satan and his family consume your hearts, give yourselves to The Goodness that Is Father God Himself, He Awaits Patiently to Heal our tormented souls. All of what is necessary to begin our healing is to believe that God Is...

255. Directions From The Holy Director

The Holy Spirit from God Himself Regularly Speaks to my heart to say, "stop concerning yourself with earthly things!" I'm Charged by God Himself to keep my concerns on Spiritual Matters; even though, I'm in the physical body. I can't stay on The Spiritual Path if I have worldly inclinations within my heart; for eventually they will sever my connection and guidance from Father God Himself! I've experienced a lot of hard knocks in this world to obtain the truth. Through the years I've truly learned how The Guidance from Father God through my heart has always been proved to have a solid foundation, so I've grown to wholly trust the leadings from Father God. There was no positive direction yielding a beneficial outcome when it came to examining myself will. Following the directions from Father's God's Will for my life has truly turned my angle in life a full one hundred and eighty degrees. I dare not to think to take any of the credit, the whole pie of glory belongs to God Himself! To the day of my last breath hear on earth, I know in my heart that I am called by Father God to be of love and service to my neighbors. I must not seek after no material riches; for they have no place in the purpose Father God Has for my life here. Every time I seek Father God from within my heart, He Always Whispers through my thoughts a deeper meaning to the purpose of my existence here upon the earth. The Spirit from The Living God Constantly Keeps me grateful and humble concerning everything that's in the realm of humanity. The Loving and Caring Father God Has Given the whole world the pathway that leads to Eternal Life; however, the behavior in people must develop into the total opposite of what is being practiced in the world as a whole.

These words will be a blessing to those who need to further build their faith, and with diversity these same words will be a dagger to the hearts of those who don't belong to Father God! As it is written the sheep will listen to the voice of The Shepard, but won't listen to the voice of a stranger.

256. The Compassion That Flows

Compassion flows through my heart like a great river whenever I contemplate on the masses of people throughout the world who are blinded and deceived by The Evil Forces that be! My heart won't allow me to stand by and do nothing, so I asked Father God how could I be of help to them? Father God Has Answered my prayer by having me to constantly pick up a pen, and wholly write the truth about things! This condition of writing about the truth will be the position I will uphold until The LORD God Himself Allows me to breathe no more. I have found my lot in this life by asking The LORD God from my heart; how can I help my neighbors? I can't explain the joy I feel when I pick up a pen and share my experiences; for I know in my heart that it will help out someone somewhere in the world! The Trinity Will Never Leave your prayers unanswered, all things are possible through God Himself. The Holy Spirit of God Has Developed me into a compassionate being, whereas I was once enslaved by The Evil Forces that be, and close at hand was my physical death and enslavement was to be the fate of my soul for forever; however, I literally cried out to God and Jesus Christ, and from that night to the day of this writing They Brought me out from the bondage Satan had over my soul! So you see The Invisible God Is Reality for me and I wholly trust The Trinity, and nothing else in this world will ever get my total trust! The deep compassion I have for the masses of people will never fade away; for The Holy Spirit of God , Flows Through my soul Constantly, I belong to God! I've learned to patiently wait for God's Directions, instead of taking matters into my own hands and saying to myself that it's up to me to take whatever actions necessary to achieve a desired result. I've made so many mistakes that way before I started to look to Father God for answers. Now, waiting on Father God Himself is the way I've lived my life for the past fourteen and one half years, and I've hardly made any major mistakes in my life personally, or in day to day living. The results speaks for itself, just as the truth needs no defense. So I will continue to seek Father God Himself, and pass on the truth about things to my neighbors; so that one day maybe they might seek The Unapproachable Light that Is Father God for themselves.

257. End of my Search

Being of love and service to each other always is the foundation of order in The Kingdom of Heaven. This is also a commandment to all of us upon the earth; however, we have something that gets in the way of God's Decree for our lives, and that something is The Evil Forces that be! Satan and his family members have been causing confusion and corruption for all of humanity fore thousands of years, and the evil will continue. This is the reality that is now, two thousand and thirteen years after the crucifixion of The Lord, and Master Jesus Christ, and all of humanity is still many blood years away from God's Perfect Order of Things. This might not be the case though; fore Jesus Christ Himself Said, "no one knows the day, or the hour when The LORD God Himself Will Come and Judge all the earth." I believe with all of my heart, soul, mind, and strength that The LORD God's Will, Will Be Done. I must continue on a day to day basis to humble myself under The Mighty Hand of God, and be committed to be of love and service to my neighbors and always watch for the coming of The LORD. The LORD God Himself Has Blessed my soul to see the truth as it was written, and now God Has Empowered me to carry out what The Holy Scriptures Meanings are! By seeking The Kingdom of God on a daily basis, The Holy Spirit From God Has Begun to

Enlighten me on what I must do from one day to the next, oh, how truly blessed I am! God's Plan for my life is already set, now I must fulfill Father God's Will for my life. God Is The Architect, and I must do the work He Has Laid Out before me. All of my past days before I sought The Kingdom of God, makes perfect sense to me now. I was trying to fit into a slot where I didn't belong; for before I came out of my mother's womb, Father God Had the blueprint of my life, and God Protected me all of my life, even until I came to end of myself, and He Will Protect me for forever; for I am God's Son, God Himself told me so! My long search is over to why am I here?

258. No Souls Can Imagine

All that is seen by the physical eyes here on the earth, and all that's in heaven above that can be physically seen consists of a great amount of matter. All of which belongs to God Himself, and The Lord Is Oh, So Kind and Generous. I know within my heart The Lord God Himself Made The heavenly bodies for humanity to live on and prosper from. God Knew that one day we would outgrow this planet; however, mankind is plagued with The Evil Forces that be, and they are the soul contributor to confusion and mistrust amongst the nations. Having chaos such as it is in our world will only continue to breed evil, and soon to follow desolation. I am only one soul who has been blessed by Father God Himself to write these words of truth, I will constantly empty out my heart with words of encouragement to the masses of humanity. Only Father God Himself Can Rid this earth entirely from the influences of The Evil Forces that be. It's only in the confines of Father God Himself, as to when He Will Step in, and take action against The Evil Forces that be! So life goes on; even though, The Evil Forces that be are running rampant . We who believe in Father God, and trust Him, must continue to live by every word that preceded out from The Mouth of God; for the words from Father God Is Seed of Knowledge for our lives! God, Doesn't Lie, He's The Only Good; however, Satan does lie, and he is The father of lies. Satan constantly looks to misguide the innocent, Satan wants so desperately to be God, and acquire all of God's Glory! Satan and all his family members have already been sentenced by God Himself, all that is required to fulfill their sentence is time, and only God Himself Knows when that time will come to pass! So I say to my neighbors, live your lives in full obedience to The One and Only God, our Precious and Oh, So Kind Creator. This comes from God's Own Words, "No souls can imagine what rewards I Have for those who Love Me and endure to the end."

259. Personal Instructions From The Trinity

My Older Brother Jesus Christ Strengthens me with each passing day and night. Power is starting to be noticed by people who are regular associates. One person said he feels something inside of himself every time he hears me speak, that my words make him cry! All I can do is praise God Himself, my Precious Maker; It's Father God's Will why I'm growing in this way. The Lord, and Master Jesus Christ Constantly Whispers to my mind by Saying "let go of worldly concerns, and continue to trust Father God." My Older Brother Jesus Christ Truly Cares for the wellbeing of my soul. Woe unto me, if I ever fall away from The Trinity; fore I would truly die, and I know this with the fullness of my heart. The Lord, and Master Jesus Christ Has Watched me all of my life and He Knows my heart better than I do myself, and that's the honest truth. Being Guided by The One Who Sits at The Side of The Creator of All Existence is the highest honor I'll ever receive in this life! No praise from man can ever equal the calling I've received from The Trinity, my base is set in place for Eternity. I live now to serve The Trinity; there is no other reason for my life now that has a greater meaning than love and service to God first, and my neighbors second. Before I sought out The Trinity for help, I didn't know how to be of love and service to anyone; for I was extremely selfish and The Trinity Had to Guide me on what I needed to do. At first it was minute by minute; fore I was so wrecked in my soul, and this was the basis for my recovery for at least three, or four years. I truly discovered by The Grace of God, and by God's Great Mercy how I was a very sick person for many years, and how only God Himself Has The Power to Heal me and Redirect my life, so eventually I would become holy and acceptable to God Himself! After seventeen years of seeking The Kingdom of God; Father God Has Called me to seek out The Lord, and Master Jesus Christ. Never have I felt this blessed in all the days and nights of my life, all praise is due to Father God, for, forever!

260. The Allowance From God Himself

The words trust God, echoed within my mind, this was my experience upon awakening, now it's late in the afternoon and the words remain constant within my mind. In my experience concerning spirituality, I mustn't ignore this message; fore that's exactly what it is! The Lord, and Master Jesus Christ Truly Speaks to my soul, in the manner I just described. Once again The Awesome Trinity Has Shown me that I belong to Them; now my calling is solidified for my heart has answered "yes" to the words--

-- trust God! No longer will worldly things have weight on my Eternal Soul; for years I worried about such things. For years I sought The Kingdom of God, now God Himself Has Allowed me to enter into it! I will keep my head bowed in prayer; for I don't know how to live in The Kingdom of God. The LORD God Has Blessed me with this Allowance. I truly thought I physically had to die, to experience it. Oh, how ignorant and blinded I was my whole life until God Himself Blessed me! The Evil Forces that be had me cloaked in darkness for more than four decades, Only by constantly seeking The Kingdom of God, have I been Allowed To Enter Into The Kingdom of God! I truly know what it means to be reborn. The Holy Spirit From God Lights the pathway I am to travel as I seek out my neighbors who are still cloaked in darkness. I know the road to salvation, and Father God Has Taught me over the years step by step by step. I've seen how Father God, Jesus Christ and The Holy Spirit From God Have All Been So Nice and Kind to me all of my life. Now my position has been set in place within my heart by Father God Himself. I know by what Power I am Empowered By, and I am loyal to that Power for forever, nothing is more important than Father God Himself!

      The End ----- Is The Beginning.

      By

      Minister Wayne Beverett

ABOUT THE AUTHOR

Minister Wayne Beverett was born to Mr. and Mrs. Buford and Patsy Beverett. The year was 1962 on December the 12th. He graduated from Chancellor Avenue Elementary School in Newark, New Jersey. He also graduated from Weequahic High School in Newark, New Jersey. He attended one half of a year at New Jersey Institute of Technology before leaving to start working in his career.

www.ingramcontent.com/pod-product-compliance
Lightning Source LLC
Chambersburg PA
CBHW050328230426
43663CB00010B/1775